WINDS
OF
CRETE

DAVID MACNEIL DOREN

ATHENS

First published in England
by John Murray (Publishers) Ltd in 1974

First published in Greece
by Efstathiadis Group, 1981

DISTRIBUTED by
P. EFSTATHIADIS & SONS S.A.
Athens, 14 Valtetsiou St. Tel. 3615011-3600495
Thessaloniki, 34 Olympou-Diikitiriou St. Tel. 511781

EFSTATHIADIS GROUP
14 Valtetsiou St. - Athens - Tel. 3615011

For Merhl —
the freest spirit

Contents

Illustrations

from the author's photographs

Illustrations

From the author's photographs

Author's Note

All of the people and incidents in this book are real, but I have taken the liberty of changing a few names and of moving some events from one village to another. Many of the Cretans who helped us and gave us hospitality during our six years on their island are named in the text; I owe them all a debt of thanks.

I would also like to express my thanks to the Ingram Merrill Foundation for the generous Award for Aid in Writing which enabled me to finish the book. My special thanks also to David Jackson, who provided encouragement and help at a critical time; and to Dorothy Andrews, an extraordinary friend, companion on outings and source of Cretan lore.

My debt to Inga, companion of all these pages, is too great for words: the book itself stands as my acknowledgment of it.

There seem to be no rules for the English spelling or Greek words. I have chosen the variants that appear to be most commonly used by English writers on Greece.

David MacNeil Doren

Uppsala, Sweden
'After all anybody is as their land and sea and air is. Anybody is as the sky is low or high, the air heavy or clear and anybody is as there is wind or no wind there. It is that which makes them and the arts they make and the work they do and the way they eat and the way they drink and the way they learn and everything.'

GERTRUDE STEIN

'I'm not a Greek—I'm a Cretan!'

NIKOS KAZANTZAKIS

I

A House in the Wind

Our first year in Crete we lived on the top floor of a house that was played upon by all the winds. In winter there were the hard northern gales, when the sea turned grey, more like the North Atlantic than the Aegean, and the bitter chill came in through the cracks under the doors; and on the coldest days in the unheated room with the stone floor there was nothing to do but put on all your clothes at once—long underwear, sweaters and jackets and scarves—and then go to bed and pile on the blankets. Came spring, and Africa had its voice in our affairs: 'the Big Tongue' as the old women of Crete call the hot, dust-laden *sorokos* that comes howling up from Libya. We would see it coming through the gap in the mountains to the south—a distant finger of haze drifting into the still blue gulf of Merabello. Innocent it looked, but the fishermen knew it for the devil it was, and when they saw it coming they made for port at once. It arrived all in a rush, churning the sea to angry foam, blowing the salt spray right up on to our terrace, raising little tornadoes of dust all over town. The first day of a *sorokos* was bad enough; the second was even worse; and by the third you were ready to commit murder or suicide. The air became clogged with yellow dust, you felt restless and often had a headache, couldn't work, couldn't read, couldn't do anything. Tempers wore thin, quarrels flared, domestic peace was threatened. There are archaeologists who say that a south wind was blowing when Knossos burned about 1400 B.C; and to anyone who has lived in Crete there is nothing surprising about this, for it is easy to believe that all bad things happen during the southerly storms.

But the essence of the Cretan climate is the imminence of sudden change; and so the south wind would leave as quickly as it had come, and then for a few days peace and calm seas and blue skies were ours. But never for long—always another wind would come, and some of them, like the cool *meltemia* breezes that blew steadily from the northwest for forty days in summer, were most welcome.

11

Winds of Crete

We used to sit on the terrace and look over Merabello Bay towards the Sitia mountains, lords of wind and weather, aware of every change in the colours of the moutainsides and of the surface of the sea. The peaks were less than five thousand feet and did not rank among the highest in Crete, but they rose directly from the eastern shore of the bay and so they looked higher than they were. Our house faced a tiny cove where I swam all through that first winter. (I became a bit of a legend—the crazy foreigner who went in the sea in January). On calm mornings I swam before breakfast, paddling out into the deep blue-green water with the mountains in front of me, about ten miles away but seeming much closer with the sun rising behind them. A little later, we would eat breakfast outdoors and watch the mellow morning light give way to the bright white light of full day. But in late afternoon the intensity and variety of the reds and violets on the mountainside would return. We never tired of just watching those mountains. In winter there were a few weeks when they had snow-caps; in summer shepherds' campfires glowed on their flanks. On windless evenings in late spring, when the moon was dark, fishermen rowed into our cove to spear octopus and squid by the light of flaring carbide lamps fastened to the prows of their boats. At such times, looking at a sky full of bright stars and the dim outlines of the mountains beyond the shadowy bay, we felt the earth moving in its orbit, and were conscious of being passengers in space. Our terrace became the bridge of a space ship, and we had the illusion that all humanity should feel at home anywhere from stem to stern of this old reliable vessel.

That little top floor terrace of ours was an ideal vantage point for viewing the continuous parade of Cretan life and the cycle of the seasons. We watched our neighbours below and on the nearby hillsides as they cultivated their winter gardens; we saw the grass and the plants wither away in the glare of the spring sunshine, and by June all was barren and brown where once green grass and bright blossoms had flourished. In autumn, after the first long-awaited rains, the green crept back and the flowers reasserted themselves.

Most of the time we were more aware of the elements and the landscape than of humans. Our poverty and our simple joy at just being there, in the sun by the sea after so many pent-up, claustrophobic years in northern climes, made for us a bed-rock existence whose elements were as bare as the rocks of Crete. The landmarks of our life were the bay and the mountains in all their aspects, our little three-room abode with its peeling plaster walls of yellow and rose hue, the few books we had brought with us from the north—classics which at last we had the time to read—and above all the relationship between us. This was the honeymoon, with one another and with Crete. Later, as our marriage to each other and to our adopted island wore on, we discerned faults in each: and loved all the more despite them, or perhaps because of them.

We came to Crete because we wanted freedom to breathe, time to think, to read and reflect, to get back in tune with the rhythms of the earth and the seasons. Simple things, but difficult of attainment in the hurly-burly of modern life. Most people go through life without ever finding the time to know themselves, much less others. When the age of retirement arrives they leave their office or shop only to find bewilderment and idleness; their lifelong habits of hurry and worry do not leave them so quickly. Inga and I were in our early thirties when we came to Crete—an early age for 'retirement' perhaps, but not for trying to find ourselves.

*　　*　　*

We were not rich—far from it: when I arrived on our island home I had but fifty dollars in my pocket, just enough to live on for the first month. Inga would receive a small monthly sum from Sweden, barely enough for one person to live on. Neither of us could count on family backing, and we had no money in any bank. It was a gamble, based on our knowledge that living costs in Crete are among the lowest in Europe, and my hope of earning a little money from certain trades that can be practiced anywhere: writing, free-lance journalism, perhaps photography.

Common sense was all against our making such a move, but I remembered the words of Thoreau: '. . . if one advances confidently in the direction of his dreams, and endeavours to live the life he has imagined, he will meet with a success unexpected in common hours'. It wasn't common sense that would decide such a matter, but uncommon sense—in other words, intuition—and it told us we should grasp the opportunity to have our quiet Mediterranean island life, for it might never come again.

Inga was Swedish, I American. Neither of us had found harmony, or joy, or satisfaction in our native lands. The meeting between us was, like so many of life's most important events, purest chance. Both of us happened to be staying at the same time in the unique youth hostel of Stockholm which consists of an old sailing ship moored to an island. Something about each other drew us to exchange 'Good mornings' as we stood waiting for breakfast coffee, and we found ourselves sharing the same table as we ate. We arranged to meet again, and a few days later I went to visit her at her home in the old university town of Uppsala, where she was studying Art History. We found that we had much in common: a love of books, of nature, of solitude; a sense of humour that had us laughing at the same things. Neither of us realised that something serious had happened between us until the moment that we seperated. She was going off to Greece on a trip partly inspired by my anecdotes, and I was going to Germany to take a job on a magazine—a temporary expedient to keep me in Europe until I could save enough money to travel southward to a more congenial milieu. The sudden and totally unexpected intensity of the pain of separation told us that something had indeed happened; and from that moment our letters were full of anticipation of our next meeting.

On her way back from Greece to Sweden, she stopped off in Wiesbaden to see me. Suddenly we were plunged into a passionate love such as neither of us had ever known before. We were together for one whole intoxicating month. I neglected my work (the editor was on vacation and I had been left in sole charge of the magazine— which gave me a perfect chance to slip away on long three and four day weekends). We spent much time out in the country, walking over the hills and through the woods of the Rheingau.   It was lovely country, and a lovely time for us, yet somehow we felt beleaguered, alienated from the bustling moneymaking life around us. We wanted more time for ourselves, more freedom from the intrusions of the world. We began to hatch our plans for an escape to the south, and we felt that we had to find a way to do it, that we had to go soon, or we might never make it.

For there was a shadow over it all, a cloud of which we were always aware, even—especially—during our most joyous moments, and that lent an even greater poignancy to them. For Inga suffered from a serious heart condition: had already been through one —unsuccessful—operation, and knew that eventually she would have to have another, or face the certain prospect of a slowly worsening condition leading to invalidism and early death. Two valves had been damaged by rheumatic fever, and it was not yet within the ability of medical science, despite the many recent advances in heart surgery, to do this kind of operation. She had to be careful—couldn't over-exert herself, had to go slowly and pause often for breath when walking uphill, and had to be very careful not to catch a throat infection which might lead to a recurrence of the rheumatic fever. She could not hold any job; fortunately, being a citizen of Sweden, she was eligible for a pension that gave her just enough to live on, if she lived frugally.

I think it was precisely this condition of Inga's, this awareness of ours that our passionate love might not last, that she might be taken away at any time, that gave it such an intensity. Aware of how our days together might be cut short, we wanted to concentrate our lives on essential things, not to be burdened and encumbered with trifles, not to waste our precious minutes on profitless occupations.

Inga was fantastically proud and stubborn and courageous about her condition—that combination of qualities for which the Finns have a special word, *sisu*—and it was no coincidence that she actually had Finnish blood, on her mother's side. She refused to use her heart as an excuse, and would sooner exhaust herself, and suffer later in silence, than to mention to anyone that her heart was bothering her. It was this attitude that determined her response when I asked her to marry me

'I will not marry you,' she said, 'because the purpose of marriage is to have children, and I can't have any as long as my heart is like this. But I will live with you, if you want me to, and I will go wherever you want me to.'

Those were the terms of our 'marriage' and the terms under which we are still living together. We have never gone through any ceremony, public or private, yet we are as true and faithful to each other, as truly married as it is possible to be. And I shall refer to her in these pages as my wife, as I do in conversation, and as I regard her in my own mind—the only wife I ever have had, or ever want to have.

* * *

We chose Crete because, quite simply, there is no other place like it in the whole world. I had visited the island once before, briefly, and even during that short time had felt its fascination. As the old island steamer carried me along the Cretan coast I had an eerie feeling, as of being a million light years away from all that was familiar. Sailing into those ancient harbours was like entering some remote port on the far side of another planet. The journey had a dream-like quality that I have never experienced anywhere else, and it inspired another dream: to live in the midst of that lunar landscape, by one of those harbours. The people, too, impressed me even on short acquaintance: vigorous, proud, curious—above all, they gave the impression of being *free*. The Cretans—at least those who live in the country and not in towns—seem still happily wedded to nature and to the rhythms of the sun and moon; whereas we of the modern cities have for long been unhappily divorced from all natural forces.

These were first impressions, but powerful ones, and in any case I have always believed in first impressions and been willing to put my faith in them: they represent true intuitive reactions, unmodified by later considerations of logic or social pressure.

Inga, too, had been fascinated by the island. Her recent trip, which had been planned to include most of Greece and the islands, had turned into a four-month sojourn solely in Crete. Most of her time had been spent at Ayios Nikolaos, a fishing port in the eastern part of the island. She had made some friends there, and its setting seemed right, so it was there we decided to settle at first, intending to move westward later to a village and to make trips of exploration all over the island. In December of 1960 she preceded me to Crete to look for a house, while I remained a few weeks in Germany to finish up my employment. It was early January when I arrived in Athens to find a stack of letters waiting for me, including one that said: 'I have found the house! I hope you like it, for it faces the sea and is cheap'.

I took the next boat for Crete, and arrived on the morning of January 6th, the Feast of Epiphany when the waters are blessed, which seemed a good omen. At seven in the morning I was standing on the top deck as we moved in towards the harbour of Herakleion. The sea was calm and dark blue, the sky clear. The sun coming up beyond Mount Dikte poured warm golden light over the winter-green folds of a landscape that recalled the painted robes of El Greco, a native son of the town we were approaching. High to the south rose the snow-crowned bulk of Mount Ida where the young Zeus was hidden and brought to manhood. A Cretan landfall is always memorable—this one above all for me—and to top it off the lightning-fast notes of a lyre filled the air, playing the *pentozali* or Cretan warriors' dance. The effect was genuine, despite the prosaic fact that it was Radio Crete's morning broadcast of folk music, coming over the radio on the ship's bridge.

Distant white buildings materialised into the old houses around the harbour, and soon we were gliding in past the fortress at the end of the Venetian mole, with the Lion of Saint Mark still guarding its gates. I discerned the figure of Inga, slim and blonde, waving on the quay, almost lost among the press of Greeks. Docking procedure was the usual chaos and curses, and then we were in each other's arms, playing our little drama of reunion before an approving audience of Cretans who stared and smiled unabashedly. More than anything they love these arrivals and departures with their rich blend of melodrama and confusion.

16

And there was to be much more of it that day, for the flags were out and the narrow streets of the old port were decked with the blue and white of Greece. It was a national holiday, and the town was full of people in noisy and light-hearted mood. Inga and I had coffee together and then strolled hand in hand down to the quays to watch the parade and the ceremony of the Blessing of the Waters. We saw the Archbishop in his golden robes and top-heavy mitre, a bearded, massive figure of patriarchal authority leading a squad of lesser ecclesiastics and a guard of honour from the army and navy. They all piled into small boats and were ferried out to a tugboat in the harbour, where half a dozen boys waited, shivering in bathing trunks in the crisp January air. The Archbishop raised a silver cross high in the air for all to see, and then tossed it into the water—but he had taken no chances on losing it, for it was fastened securely to the end of a long string, and he held on tightly like a fisherman with a good bite. The boys all plunged into the water, and a few seconds later the winner emerged with the cross held triumphantly aloft: he would be a new hero for a while. Church bells rang out, ship whistles blew, people shouted and cheered. The sea was now considered to be purified, and the brown harbour water was dipped up in thousands of buckets and pitchers, to be taken home and carefully preserved to ensure good luck in the coming year.

That afternoon there were more good luck rituals on the way to Ayios Nikolaos in the ramshackle bus. The first part of the road led eastward along the coast: then after about an hour we climbed into a spur of the Lassithi mountains. Halfway up the first pass the bus stopped near a small chapel, and all the passengers hurried over to present their offerings to Saint George. His icon was festooned with hundreds of votive offerings, crude tin representations of legs, eyes, sheep, even trucks and cars that the petitioners wanted cured, repaired or blessed. This stop at the chapel is an iron-clad local tradition; and we were solemnly assured that should any driver be so rash as to ignore it, whether out of haste or impiety, he would surely meet with an accident before the trip ended. Actual cases were cited as proof.

And so as the bus wheezed up the last grade and then started the long drive down the valley, at the end of which gleamed the blue of Merabello Bay and our new home, we felt that we were absolutely loaded with good luck. The omens were propitious; and above all we were together again, and in the sun. The rest would take care of itself—and never mind where next month's meals were coming from. We felt instinctively that Crete would not let a stranger starve.

2

Bean Days

The luckiest thing that happened to us at the beginning of our stay in Crete was that we were so poor. If we had had more money, we would have looked abroad for our amusements, travelled about more, doubtless fallen in with other foreigners. As it was, our poverty compelled us to stay at home most of the time, to look within ourselves for resources to sustain our spirits, and to turn to the Cretans for companionship when we needed it. We had brought a few books with us, and these we devoured with greater attention and comprehension than anything we had read for years amid the distractions of other environments. At last we were able to read books as Thoreau said they should be read—'as deliberately and reservedly as they were written'. (And one of the first books we read in this way was *Walden*. I read it aloud to Inga during a succession of long winter evenings—thus passing along a love for this book that I had first acquired, long ago, when I was a boy and my grandmother had read it to me when I was staying at her farm. It's a pity that the old-fashioned habit of reading aloud is so little practiced nowadays. There is no better way to share an author's thoughts and feelings —and no sterner test of a writer. Only the very best of them have written sentences of such pith and vigour, so free of falsity and posing, that they can be read aloud without boredom or embarrassment. I know of no writer who can stand up to this test as well as Thoreau.) We felt that we knew our authors personally—that Thoreau and D. H. Lawrence, and Yeats and Hardy and Henry Miller were the companions of our days. An odd and ill-assorted collection of authors, perhaps, yet in each we found something that was grist for the mills of our spirit, some support for what we were doing, some echo or confirmation of our own deepest intuitions and needs. The groundwork of our life here in Crete had been laid long before by these writers: by Lawrence with his belief in the sacredness of the love relation between a man and a woman: by Thoreau with his insistence on the need for an individual to lead his own life, and to simplify that life so as to extract the most from it; by Yeats with his sombre stately music which, read aloud, accompanied us to many an improbable setting; by Hardy with his fatalism and belief in the overwhelming power of the natural forces; by Miller with his sharp criticisms of modern society and his paean of praise to the life still to be found in Greece. Now, re-reading them, we found the encouragement and support that we needed; they were the trusted advisers and daily friends of our inner life together.

As for the Cretans, the companions of our outer lives, we learned now at first hand of one of their best qualities: their generosity and goodwill towards strangers. During those first months in our new house various neighbours used to come up to us in the street and press upon us small gifts of food—eggs, cakes or fruit—and sometimes a bouquet of wild flowers. And whenever we went for a walk in the country, people called us into their fields and gave us such quantities of oranges, lemons and vegetables that our shoulder bags would not hold them all. This casual generosity to strangers, springing from no motive but the sheer pleasure of giving, was a characteristic of all the Cretans we met. It was impossible to refuse anything, or to attempt to pay—that would have been an insult. (Indeed, there are ways of repaying, such as taking people's photographs—Cretans invariably regard that as a personal compliment and respond to it with delight and pride—or making some small spontaneous present like candy for the children or cigarettes for the men or some item of clothing for the women. But these gestures have to be in kind: that is, proffered in the same spirit in which the initial offering was made.) I believe that encountering so much generosity must be good for the soul; for in addition to making one well-disposed towards humanity, it imposes a test of one's own spiritual state: for giving and receiving are two sides of the same coin, and it takes an open and generous spirit to be able to accept gracefully.

Generosity helped our household economy, and so did credit. We soon became known to the shopkeepers along the little treeshaded main street, and all of them were quite willing to extend apparently unlimited credit to us immediately. Thus we were enabled to set up housekeeping at the very start, by buying a small gas stove with three burners and a bottle of Italian gas on the instalment plan. The stove and gas together came to a little more than £7 (twenty dollars), but for us it was a great sum, and without the credit we would have had to cook over charcoal in the little fireplace in our kitchen.

We found one grocer, Petros, who was especially friendly. He was a little man who looked something like Charlie Chaplin, with some of his wistfulness; in comparison with him, his wife resembled a mountain range. From their little den of a shop, smelling of garlic and sweat, they dispensed eggs, vegetables, fruit and other staples to us, and never hinted at payment even when the bill was running high. It was the same with the keeper of the wine-shop next door: a short, plump man with a face perpetually rosy from imbibing his own wares. He sat all day behind a high counter in the narrow shop lined with huge black barrels full of wine and *raki* (the Cretan version of schnapps) and whenever he saw us passing by he would smile and beckon to us, using that Greek come-here gesture that became so familiar: the arm extended, palm down, the hand sharply dropped as though swatting a fly in mid-air. And the insistent *'Ella, ella'* (Come here)'. And there was nothing for it but to go in and have another free sample He seemed to take positive delight in giving us credit, and thanks to him our huge wicker demijohn was always well-supplied with the sharp, dark red wine of Sitia. We quickly acquired the local habit of drinking wine with all meals, not only because we liked it, but because it was cheaper than anything else. Neither of these tradesmen, nor any others, even made us feel guilty about our credit; on the contrary they seemed honoured that we asked for it.

We began to feel that we had joined the best and biggest company in the world—the blessed poor, who are the salt of the earth. Greece is a wonderful country to live in when you are short of funds, for poverty here is the normal condition, whereas in the north it is regarded as a sign of failure or of moral deficiency. Of course, Inga and I were only poor in a relative way; compared with the really poor we were wealthy indeed, for we never lacked hope and the possibility, the expectation of more income was always before us. And to live thus, young and optimistic, is quite another matter from being totally bereft of all hope, which is the lot of most of the world's poor.

In Crete there is hardship, there is austerity, but no one is made to doubt his own value as a human being because of it. Then, too, the Cretan peasant eating his beans, his vegetables and his dark bread is partaking of richly nutritious foods straight from his own soil. Even the poorest have their olive oil, their lemon juice to sprinkle liberally over everything, and their wine—even though it may be rough and sharp. These are the necessities: and it is a rare Cretan indeed who hasn't got them. Cretan poverty can be survived: it does not break the spirit. Nikos Kazantzakis expressed it well when he quoted an old islander who said: 'A poor man is someone who fears poverty. I do not fear it'.

Our combined income never exceeded £18 (fifty dollars) a month during our first half-year in Crete; after that, I began to sell a few stories and articles, and our income rose gradually until finally we became almost rich—by local standards. Fifty dollars a month may not seem much for two people to live on, but in Greece that is fifteen hundred drachmas; labourers were earning only fifty drachmas a day, out of which they had to support their entire families—and they didn't work every day, either. After paying our rent we had twelve hundred drachmas, £14 (forty dollars) to eat on, and it was enough. We were never hungry and never badly nourished. We ate the foods of the country, and loved them. We quickly discovered which foods were cheap and tasty: the little fish called *marides* which were delicious when fried and eaten whole, heads and bones and all, and were so cheap that an ample supply for two people could be obtained for about five drachmas; and octopus and squid and other inky fish which were fine either fried or else stewed in their own ink; and yogurt and goat cheese (*feta*) and the sort of cream cheese called *myzitra.* Olive oil, the best we had ever tasted, replaced butter in all our cooking—like so many other elements of the Cretan diet, it was not only less expensive than what we had been used to before, but healthier. Fruits and vegetables were always plentiful, varying according to the season. Late in the winter oranges, the sweetest and juiciest imaginable, were hawked for next to nothing from the backs of trucks that brought them from the orange groves of western Crete. And we learned to love the wild greens that Cretan women pick. Some of these, such as dandelion and mustard greens, were known to me from boyhood visits to my grandparents' farm, but there were many others we had never seen before. All went under the blanket name of *horta*—though each variety had its own name too. Eventually Inga learned to identify many of them, and often went out to pick them herself. Cooked and served with olive oil, garlic, and sprinkled with lemon juice, they were enough to make a whole meal, together with plenty of bread and wine (and in fact the poorer peasants eat little else, for months on end).

Preoccupation with food is part of the price that must be paid for poverty. Starving men are said to dream of huge meals. Perhaps that is why the Cretans take every opportunity to nibble at something— because they know what it is to be without. They chew on dried chick peas, roasted pumpkin seeds or sunflower seeds, fruits, even rusks or bits of hard bread '*paximadia*' when there is nothing else. The women constantly pick, pick, pick away like so many hens grubbing for their chicks; in the country, you come upon their black-clad figures everywhere—old and young, they search for *horta* or harvest snails on rainy days, or gather wild fruits. The men, too, play their part in the endless food ritual: they are the ones who usually buy the meat for special occasions, and they love to select choice fruits when they are in company, peeling the pears or apples or oranges expertly, then dividing them into little titbits and distributing them to every member of the company.

Taking our cue from the poorer peasants, we ate little meat: as a cheap and tasty substitute we could always have a sort of stew of beans or lentils, mixed with tomatoes, parsley and, of course, garlic. Eaten every day, it might have become monotonous, but it was comforting to know that when the cupboard was bare of all else, we could fall back on the familiar beans and lentils—and 'bean days' became our designation for those times when money was running low and we had to count every single drachma. And, of course, if a meal was short on other things, it could always be filled out with bread: in Crete it is still truly 'the staff of life'. It must be eaten with every meal, even when the bulk of the meal is something starchy, like macaroni or potatoes. To the Cretans, bread *is* the meal, everything else mere dressing. Nearly every aspect of its baking and eating is governed by some ancient ritual or superstition. Unfortunately, bread has become mixed up with social and economic striving, so that the middle-class townspeople—and those who aspire to that exalted status—despise the coarse, whole-grain country bread, favouring instead a tasteless white loaf that tries hard to be as insipid as American bread. The dark bread, which ranks with the best in the world, actually costs less than the inferior white kind—which is perhaps one reason why the poor villagers are healthier than the town-dwellers. (It is necessary to distinguish between the different kinds of dark bread available in Crete. In the towns, a dark loaf is made by the bakers that is usually quite wholesome and tasty, but which contains some white flour mixed in. The best bread of all—to our taste—is found only in villages; and the more remote the village, the better the bread. This country bread or *starenyo* is baked by the peasant women in their own ovens, using only whole-grain flour made from wheat grown in their own fields, and ground at the nearest mill. Some of it is baked into thick, round, heavy loaves that last for weeks; while some is dried into *paximadia* or rusks that will keep indefinitely—they are rock-hard until soaked in water, when they become soft and edible. We liked both kinds—though we never once met a villager who believed us when we said so.)

Bean Days

We first learned about Cretan food habits, and attitudes and opinions in general, from the family that shared their house with us. We rented the top floor two rooms, kitchen and terrace—and the ground floor was occupied by the Levendis family and by tenants in two or three small rooms, mostly schoolchildren from outlying villages who lived in town during the gymnasium term. 'Levendis' is a sort of honorary nickname bestowed on a man who has spirit or *kefi* plus good looks, bravery and perhaps a sense of honour. The father of the present head of the household had earned the name for his personal qualities and had passed it on to his progeny—while neglecting to bequeath the characteristics that went with it. The current Levendis was a stoop-shouldered little man with white hair and a quick, furtive glance, perpetually harried and bullied by his wife, Kyria Ireni. Inga, with a typical woman's perception of the telling domestic detail, was the first to notice that one could always tell when Kyria Ireni was addressing her husband: her voice became a note shriller and took on the insistence of a pneumatic drill hammering at a hard pavement. The couple had two children. The daughter, Photinoula or 'Little Light,' was thirtyish and plump when they finally married her off, on the very day of our arrival, to a curly-haired man named Costas. The son had been married for some time and had a little boy, Ioannis, who was often with his grandparents. He seemed to have inherited some of Kyria Ireni's formidable will power plus his great-grandfather's Levendis spirit, unfortunately expressed at this stage of his development in screams and tantrums that were the despair of the whole household. Their greatest worry was that he never wanted to eat, and this caused the utmost concern to all—including neighbours and tenants—for Greeks like to display fat children; it adds to their social prestige and is a mark of affluence. Kyria Ireni, fat though she was, had to chase after him at mealtimes with a plate of food and a spoon; sometimes she would catch him on our terrace, where he had taken refuge, and there she would force-feed him as Alsatian peasants stuff their geese.

The Levendis family had a small shop in town where shoes were sold and repaired. Whenever we passed that way, the old man would call us in and send out for coffee or drinks; and then he would ask a hundred questions about life in our countries—Sweden and America. Did we have coffee-houses where the men could sit and read the papers and play cards? No?—But how did the men pass their time? We told him they sit at home in the evenings. 'What, with the women?' he exclaimed, but I don't think he quite believed it. He was equally surprised to hear that daughters have no dowries in the odd north: 'But how do their parents find husbands for them?' We said they marry for love, and he said 'Po-po-po' which is Greek for 'Tch-tch-tch', and gave the gesture of wonder and disapproval, shaking his right hand as though he had washed it and didn't have a towel.

Levendis spent most of his time in his favourite *kafeneion*; on the rare occasions when a customer came in and wished to look at shoes the shop was usually empty, and neighbouring tradesmen would shout across the street for the old man. How this languishing business could support a family of six or more was a deep mystery. But of course, like so many Cretans, they had varied resources: the rooms they rented out; their garden; a goat that gave milk; the inevitable chickens; a boat used for fishing. And pigs—penned up somewhere in the labyrinth of rooms and stables beneath our kitchen. When the weather was damp, we smelled them. Every now and then Costas and Levendis selected a pig to be butchered and sold. Then they had to push and pull the screaming beast out of the narrow passageway and into the street, assisted usually by Kyria Ireni and the little grandson and any other children who happened to be about. The grunts and whimpers would fade away as they drove the doomed pig up the rocky hill across the way, walking the last mile to the slaughterhouse which was (mercifully) out of sight beyond the rocks.

There was a yellow kitten in the Levendis garden, a derelict with a limp, perpetually afraid of the big tom-cats that prowled through like lions on the hunt. He more or less belonged to the household, but they took little notice of him. 'It will die,' said Kyria Ireni with a shrug. We called 'Puss, Puss' and he learned to come to the garden corner below our kitchen, where he looked up and meowed for his handout of food. He was timid at first, and for a long time he wouldn't come up on our terrace, but one day we lured him there with a dish of yoghurt, which he loved. It was a great occasion when, a few days later, we coaxed him inside the house. After that our relationship grew apace. As we were now indisputably in possession of a cat—in so far as anyone can ever 'possess' one of these independent creatures—we thought we had better give him a proper name. I happened to be reading Pushkin just then, and as that sounded something like the 'Puss, Puss' he had grown used to, we promptly baptized him after the Russian poet.

Just a normal, cute kitten might have bored us, but Pushkin had a personality of his own; he was a character—a Thurber cat. The interesting thing about him was that he was neurotic; all that bullying by bigger cats, those nights of terror holed up in a bush or under rocks, had left their mark on him. We thought he would never learn to hunt. But one day when he was half-grown he disrupted our midday meal by leaping through the open terrace window on to our table with a live rat dangling from his mouth. During the vivid moments that ensued, I chased him into the bedroom with a broom; the rat broke loose and ran squealing under the bed; and finally Pushkin recovered his prey and disappeared through the window in one great leap. At the top of the stairs he paused to look back with hurt pride and reproach. After that we ceased worrying about him.

Our life was taking shape: we had a family; we had a cat; nor did we lack for friends. The first and best of these was a doctor named Zographakis, who had a practice in town although he came originally from the nearby village of Limnes. Though he had never been out of Greece, having received his medical education in Athens during the war, he spoke German well and English passably, and he made almost a hobby of 'collecting' foreigners—a hobby which, in those days, he had little opportunity to practice, for tourists strayed through only rarely.

'Doc'—as his foreigners called him—was a middle-aged, slim, dark man with kindly eyes that twinkled with humour but also had a touch of sadness that made him attractive to women. The look of melancholy might have had its origin in a long-drawn-out and frustrated love he had borne for a lady of the town. In love with each other for years, they had been kept apart because her father—a rich businessman—was against her marrying a former village boy. Finally, when the father died, Doc was close to fifty and the lady had reached the mid-thirties; but still they had to wait a year, the minimum period of mourning. They were married at last, towards the end of our first year there; and within another year they had a son. Fatherhood, especially of a boy, is the ambition of every Greek; the final crown of manhood and proof of virility; and to achieve it at forty-plus is especially gratifying.

The doctor's office was on a side street just off the main square. It consisted of a front room with a door that was always open directly on to the street, and an inner examination room with windows looking towards the distant sea. The front room had a desk, two bookcases and some chairs; its chief ornament and attraction was a collection of seashells, starfish and other marine curiosities displayed atop the biggest bookcase. This was the consulting room, waiting room and place of general sociability. Doc had no nurse and no secretary, so contact with patients was direct and immediate— they just walked right in off the street and started talking to him, without waiting their turn. Privacy is not a commodity that is valued in Crete, and so the patients seemed not to mind expounding their symptoms before a roomful of people. Some seemed positively to enjoy having an audience, and would act out their ailments with appropriate groans and gestures. The old village women would hobble in, full of aches and moans, and after several minutes of complaining about their miseries to the company at large, they would listen to a few words of sympathy from the other patients and advice from Doc, and perhaps accept a few pills, and then they would leave, looking better already. It was almost like group therapy.

Many of the pills which Doc distributed so liberally to his friends were free samples sent by pharmaceutical companies; they were scattered about the office and in the drawers of his desk—a sample for nearly every type of malady that could occur locally. Actually, a Cretan doctor does not require an extensive repertory of remedies, for most of the island's illnesses are of the upper respiratory type, and various intestinal infections. 'Grippe' and colds are prevalent in all seasons, especially in spring and autumn. Cretans are generally very healthy specimens indeed, apart from their perpetual sniffles and sneezes. These illnesses, like the cold weather and the winds, came as a surprise to us; I suppose that, like most northerners, we had imagined the Aegean climate to be subtropical. The constantly changing weather, plus the universal lack of any concepts of hygiene, probably accounts for the prevalence of colds. (Men spit on floors; people sneeze in one another's faces; hands are seldom washed and yet the ritual handshake occurs every time you meet a friend on the street and when you enter and leave a house—practices that do not exactly inhibit the spreading of germs.) Inga and I, though generally healthy, had our share of the cold bugs; in particular, we came to dread a sort of virus that stole upon us insidiously and then lasted for weeks; you felt below-par all the time, without actually being ill enough to go to bed. We named this mysterious malady 'the Cretan Grippe', but Doc called it 'the Sun Grippe' because, so he claimed, it was caused by sitting in the sun in mid-winter (always potent, even then) and then going inside, where you immediately became chilled in the unheated rooms with stone floors.

Most of the loungers in Doc's office at any given time would not be patients, but friends and acquaintances who had dropped in for a chat. Invariably these callers would be offered something: a Turkish coffee, a glass of *ouzo* (aniseed-flavoured liquor) or *raki,* or a *gazoza* as carbonated drinks were called. Just down the street was a *kafeneion* which must have derived a substantial income from Doc's patronage, for at all hours of the day and night waiters in their white aprons were dashing back and forth with their little trays. Doc could always summon a waiter simply by hailing a passing boy; the young lads and teenagers are the universal messengers and errand-runners of Greek towns.

Doc loved to discourse with foreign visitors on his favourite topics: cameras, Cretan handicrafts, Greek foods and how to eat them, peculiarities of the peasants. Of cameras we heard a great deal in those early days, for Doc wanted to buy one, but couldn't decide which make would be best. He sent for literally hundreds of brochures from all the leading photographic manufacturers of the western world, plus Japan, and kept them all in his desk ready for perusal at odd moments. The foreign visitor, five minutes after being introduced, might be asked to render an opinion on the relative merits of Brand A and Brand B; and if he had a camera of his own, Doc would examine it with a minute care that few of his patients received. This whole problem was solved finally when a group of his friends got together and presented him with a 35 mm camera on his name-day. The solution, however, proved temporary, for he was soon in the throes of deciding about 'moving up' to a more complex model.

The Cretan handiwork was of greater interest to most visitors. Colourful woven handbags, rugs, blankets, pillow-covers and shawls in intricate designs that varied from village to village comprised the collection; some of them were more than a hundred years old and of great beauty. They were stored temporarily in drawers in the examination room, but the doctor's ambition was to house them in a museum.

Doc was a man of natural generosity and kindliness, one of the few people I have ever met who could truly put himself in the place of others, and therefore anticipate their needs. He was beloved of the peasant patients, of whom he saw many; for, in addition to his private practice, he served as the official doctor, which meant a heavy load of people too poor to pay and being treated on their government insurance. Cretans personalise everything and so Doc, even though he treated them in his official capacity, was the beneficiary of a constant stream of offerings from the grateful villagers; choice cheeses, baskets of juicy snails (Cretan snails are famous all over the Levant, and formerly were exported to Smyrna and elsewhere), oranges and lemons and various vegetables. Many of these items he promptly passed along to us in our time of need; without his generosity, we would have had many more 'Bean Days.'

3

The Town of Tired Heroes

Ayios Nikolaos is fortunate in its setting. It occupies a promontory jutting into Merabello Bay, with the Sitia mountains facing it to the east, and the foot-hills of the Dikte range rising behind. From a distance it looks like everyone's dream of a Mediterranean fishing port: a cluster of pastel-tinted houses around a miniature harbour where high-prowed caiques line the breakwater. But as you approach closer a feeling of vague and ill-defined disappointment takes over. Somehow the style, the grace and colour that you would expect to find in a small port on one of the Aegean islands, or in a French or Spanish fishing village, are missing. Partly this is because the town is new, having been built up within the past hundred years; one misses the picturesque quality that other Cretan towns—Herakleion, Rethymnon, Canea—derive from their Venetian and Turkish houses and fortifications. Under Venice, Ayios Nikolaos was only a minor port with a castle, of which nothing remains; in antiquity it was merely the harbour of Lato, a Dorian city on a hill a few miles inland. The older houses, dating from the turn of the century or thereabouts, are nondescript: two-storey, square and solid, with iron-railed balconies and roofs of tile. Here and there a modern horror has intruded, garish with clashing colours, often featuring the egregious pseudo-Minoan columns inspired by the restorations of Sir Arthur Evans at Knossos. One of the most eye-searing of these monstrosities is the home of a local architect. There is also a cinema house that is a collection of candy-box tints ranging from peppermint pink to pistachio green—the result of someone's misuse of a 'colour wheel' sent out by a sadistic German paint manufacturer.

The main street is pleasant: a clean, quiet, acacia-shaded avenue of shops and cafés that runs from the little square on a hill where the buses stop, down to the harbourfront. But step one block off it, and you are confronted with dismal dusty squares piled with rubbish, with streets that peter out in a no-man's-land of pot-holes and backyards. Half a block in another direction, north of the main street, there is a little lake, nearly enclosed by steep rocky sides, connected with the harbour by a narrow channel that passes under a bridge. This lake of Voulismeni, said to be bottomless, is the Local Beauty Spot, and it is regarded as such a curiosity that people come from other towns in Crete to look at it. Around one side a charming little park with paths and benches and peacock pens has been built; and a tasteful and unobtrusive stone building houses the tourist information office. Boats are tied up along the seaward bank; a palm tree rises on the quay. It is all very pleasant and peaceful—or was, until the town fathers conceived the grandiose idea of 'illuminating' the lake; for now its banks are festooned with glaring light bulbs, and it has become a magnet for noisy crowds.

If you wander about Ayios Nikolaos looking for hidden corners of beauty and charm, you will give up in half an hour and return to the port, depressed by the ugliness that lurks everywhere, ready to pounce on you unawares. The local people are not affected by it; they seem crippled in their aesthetic sense—and in fairness to them I must add that this condition seems to be the rule all over modern Greece. They have other criteria for judging their community. Take, for example, that foul-smelling olive oil factory that stands on the edge of town, polluting one of the best beaches with its black effusions. Most foreigners are shocked by it; but the natives swell with civic pride every time they pass—because a real factory with smoke-stacks and all is a mark of the town or city; mere villages don't have such industrial wonders.

Although its population is less than four thousand, Ayios Nikolaos is classified as a *demos* or municipality by virtue of its position as the capital of the Nome of Lassithi (one of the four provinces into which Crete is divided); and the fact that it is by far the smallest of the provincial capitals, and that it is exceeded in size by a number of country towns and even by some villages, only makes the townspeople more sensitive about their status. Greek local pride is always intense and touchy; and it was all the more so in this town 'on the way up'. It was afflicted with that deadly fever, so well known in America: the 'booster spirit'. From the Mayor on down, all the leading officials and businessmen were burning with a desire to build up the town—and incidentally to make some profits while they were at it. And I am bound to add that their efforts have been successful, especially in the years since we left, which have witnessed the construction of the first Cretan beach-bungalow hotels and with them a tremendous increase in tourism. In fact, the sleepy port that we knew has been transformed into a thriving tourist centre.

Winds of Crete

It was some time during the latter half of the last century that the town first became known as a refuge for tired heroes—that is, for fugitives from vengeance in the blood feuds of other districts. Among the present population, there are a number of families that 'emigrated' from Sphakia, a region of western Crete still famous for its outlawry and feuding. Some of them were told by the police that they had to leave, and so rather than abandon Crete entirely they travelled as far east as they could on the long, narrow island, putting a hundred miles or more between themselves and the scenes of their misdeeds. One of these Sphakians, a plump, short man of middle age with a dainty curl over his forehead and the mild manner of a clergyman, was rumoured to have killed several men. The only killing he makes today is on the tourist trade, for he owns a *taverna* right on the best beach, a place that was quite deserted until a big international hotel company moved in and built the bungalows. Even before this bonanza, the Sphakian displayed a tendency to overcharge the occasional foreigners who strayed into his web; at one time the situation became so outrageous that the civic leaders talked to him about the need for charging only established prices, for the long-range good of the business community as a whole. He mildly agreed, and went on overcharging; for the one thing no Cretan will ever do is to sacrifice a temporary advantage, however slight, in the interest of an uncertain future.

A nearby *taverna* was run by another refugee from the wild west of Crete, but he was of another sort than the Sphakian: sly upon occasion, quite capable of cheating but equally capable of lavish generosity with his food and drinks if he took to you. I like to think that he was a more typical Cretan, in that his natural warmth and good humour balanced the lies and trickery. For these, we couldn't blame him: all Cretans live by them. An 'honest Cretan' is a contradiction in terms, for a Cretan is by definition a liar and always has been. The tradition goes all the way back to ancient times, when Epimenides posed the riddle:'All Cretans are liars; Epimenides is a Cretan; is Epimenides a liar?' The answer is Yes, he was a liar if he was a Cretan—and never mind the riddle, which is just a clever bit of typically Cretan trickery designed to hide the truth. 'A Cretan needs lies as he needs air,' we were told on more than one occasion. Everybody lies to everybody else, continually and effortlessly. Parents lie to their children every hour of the day; workers lie to their employers; teachers to their pupils; priests to their flocks; and the politicians to everybody. If George Washington had been a Cretan national hero, that little fable about the cherry tree would have ended differently; in the Cretan version, he would have said: 'Father, I cannot tell a lie: I didn't chop down the cherry tree—it was the neighbour boy who did it.' The only Cretans who do not practice deception are the very simplest sort: some fishermen and some of the poorer shepherds and others rustics—and they only because they haven't the sophistication for it. The Anglo-Saxon in me never quite accepted all this trickery; I always liked the honest simpletons best.

Perhaps that is one reason why we preferred their company whenever we had a choice. In Ayios Nikolaos, around the harbour, there were some smoky little *tavernas* patronized by fishermen and sailors—places with sawdust on the stone floors, raucous with the voices of bronzed and mustachioed men in high-necked, dark blue wool sweaters. They made a great deal of noise as they slammed their cards on bare wooden tables (there were always several games going on), tossed down their drinks, and called for more. From scratchy phonographs the *bouzouki* music—named after the mandolin-like instrument that accompanies it—wailed forth its erotic caterwaulings: monotonous and rather oriental to western ears, but rich in rhythmic and sensuous appeal. Often in the evenings the seamen would do their strange gyrating dances, either alone or in circles with hands linked. No one (except foreigners) took any note of the solo performances; anyone was free to get up on the inspiration of the moment and launch himself into what, to the eyes of the uninitiated, looked like some old form of yoga exercises done to music. The dancers' faces usually had a look of rapt concentration, and there was a trance-like quality in their agonised contortions as they turned, twisted, bent over nearly double: always in slow motion, snapping their fingers and never losing the sense of rhythm and balance. The purely Cretan dances were seldom seen in these taverns; the spirit was cosmopolitan, part of the great Greek waterfront that extends throughout the islands and into every harbour of the watery kingdom.

Natural psychological releases seem to be built into Greek life in many ways. Those dances, for instance: what a wonderful release of tension and frustration! Real dancing—that is, with plenty of rhythm and movement, not just a public display of adolescent sexuality like most of our modern dances—has always been an essential activity of man, a means of expression available to all. Greece and some other Balkans countries still have it; and they need it, for theirs are restless, active spirits. The twiddling of amber or black rosary-like 'worry beads' *(komboloy)* is another harmless activity that keeps men occupied. Yet another is eating roast pumpkin seeds—*passatempi* or 'time-passers'—; it requires considerable skill to open the narrow hulls with one's teeth and extract the seed, using only one hand—or in the case of some experts, no hands.

These waterfront places served up wonderful snacks of grilled octopus or fried baby squid, and fresh salads with good dark bread and strong red wine. (The resinated white wine of Attica is less popular on Crete). Two could eat well for less than twenty drachmas, and drinks of *ouzo* or fiery *raki* cost a mere one drachma each, and the price always included a little snack known as a *meze* which might be a bit of grilled octopus, a piece of cheese or a tomato or cucumber impaled on toothpicks. The Cretans never drink without eating. There was surprisingly little drunkenness in these cafés, although the men certainly drank a lot by most standards. The food they consumed with the drinks, the activities of dancing and moving about, and the purity of alcoholic beverages distilled naturally without additives—all combined to make drinking a more healthful activity than it usually is in other countries, and less fraught with danger of a hangover.

Those were the places that throbbed with life and colour. There you would meet fishermen and the like; but never, under any circumstances would you encounter one of the town's business or professional men. They had their own cafés, which presented a striking contrast to the waterfront establishments. No dancing here, and no *bouzouki* music either; but there was plenty of card-playing, newspaper-reading, and drinking of tiny cups of black Turkish coffee. The patrons were for the most part well-fed, white-faced, soft and often stout; clad always in dark suits. Some of them sported little finger-nails that had been allowed to grow two or three inches long, as a mark of their superiority to manual labour. Dark glasses were favoured by many—even indoors, even after dark (how they managed to read the fine print of Greek newspapers, in the dim light of a café, is a question that perhaps could be answered only by their oculists).

Then there was the Club. It occupied a square stone building, rather new and being added to and repaired most of the time we were there, facing the waterfront 'boulevard' a couple of minutes' walk from the harbour—but worlds away in mood and spirit. Here, in an atmosphere of fearful gloom and boredom, aspiring bank clerks could rub shoulders with the local Four Hundred—and could hope to meet their daughters, with their enviable dowries. Here, on week-ends, Lola the daughter of the richest man in town played the piano while everybody else played cards. She was a sad-eyed, thin-faced, thirty-ish virgin pining away in a country where sex morality is regulated with utmost rigour and a girl is never left alone with a young man for a moment, where 'dates' are unheard of. The poor girl had no prospects of finding a husband because there was no available male who could match her dowry. An admiring bank clerk sent her notes and gazed with moonsick eyes upon her, but he was not considered a good match because he came from a humble village family, though he was bright and could expect one day to become a bank director in some provincial town. Poor Lola—she was like nothing so much as one of Chekhov's Three Sisters, lost and forlorn among the army officers, the provincial governor and his staff, the doctors and lawyers and the local beauties.

Early during our stay we noticed that everything seems to be intensified in Crete; just as the potent sunlight brings out colours and patterns of landscape that would be lost in the dimmer light of more northerly climes, so human qualities, passions, peculiarities are thrown into sharp relief against the basic primitivism of the island's life. Everything tends to be reduced to its basic elements, to black-and-white, bedrock simplicity; as a sculpture by Brancusi of a bird or a fish reveals the essence of all birds and all fish, so human character is revealed in Crete. Taste Cretan rage, Cretan joy, Cretan perfidy, and you feel that you have sampled the essence of those qualities that would be diluted elsewhere. A totally unexpected effect of this was that Ayios Nikolaos, which should have been an ordinary provincial capital, one of tens of thousands the world over, became the epitome of all such towns: the most bourgeois place in the whole world; bourgeois—that is, pretentious, money-minded, hypocritical, hostile to things natural or aesthetic—to the point of caricature. Even a man who was rumoured to be the local 'Red Boss,' a man who had spent time in prison for his leftist activities during the civil war—even he turned out to be just another dry goods merchant with the soul of a merchant, whom a kinder heart and perhaps a keener intelligence than most had turned into a socialist of sorts, and yet the most *bourgeois* socialist I have ever met.

The townfolk came into their own on the Sunday evening *volta* or promenade. The men would be in their dark suits, white shirts and ties, and their narrow pointed shoes were always shined to a high gloss. The women put on their most expensive dresses and high spike heels, and they all carried enormous handbags: white in summer, black in winter. The children in their white nylon dresses and miniature men's suits were like little dummies of their parents. Then

33

they would stroll out along the harbour boulevard, towards Ammoudi beach, past the *tavernas* and the Club, past the town toilet which had been boarded up because nobody knew how to use it properly and after its first week it had looked like a barnyard and smelled worse, past the pseudo-Minoan columns of the architect's showcase house—and then a sudden about-face and back towards the town. Nothing free or rambling about these walks; the course was as rigidly prescribed as the uniform. Back and forth they would go, arms linked, chatting and laughing, greeting friends. It was similar to the *paseo* in Spain or the *corso* in Dalmatia; the formal public walk is a general custom in Mediterranean lands. My first reaction was to think how charming it was—how much healthier and saner than the American habit of piling into cars and roaring about on crowded highways. But after participating in it a few times, I came to loathe the *volta* and could not be dragged to it; if some engagement required me to venture out on those nights, I would take elaborate detours over back streets to avoid it. What I couldn't stand was the naked pretence, the arrant display of clothing and jewellery, the arrogance of rank and social position, real or fancied. Cretan intensification again: these qualities are present in every society, only here it seemed more so. I can see them still, parading up and down, while dusk falls on Merabello Bay, while the sunset gold creeps down the unearthly Sitia mountains—unnoticed. No one is less aware of nature than the modern town Greeks: they are far too busy studying one another or staring at strangers to notice sunset effects or any other natural thing.

Classical scholars, travel writers and others tend to wax romantic about the similarities between ancient Greece and the modern country that bears the same name. The game of parallels between ancient and modern is a fascinating one, which I have played often myself: but is there any truth in it? On *volta* nights I found it hard to believe that there could be any relation between these strutting snobs and the free artistic souls that created the Acropolis or, on this very soil of Crete, the Knossos frescoes. But perhaps there is more in this than meets the eye, for a careful reading of certain classics (the books themselves and not the commentaries on them by writers starry-eyed about the past) reveals that the ancients did possess qualities in abundance that are shared by the modern mob. We know that loved display and ostentation (the Parthenon was gaudily painted; Olympia was as vulgar and commercialised then as it is today). Thucydides above all is the great source for their political characteristics (and for the characteristics of politics everywhere).

He makes quite clear how they envied their superiors, and in many cases were not content until they had pulled them down. Then as now the Greeks tended towards extremes and were ever susceptible to the oratory of demagogues. Their periods of democracy alternated with spells of tyranny. We are inclined to forget that Spartans were just as much Greeks as Athenians—and even Athens became tyrannical, as Thucydides is honest enough to show us. Perhaps we are all too romantic about ancient Greeks, as D. H. Lawrence was about his Etruscans. Would-be social critics and prophets find these safely-buried utopias useful as examples for scolding their contemporaries. And escapists who go off to live on remote islands make a similar error when they idealise the 'happy natives'. I was determined to avoid that pitfall—and Ayios Nikolaos with its Club and its *volta* nights, and the unconscious Aristophanean buffoonery of its bourgeois élite, was making it easy for me.

4

Merabello Villages

But for consolation there was the countryside. Hardly a day passed without our taking a walk somewhere, and as spring advanced we explored the whole district of Merabello in a series of short, one-or-two-day excursions. We would pack a little food—bread and cheese and boiled eggs—and a bottle of wine in a knapsack, and set out on foot. Sometimes we were offered lifts—there was little traffic on the roads, but the few cars that did come along invariably stopped for us.

The first of these spring excursions occurred on a bright day in mid-February. Already the worst of the winter gloom was behind us: the days were lengthening, the midday sun was warmer, and the quality of the light was changing, growing more intense. In the glory of returning spring we walked out through the town—past the roaring electric generator, past the slaughterhouse and the olive oil factory—and then suddenly we were surrounded only by silence and sunshine, with thyme and marjoram scenting the air. We passed the little chapel and graveyard with its slender cypresses, and came upon a white shingle beach backed by shady tamarisks and a solitary stone hut that was occupied by a blind man who sold *ouzo* and wine to the fishermen who frequently came here to draw in their nets. The clear water gurgled on the rocks—inviting even in February. This was one of our favourite swimming places; but on this day we were bound farther afield, and so we walked on, and soon came to a wide smooth sandy beach with springs of brackish water and a forest of tall rushes where many sea-birds dwelt. There was a lone palm tree, and a chapel on a hill, and nothing else—except for some obscene squatting pillboxes of grey concrete: relics of World War Two. The Venetians ruled Crete for 465 years; the Turks for 200; the Nazis, boasting of their '1,000-Year-Reich', barely managed to hold the island for three years. But even during that short time they were able to erect hundreds of indestructible gun emplacements—monuments of German efficiency that probably will stand as long as Knossos, and may puzzle archaeologists of the fiftieth century. Perhaps they will be 'restored' in bright colours and opened to tourists; for the present, they serve as latrines for the whole countryside, and as occasional shelters for sheep and goats.

Here we picked up the main road—if such it could be called, for the principal east-west highway of Crete was unpaved from Ayios Nikolaos eastward, and as we hiked along the winding gravel road, with no signs of traffic from either direction, we felt far from the main streams of the world's commerce. An hour's brisk walking brought us to Kalo Horio, the 'Good Village'. It lay back from the sea, like many Cretan communities, for through long periods of its history the island has been plagued by pirates; to live near the coast was to invite pillage. Down by the sea, there was nothing but a long sandy strand, a semi-derelict stone pier, a chapel and some huts used for sheltering animals. And almonds—thousands of the little trees in full blossom. Whiter than the white chapel in the blazing light of midday, they would take on a pinkish-violet cast when seen in the warm golden light of late afternoon. We wandered among the groves, intoxicated by their smell, lulled by the buzzing of bees out gathering the incomparable almond honey.

In the distance we discerned a group of people working among the fields. One or two of the men shouted and waved at us. We were worried—could it be that we were trespassing on someone's land and they were warning us to get away? Our apprehension increased when one of the men came bounding over to us, all the time waving and shouting, 'Come here, come here!' Hardly knowing what to expect, we followed him back to his field. About a dozen peasants stood about waiting for us. The whole family was out planting onions: grandfather and grandmother, several brothers and sisters, and a baby lying contentedly in a basket among the spring flowers. Far from scolding us for trespassing, they wished to invite us to join them for their midday meal. The women spread thick white woollen cloaks on the ground and motioned us to be seated. They had built a fire and were cooking lunch in a huge blackened pot. When it was ready, they gave us spoons and offered the usual words of welcome: *'Kalos orisate!'*—to which we responded: *'Kalos sas vrikame!'* ('It is well we have found you'.) These ritual words of greeting and response were among the first Greek phrases we had learned; it would hardly be possible to travel in Crete without them.

The main dish was a stew of beans, onions, garlic and tomatoes, with plenty of dark bread and red wine to go with it. Fresh lettuce was picked on the spot, washed with water from a big earthen jug, and served plain with coarse sea salt; a better salad couldn't be imagined. Though some might have called the meal frugal, for us it was sumptuous—for food never tastes as good as it does out of doors, when you have been walking or working. We felt grateful to these people for the food and the welcome, and they in their turn seemed equally grateful to us for breaking the monotony of their work and providing a topic of discussion. As we strolled away— after the usual formal handshakes all around—we heard them analysing our peculiarities.

Beyond Kalo Horio the south side of the bay curves around to meet the mountains, and just before the shoreline makes its sharp turn northwards, where the road to Sitia snakes high up on the mountainside, there is a fishing village called Pachia Ammos (literally, 'Thick Sand'). This is the narrowest part of Crete, where only a low-lying isthmus less than ten miles wide seperates the Cretan and Libyan seas. Through this gap in the mountainous spine of Crete the sirocco winds blow with the fury of hurricanes; we had often sat on our terrace and watched them coming from afar. Now, on this day which had started so clear and blue, we saw ahead of us the first sign of south wind: a puff of cloud blowing past Pachia Ammos. But we were still sheltered by the mountains, not having reached the isthmus, and so we felt little wind as we watched the clouds fill up the whole pass, and the dust-laden mass rushed northward into the bay and churned up a mass of white-caps.

Before Pachia Ammos, the road sweeps around an apparently deserted hillside. This is Gournia, where the American archaeologist Harriet Boyd, with her colleagues and a crew of Cretans, uncovered in the early years of this century a complete Minoan town. We followed the ancient streets up the hill, to the small square and the foundations of a modest palace. These tiny houses, cramped close together along narrow alleys, had been the homes and workshops of craftsmen and artisans—carpenters, coppersmiths, potters—whose tools and products are now on display in the Archaeological Museum in Herakleion. The distinction of Gournia is that it is such a humble place, in contrast to the grandeur and wealth of the Minoan palaces at Knossos, Phaestos and Mallia. At Knossos they found jewellery, a throne, a royal bathtub; at Gournia, axes, saws, chisels, a forge, an olive oil press. It requires little imagination to picture it as it must have been some 3,500 years ago: very like any modern Cretan village of the poorer sort.

The site itself was lovely on that hot spring day with a breath of south wind in the air, and we spent a couple of hours wandering among the ruins, all alone, seeing them much as the first archaeologists must have. The air was silent save for the tinkling of goat and sheep bells and the buzzing of bees among the millions of bright red anemones and yellow ranunculi that grew everywhere, in all the crevices of the walls and in the foundations of the houses.

* * *

By the middle of March the returning sun had become so hot that the peasants regarded it as an enemy that would burn and blacken their skins. When we began to swim and sun-bathe, Inga's rapidly acquired sun-tan, which would have been the envy of anyone just arriving from the cold north, aroused much worry on the part of the neighbour women. Photinoula, our landlord's daughter, lamented: 'Oh, *why* must you go in the sun when your skin is so white? White skin is more *aristocratic*'. She herself took no chances on losing her pasty complexion—she never ventured out without covering her head with a scarf. Children were protected from the sun by having red ribbons tied around their necks or wrists.

All through the cold weeks of winter we had sat in our house, swathed in sweaters, hunched over a little *mangali* or charcoal burner which gave off more headache-inducing fumes than heat. We had read a great deal, and talked even more—told each other our whole life stories, shared the most intimate details of our lives in that dim period before we knew each other. During that brief Cretan winter our spirits grew together until we felt that we were but two halves of the same personality. Now, with the sap of spring in our veins, our souls expanded until the four walls of our little house were no longer large enough to hold them. The Kalo Horio excursion in February had whetted our appetites for more. In whatever direction we chose to go, something delightful and intriguing awaited us, so we simply chose a name we liked: *Elounda*.

We set our faces for the tier of gaunt buff hills that hemmed in Ayios Nikolaos to the northwest. The road led past a narrow cove where rotting hulks of fishing boats lay at their last rest, and where more war relics—rusting landing craft—were half submerged and wholly forgotten. Flowers bloomed in the dry land: the anemones of winter now giving way to the dazzling poppies and daisies of spring. An hour's hike took us to a pass at the top of the hills we had admired from afar. The houses of the town, bleached white by the morning sun, gleamed far below at the edge of the wide blue gulf. High in the west the snow-white rooftop of the Dikte range was beginning to melt in the spring sunshine. Eastward, over the water, the familiar

Winds of Crete

Sitia peaks had rearranged themselves into quite another pattern. At their base, guarding the eastern approach into the bay, was the little isle of Psira ('Louse') where archaeologists discovered a Minoan seaport.

A few steps farther, around a bend in the road, and a totally different panorama unrolled to the north: a nearly landlocked lagoon, with the Venetian fortress of Spinalonga at its entrance, and the several villages that collectively comprised Elounda stepping up from sea level towards the jagged peaks above. We had it all before us for half an hour as we walked down the dusty road. Reaching level ground at last we spied, off through the olives, a little white house under a eucalyptus tree, and some instinct guided us towards it across stony lots carpeted with flowers. The house, a primitive earthen-floored affair, was deserted as the peasant householders were out in the fields. It faced a crescent of purest sand and blue water. The temptation was irresistible: we undressed and waded in over the soft sand. The water was still cold, but it was transparent and smooth as silk on our skins as we paddled through it. We emerged glowing and rejuvenated. And just then the great idea was hatched in both our minds. Inga said it first: 'Why don't *we* find a house like this and live in it? Haven't we had enough of that town and its stuffy people?' From that moment, on all our trips we were constantly looking for the right place—but many months were to elapse before we actually found it.

*   *   *

Hardly a village in Crete has a hotel; some of the larger ones have rude inns with one or two rooms, while in the vast majority the traveller must find accommodation in some private house (easy to arrange in this hospitable land). It was surprising, then, to find in little Elounda a two-storey hotel made of concrete, standing on the quay by the lagoon where the fishing boats tied up. They were bringing in the catch when we arrived, weighing the fish in the taverna on the ground floor of the hotel. We decided to splurge a bit, and ordered grilled *barbouni* (red mullet)—one of the most prized, and therefore expensive, of Aegean fishes—for our evening meal.

Later, we sat on the second-storey terrace of the hotel and looked over the moonlit lagoon where boats bobbed at anchor. A small taverna stood, all alone and dazzling white, on a spit of land jutting into the water. Sounds drifted over: laughter, the clink of glasses, the stomping of feet to scratchy music provided by records played on an ancient hand-crank gramophone. The fishermen had made a good catch, and were celebrating. The town and its annoyances were now far away. We knew then we could be truly happy in Crete only if we found a village and immersed ourselves in its life. Time and again thereafter, weary with the mean towns and their smell of falsity, we returned and refreshed ourselves, as at a cool spring, in the pristine simplicity of the country.

Next morning we bargained for a boat—a commercial operation that was relished by all the dockside loungers—and when the price was right, embarked for Spinalonga. We chugged over the brownish water, and the old bastion loomed larger above us. The place looked utterly desolate, but a dog's bark drifted over the water, and two women in black stood waiting on the pier. They were the caretakers, whose job was to look after the chapels on the island. They were pathetically glad to see us, for they had spent some twenty years there, and seldom visited the mainland, or were visited by anyone.

Spinalonga was built by the Venetians as one of a chain of island fortresses guarding the north coast of Crete; the others were at Suda Bay and Cape Grambusa in the west. These islands remained in Venetian hands long after the rest of Crete fell to the Turks in 1669, serving as naval bases and refuges for Christian rebel bands. Grambusa was betrayed to the Turks in 1692, but Suda and Spinalonga held out for another seventeen years. An English traveller reported that Spinalonga was occupied by Turkish fishermen in the 1860s. The twentieth century found another use for it—as a leper colony. Gendarmes had orders to pick up lepers from all over Crete and send them to this hot, barren rock to end their days; many came with their entire families. Some fifteen years after the end of the Second World War the leper colony was disbanded; no one remained but the lonely caretakers, who were not lepers themselves but had spent many years as employees of the colony.

The Venetian walls, narrow paved streets, terraces and many houses are perfectly preserved. To walk among them is to enter again the world of perfect architectural harmony that the Venetians created wherever they went. The contrast with the rambling hodge-podge of nondescript structures that constitutes the typical modern town of Crete, is most striking. The Venetians planned well, and their buildings were made to last; they seem to have inherited the Roman tradition of careful and permanent work in stone.

On to the Venetian base, a top layer of lepers' tiny houses had been built. Old *palazzi* had apparently been used as clinics and as

Winds of Crete

residences of doctors and administrators. We wandered down the narrow 'main street' of the ghost town, past former shops and homes of lepers, with glimpses of kitchens that looked as though they had been abandoned yesterday. Here and there a blackened pot or a rusty spoon lay as if dropped by a housewife about to flee from some sudden catastrophe. Through grassgrown courtyards, and under graceful arches, and up impressive stairways we strolled, until at last we came out on the upper ramparts and breathed salt air from the windward side, where the channel out the lagoon gave into the open sea. Near the lonely cemetery we came upon a deep covered pit filled with skulls and bones—the lepers' ossuary. All of Spinalonga is a *memento mori* in stone; here among the lepers' bones, the message was too explicit, and we fled. Down on the quay the two crones waved a sad good-bye as the boat carried us back to Elounda—and life.

Later, towards sunset, we wandered by the marshy lagoon shore, near the peninsula which hid Elounda from the sea. A path led along the edge of the enclosed beds where sea salt was allowed to accumulate. (By summer's end the water in the beds would have evaporated and the gleaming white salt would be piled high into snowy mountain ranges. Later, in little packages, it would reach kitchens in Greece.) The villagers were returning on their donkeys from their day's work among the gardens and olive groves. We stood by an abandoned mill and watched as they passed over the high-arched bridge one by one, each in turn silhouetted against the darkening sky above, reflected in the still water below. They all greeted us shyly: *'Kalispera!'* ('Good evening') and *'Hairetai!* (Literally, 'Rejoice'—a happy salutation that can mean either Hello or Good-bye).

The Roman seaport of Olous once stood near here; now its remains lie beneath the sea, having been submerged during a gigantic upheaval that tipped the entire island of Crete on its axis. (The date of this event, which may have been caused by an earthquake or volcanic eruption of the island of Thera in the Aegean, has been variously estimated from 66 B.C. to the sixth century A.D. Its effects are clear enough: several submerged sites in eastern Crete and, in the far west, the former port city of Phalasarna now high and dry. The old water line can be seen along the cliffs of southwestern Crete, etched on the rocks some ten or twelve feet above the present sea level.) Beyond the bridge we found a Roman mosaic floor, still on dry land though it contained marine motifs—playful and realistic fishes, popular artistic subjects in this sea-girt land ever since Minoan times.

We hastened back to the village; and in the dusk there appeared on the hillsides above, not the two or three scattered villages that we had seen before, but some half a dozen of them. Drawing closer, we realised that our eyes had deceived us in the fading light: what we had mistaken for villages were in reality thick groves of almond trees in full blossom. The west wind, quickening at twilight, brought puffs of almond-scented air down to us. It went straight to our heads and we walked the last quarter-mile in a sort of ecstatic trance, knowing not to what century nor what race we belonged. But the smell of *barbouni* frying in the taverna brought us back to earth.

*   *   *

The third of our spring excursions in our district of Merabello occurred some two or three weeks later, near the end of March. We walked first to Exo Lakonia, the closest village to Ayios Nikolaos; you get there by heading straight inland on a narrow road through immense olive grounds (the major source of the wealth of some of the town's bourgeoisie—for in Crete, even townspeople often have their roots in the land). A short climb, and you come out on to a wide round plain at the base of the Dikte foot-hills. Our destination was the ancient site of Lato Etera which dominates the countryside from a steep, high hill that rises abruptly above the Lakonia plain.

Once again, as at Gournia, we enjoyed the feeling that we were the first visitors to an archaic site. However, Sir Arthur Evans had got there first—followed by the French. But we had the grassgrown ruins all to ourselves, except for the ubiquitous sheep, goats and their attendants. None of the mechanisms of modern tourism— neither gates, nor guards, nor tickets, nor turnstiles—distracted our imaginations from their work of re-creating this place as it once had been. We rambled alone up the steep entrance passage, past foundations and segments of walls still in place, and then through the main portals and on to a level where once the marketplace and town centre had been. Most of the ruins date from the third century B.C., though the place was settled before the seventh century, probably during the period between sub-Minoan and archaic Greek times. In situation and atmosphere, it differs strikingly from Gournia. Gournia lies exposed and unfortified like all Minoan sites; its craftsmen must have worked in peace, without fear of sudden invasion. But Lato breathes fear still, after all the centuries that have passed. It is closed in upon itself, and glowers down upon a hostile world like a medieval keep. Only fear of enemies would have forced men up into this eagles' aerie so far above the lush plain, several miles inland from the maritime highway. The ruins sit mostly in the saddle of a twinpeaked hill, and extend around a rather deep crater, perhaps of some long-extinct volcano. There are huge cisterns that would have held enough water to withstand several sieges, and the great walls insured against all marauders: Lato must have been well-nigh impregnable. Below it spread the variegated pattern of coffee-brown fields and olive-green groves of Lakonia; high above rose the Dikte peaks. We munched bread and olives and drank our red wine under an almond tree, whose spring blossoms had been replaced by tender green leaves. In the distance gleamed the Bay of Merabello and our town of Ayios Nikolaos which once had been the port for this fortress city.

We kept to the heights, returning to Ayios Nikolaos by way of Kritsa, which lies above Lato towards the southwest. There was a road of sorts, though more suitable for donkeys than for anything else. We crossed a dry river, and came out below the village at the isolated chapel of the Panayia Kera. The white church with its tall, slender cypresses stands beside a lane, well off the road—a landmark above the vegetation of the fertile valley with its olives, oranges, and lemons. It was built by the Byzantines in the thirteenth century, and later additions have not detracted from its architectural unity: the high dome, three peaked naves, heavy buttresses and little belfry form an aesthetic whole, pleasing when viewed from any angle. Inside, the walls are covered with frescoes in a good state of preservation, the work of an unknown artist of great talent and with a style of his own even though he conformed to the Byzantine conventions. In some of the scenes, and especially in the Last Supper where goblets, bowls and a fish are laid out on the table, his work has a 'modern' quality that makes one think of the two-dimensional effects of Braque. But far removed from the modern spirit is the serenity and dignity exuded by all of the painted figures. A modern artist could not paint the journey to Bethlehem, the faces of saints and prophets, the grieving Virgin, with such touching sympathy and faith. The key has been lost.

The chapel is very much a living place, with candles usually burning and everything kept clean by the pious village women. All over Crete there are countless such chapels, some on remote hillsides or on the summits of steep mountains; and all of them, even the most tiny and insignificant, are maintained by the women; and each has its services once a year, on the day of its saint. This Panayia church below Kritsa became one of our favourite spots in the whole district of Merabello, and we returned to it time and again, never tiring of it. For us, it was one of those magic centres of joy and peace where you feel you are standing at the very core of the universe, where you breathe happiness in great gulps, and where your faith in life, in the world, in mankind is reaffirmed.

5

Easter Passion

The return of the sun and the arrival of spring have been celebrated as long as there have been Cretans. Pagan festivals gave way to Christian observances, patterned along similar lines—just as Christian churches arose on the foundations of ancient temples. Thus with Easter: today it is the greatest celebration on the Orthodox calendar, a time when all Greece relives the story of Christ with Passion Play fervour; in ancient times, the Eleusinian Mysteries were observed at this season, marking the return of Persephone from the underworld and the restoration of the earth's fertility.

For weeks in advance, the villagers had been making their Easter preparations. Houses had been cleaned within and lime-washed without; new clothes were made; and the women spent hours preparing special cakes which they carried, in great pans on their heads, to the bakers a few days before Easter. The forty-day Lenten fast was strictly observed—no meat, eggs, fish or milk products; and no wine or olive oil during the final week—and towards the end the people were in a lean and hungry state which, however, did not prevent them from working in their fields all day and standing in church for hours every night.

On Maundy Thursday we went up to Kritsa to witness the climax of the Easter celebrations. Besides being one of our favourite villages in the district, Kritsa had associations which made it a natural choice at this season: it was there that Jules Dassin had filmed most of the location scenes for his motion picture, *He Who Must Die,* which was based on Nikos Kazantzakis's novel *The Greek Passion (Christ Recrucified).* It was an appropriate setting for the film, for Kazantzakis was above all a Cretan who knew and understood his native island as no one else has. And, although the novel is set in a Greek village in Asia Minor under Turkish domination, Kritsa fits perfectly the description of the fictional village. Though it took some perhaps unnecessary liberties with the original story, the film became an artistic and critical success; when I first saw it in New York I was especially impressed by the austere beauty of the landscape, by the white-washed village perched on a mountainside, and by the remarkably expressive faces of the Cretan extras. Now I was curious to see how the villagers had been affected by having taken part in the film; and above all I wanted to see how these people, whose faces had so impressed me, would respond to the Easter drama.

It was mid-April when we rode up in the local bus from the sea to Kritsa—a pleasant half-hour climb through the foot-hills above Merabello Bay. The country was Erin-green after the long winter rains, and the colours of the wild flowers—blue irises, violet orchids, deep red poppies—were at their most intense. Everything was saturated in mellow spring sunlight. Through this wonderland of light and colour strode the country people at their daily tasks: men in knee-high boots and baggy blue breeches, with yellow-fringed black bandannas wound around their heads; women in dark brown and blue homespun dresses, with black kerchiefs concealing their heads and lower faces. The children were there, too—and the animals: donkeys, mules, goats, and sheep. In plots of land among the olives, the people worked. The men sweated behind ox teams drawing wooden ploughs, the women carried water on their shoulders in earthenware *stamnoi* exactly like those depicted on ancient vase paintings; for life has changed little for the rural people of Crete in the forty-odd centuries since the Minoan civilisation flourished here.

We found a room in the simple village inn for a mere twenty drachmas a night— and just outside our window there was a broad terrace, perched high above the flat rooftops of the village, with a view all down the verdant valley to the distant sea and the eastern Cretan peaks beyond. We were told that we were the first foreigners who had ever slept there overnight. (The Dassin film company stayed, not in Kritsa, but in Ayios Nikolaos).

In church that evening, we found ourselves in a crowd of hundreds, the men standing in front, the women at the back, according to Greek custom. All made way for us, and we were shown to places of honour in stalls near the front; the stranger in ancient times was thought to 'come from God', and Cretans today still act on this belief.

A black-bearded priest read from the Gospels and chanted, accompanied by a male choir at appropriate moments. At one point during the services women hung wreaths, woven of sweet-smelling lemon blossoms, on the wooden cross which stood in the centre. This was the crucial moment in the Maundy Thursday services, symbolising the placing of Christ on the cross. Suddenly the air was full of flowers which women were tossing all around the cross. People pushed forward to kiss the feet of Christ. Later they went home quietly, conversing in low tones as they clumped over the cobblestones of the narrow streets. Christ was in agony, and the village mourned.

Good Friday morning found the two churches, upper and lower, filled with girls who were busily decorating coffins for Christ. Flowers were strewn on the floors; children ran to and fro, trailing paper streamers; expectation and an incongruous gaiety were in the air. There was a friendly rivalry between the two churches as to which would have the most beautiful catafalque, or *epitaphios.*

Evening came, and services began in both churches: in the big one, lower down, with its tall cypresses standing guard; and in the smaller, more intimate, white-washed upper church with its commanding view of the whole village and valley. Anticipation was on every face; they were all waiting eagerly for the grand funeral processions.

At last the processions started, one from each church. Young men carried the flower-bedecked *epitaphioi*; priests and choir boys went in advance, carrying banners and the cross; the congregations (which consisted of everyone in the village able to walk) streamed along behind. Although they were supposed to be observing Christ's funeral, the villagers appeared to be enjoying themselves in an almost pagan way. Noise welled through the streets; little boys ran ahead, announcing the event by banging hammers on iron bars; bells rang; voices rose in excited chatter. Down through the steep streets wound the procession from the upper church; upward went the parade from the other church to meet it. Resplendent in rose-gold robes, each priest led his flock: black beard on the way up, bushy red beard going down to meet him.

The processions made slow progress, for they were stopped every few yards by pious people who kissed the hands of the priests, while the more superstitious ones performed the good luck gesture of walking (or rather, almost crawling, bent over double) under the upraised biers. Whether this was genuine religious fervour or mere superstition it is hard to say; but it was popularly supposed to bring good luck for the coming year. Incense filled the air, and silver censers clanged and rattled just as they had thousands of years before, when pagan ancestors celebrated the Earth Mother's return.

Observing that I was taking photographs, the red-bearded priest from the upper church stopped his procession several times and voluntarily posed for me. This heightened camera-consciousness was the only noticeable effect on the Kritsa people of their recent appearance in a motion picture; otherwise, they were quite unspoiled.

The two processions met in a little square that crackled with light and movement. All the village jostled for a view as the two priests kissed each other. Then they turned around and started back again, to their respective churches; and finally, long past midnight, a melancholy quiet settled over Kritsa, for everyone knew that Christ had died. He had died—and he had had a glorious funeral.

Saturday dawned quiet, hushed, a day of mourning but also a day of muffled excitement in anticipation of the great event to come. The bakers sweated over their work as women brought the last of the Easter cakes to them; butchers in bright red aprons slaughtered lambs for the impending feasts; and children dyed eggs red, using tiny leaves as stencils to create gay designs.

Late in the evening everyone went to the churches, which by now had shed their funereal aspect and were decorated with fragrant rosemary, laurel and myrtle. The services droned on and on. Old men's voices joined the priests in chanting. Higher and higher rose the voices, in a rising chorus endlessly repeating the invocation, *'Kyrie eleison'* ('Lord have mercy') 'Kyrie eleison!' piped a shrill old man with white hair, 'Kyrie eleison', sighed another in a near-whisper. 'Kyrie eleison, Kyrie eleison, Kyrie eleiso-o-on!' confirmed the rich bass of the black-bearded priest.

The voices, vibrant with feeling, were reflected in the faces of the crowd: the work-lined faces of women in black; the proud features of elder men; the round-eyed faces of small children. Every one of them was privately acting a vicarious role in the Easter Drama. Like the characters in Kazantzakis's book and in Dassin's film whom they had once impersonated, they had—for a few hours at least—identified themselves completely with the figures of the Passion story. Everyone in Kritsa was a Passion Player for an evening. Now I had the answer to the question that had been in my mind before I went to Kritsa; the promise of those marvellous faces on film had been fulfilled in the flesh.

Towards midnight the voices and the faces changed. Expectation grew; melancholy gave way to hope. As the moment approached, the people could scarcely contain themselves; they shifted and murmured. Suddenly all of the lights in the church were put out. For a moment all was in total darkness—and then from behind the iconostasis there appeared one single bright light, the consecrated candle of the priest.

'Come and receive the light!' proclaimed the priest, and at once from all the dim corners of the church hundreds of hands stretched out their slender white tapers to receive light from his candle. The lighted candles were passed from hand to hand, back into the dark body of the church, and in a few moments hundreds of bobbing tapers illumined the excited faces and cast dancing shadows on the walls.

Then the crowd pressed out through the doors, into the church-yard which was already full of hundreds more, all holding lighted candles. The priest led a procession three times around the church and then, mounting a small platform, he read the Gospel passage describing the Resurrection. At the end his proclamation 'Christ is risen!' evoked an answering shout from the throng: *'Christos anesti!* Christ is risen!'

In a corner of the churchyard a huge stack of wood awaited this moment. Now it was touched off, the bonfire roared up, lighting the entire yard, symbolising the burning of Judas. Rockets and Roman candles added their touches of light, colour and noise to the night sky. Round and round the yard in the flickering coloured light the people milled, holding their candles high, repeating the joyous cry: *'Christos anesti!'* Friends greeted one another with the words *'Chronia polla'* ('Many years') and received an answering *'Episis'* ('Same to you').

The bonfire finally died down, and the people started to walk home through the dark streets. They walked carefully, for tradition has it that if you can get your candle home without it going out, you will have good luck for the coming year. Far into the night the candles flickered along the cobbled alleys of Kritsa.

The fast was broken; the feasting started, and lasted far into the early morning hours in many village homes. The next day, Easter Sunday, the hungry Cretans continued to gorge themselves on roast lamb and other delicacies. As strangers, we were offered more than we could eat. We could not walk down any street without being hailed from half a dozen doorways and invited to come in and partake of the family meals. The day passed in a daze of eating and drinking, all of it accompanied by the ritual formalities of greetings, departures, toasts, and compliments with which the peasants surround their hospitality. Payment was out of the question—even to have offered would have been an offence; as strangers and therefore guests, our time-honoured role in the ritual of Homeric hospitality was to accept everything they gave us with a show of relish—even when we were so stuffed that we could hardly eat another mouthful. Many of the people who offered roast lamb so liberally during this great feast cannot afford meat more than once a month during normal times; the generosity even of the poorest was prodigal.

Late in the afternoon, in the upper churchyard on its airy terrace high above the village and valley, the people expressed their feelings in the way that Cretans know best—by dancing and singing. Music was provided by two young men who played the *luta* (similar to a mandolin) and *lyra* (a three-stringed, viol-like instrument with little bells on the bow, held on the knee while played; not related to the ancient lyre of the same name, but a medieval instrument of probable Venetian origin, and immensely popular in Crete today). The insidious rhythms inspired young men and women to step forward, link hands in circles, and whirl about in the intricate yet graceful Cretan dances. Faster and faster went the bow across the *lyra*; the little bells danced wildly; the musicians' faces were wet with sweat. Young men were inspired to perform feats of athletic bravado when their turn came to lead the line of dancers; they did high leaps and pirouettes and deep knee bends. The Mayor of Kritsa, a stalwart fellow in high black boots and riding breeches, led a circle of men, with their arms around one another's shoulders, in the wild *pentozali* —the Cretan warriors' dance, which is said to be based on the ancient Pyrrhic dance.

Dusk descended on dancers, players, watchers; a row of boys leaning on a wall made a silhouette against the dim background of gaunt peaks and lonely valley. There was a timeless quality about the scene that made me wonder: Where have I seen this before? Then I remembered—the dancing figures on Greek vase paintings of the fourth and fifth centuries B.C.

Later, in all the taverns and coffee-houses there was singing, dancing and drinking unparalleled. The shepherds had come down from the heights of Mt Dikte for this occasion; lean and tall, they wore their black and yellow kerchiefs at defiantly rakish angles over their brows. When they danced, they did it with demonic vigour, stomping, whirling, slapping their boots as they leaped in the air, while the watchers whistled loudly and shouted an approving 'O-pah!'

A little man with a wispy moustache, who had been singing with angelic devotion during the preceding days and nights in church, suddenly blossomed as a rollicking shouter of bawdy songs. Hoarse-voiced and bleary-eyed, he sang and sang, while his mountainous wife sat silently smiling, occasionally refilling her husband's glass with wine.

51

Winds of Crete

Several young men, home from the army for the holidays, strolled the streets playing a violin and a mandolin and singing *mantinades* (rhymed couplets, both traditional and impromptu, sung to ritual tunes). At midnight we went to bed; at 2 a.m. we heard the strolling singers, and again at 4. All night long the insistent, insinuating music drifted on the air above the darkened village, telling of love, war, death and the struggles of Cretans for freedom. The next morning when we went out for coffee they were still at it, sitting under an old plane tree, singing their hearts out.

In the mauve light of Easter Monday morning we followed the villagers down the hill to the graveyard. There, under tall cypresses, beside a white chapel facing the long valley leading to the sea, the people were assembled near their family graves. The living had feasted; now the dead were to have their meal. Like reanimated figures from an ancient *lekythos*, the women of Kritsa had come with baskets of food to the graves. The baskets, covered with white cloths, lay on the graves while services were conducted inside the chapel.

The wind blew up the valley from the sea, rustled the cypresses and ruffled the hems of the women's brown homespun dresses. It blew gently over the crowd like a sigh and then died away, leaving the old mourning men and women leaning against trees and against the chapel wall in absolute silence, unbroken by any sound save the muffled chanting of the priests. They were remembering—remembering those who had gone, the ones they were honouring with gifts of food and with the silent dignity of their presence in this place where they would all rest some day.

The winds of Crete change quickly, and so it is with the moods of the people. Services ended, and the mourners were transformed in an instant from their mood of sadness and gravity to one of light-hearted generosity. The women opened their baskets and handed the cakes and red eggs to one another and to children and beggars who clamoured for their share. There was animated confusion as everyone hastened to give away her basketful of food. A ragged beggar sitting alone near the chapel saw the lap of his cloak fill quickly with cakes, bread and eggs. Within a few minutes all of the baskets had been emptied.

Then they all walked back up the hill to the village.

6

On the South Coast

The days lengthened after Easter and the sun became all-powerful. Spring's flowers withered, and green gave way to brown. By mid-May we might have been living in a desert, and we were to feel no more rain until October. The sea became lukewarm, a tepid bath by the beginning of June, yet still the local people refused to go into it; they claimed it was too cold, and they said they would start bathing 'in summer'—by which they meant July and August only. Suspended between sea and sky on our second floor, we passed our days in a haze of swimming and sunning. Early morning and late afternoon were for reading and writing, walking and marketing. From one o'clock until four the whole world closed up shop and went to bed— a custom we were quick to adopt, for in those hot hours there was nothing else to be done.

It should be possible to draw up a Cretan calendar with pictures of different fruits instead of days and weeks; any local resident would understand. We watched the progression of the seasons, counted days by the appearance and disappearance of fruits and vegetables on the market stalls. By the middle of May the last of the oranges had been seen; they would not reappear until late autumn. For a time we gorged on medlars, the rottener the better—deliciously sweet as one chewed out the juicy pulp and then spat out the pips. Then in turn came apricots, plums, cherries (by now we are well into June), pears, apples. Of the vegetables, artichokes were a daily staple for months in late winter and spring (we loved them raw, with lemon juice and salt, as a *meze* with drinks). They were gone by early June, as were winter's beets, lettuce and wild greens; but along came egg plant, green beans and tender little squashes to take their place. With the advance of summer came the luscious melon season, and every day we had our fill of watermelons and sweet cantaloupes. Figs and grapes ushered in late summer and autumn; the abundance of them was unbelievable. All of these good things were so very cheap that even we didn't have to think twice about buying all we wanted. And at all times and seasons, too, came the stream of gifts from 'Doc'—

especially during the almond and grape harvests, for his village of Limnes was rich in them.

We would have liked to travel more, to take trips all over the island, but our economy was so precarious that we could not afford even the ridiculously low fares on Cretan buses, or the rates in country inns. We hardly cared, for we were hypnotised by the healing heat of the sun; as long as we had that, nothing else mattered. We had no idea how long we could hold out, when we would have to go north in search of work, whether we could make any money at all from my writing.

In mid-June the break we had been hoping for finally came: a little magazine in Paris accepted my first story. The payment of $35 added up to more than 1,000 drachmas in local currency—a small fortune for us. We immediately made plans for more trips around our part of the island, and we dared at last to entertain hopes that I might be able to earn more money from my writing and that we would be able to stay on in Crete.

There is a certain similarity about all Cretan bus journeys. Well before the scheduled hour of departure the first passengers—usually old women laden with baskets and parcels and wicker demijohns— arrive to claim seats. The buses are usually ancient and decrepit. The freight is piled on top in the racks and, if the weather is threatening, is covered with canvas tarpaulins. Chickens, goats, lambs are strapped carelessly—and often cruelly—to the racks. There always seem to be more travellers than there are seats, but little wooden stools are put in the aisle for those who failed to get proper places. People double or triple up, sitting on one another's laps if need be. If a foreigner appears he is invariably given a seat, generally the best on the bus. There is an air of excitement, of anticipation, and spirits are high. Everyone laughs and jokes; the crowding and last-minute delays are taken in good humour.

These departures are little dramas—melodramas, rather, or one might almost say miracle plays—and they always seem to have the same cast. The hazards of travel must be forestalled by certain ritualistic enactments. We soon learned to recognise the archetypical characters. There is the old woman who is sure she will get sick; and, being sure of it and indeed *wanting* it, she invariably does get sick—sometimes within minutes of the time the bus gets under way. The others may smile in a superior way (male reaction) or cluck sympathetically (female), but all have benefited by the ritual expiation of their own inner doubts and fears before the uncertainty of the journey. The sick woman basks in the attention of an audience; she reaps the reward of actors. Then there is the man who is always late. He doesn't appear until the bus has already started moving; then he comes running pell-mell from a coffee-house where he has been sitting all the time. He shouts and pounds on the back of the bus. Will he make it? Will the driver stop in time? The whole bus is in suspense. All of their own bad dreams about missed buses and appointments are being re-enacted. The sigh of relief is audible when the driver pulls up—as he always does—and admits the late-comer, who is sweating and complaining. But he, too, wears the look of satisfaction of an actor who has performed well. Another arche-typical passenger is the trickster who tries to get out of paying his fare—claims he has lost his ticket, or any other bald strategem. The sympathies of the audience are divided: on the one hand, they are for him, and secretly hope that he gets away with it— for deceit and cleverness have always been much admired in this country that has made Ulysses, prince of tricksters, its national hero. On the other hand, there are the claims of law and order, backed up by the envious wish that no one else should get away with anything that we can't. On the whole, the reactions are of satisfaction when the trickster is exposed and made to pay—as he usually is.

As foreigners, we always attracted the interest of everyone on the bus. Any of them who knew a few words of English would be sure to try them out on us, while the whole bus listened. When they learned that we spoke some Greek, they all expressed surprise and admira-tion, and our words would be relayed from one to the other. And even though they knew we spoke Greek, they didn't hesitate to discuss our personal peculiarities in our presence—or to ask about them outright, for that matter. Shortly after coming to Crete, I had started growing a beard. It had grown rapidly and had taken us quite by surprise by turning out to be reddish in colour—though my hair is dark brown! Possibly a throwback to Scottish ancestors. Inga admired my new beard, and I rapidly became rather vain about it; but my vanity was always punctured by the Cretan reactions to it. They were outspoken, to say the least: 'Why do you grow that ugly beard? You're not a priest'. Thus to me. And to Inga: 'Can't you get him to shave? How can you stand to live with such a beard? It seemed impossible to find a satisfactory answer to their queries about the beard. If I said that it was a Cretan custom I had adopted, they would reply that only old men wear them now. If I said it was a new fashion in Europe for young men to grow beards, I was greeted with a look of total disbelief. It was not until much later, after the assassination of President Kennedy, that I finally evolved a satisfactory—though in the long run, temporary—answer to the beard questions. In Crete it is customary for a man to wear a beard for some months, or even for a year, after the death of someone in the family or some revered leader, as a mark of mourning. After the President's tragic death, I always answered their questions by saying that the beard was 'for Kennedy'. They accepted this immediately, with understanding nods and expressions of approval.

Do not imagine that anyone is allowed to sit introspectively lost in his own pool of silence on a Cretan bus. These journeys are communal affairs, with general conversation and lively give-and-take in which all participate—including the driver, who often takes both hands off the wheel to illustrate a point. You may wonder whether there are many accidents on Cretan roads: the answer, not surprisingly, is Yes—we have seen quite a few ourselves, and heard of many more. Those little saints and icons dangling from the driver's window are often needed. The pious old ladies help them along, crossing themselves and murmuring prayers at every dangerous intersection or hazardous encounter with another vehicle—and sometimes calling aloud on the Virgin to intercede. Another of their regular jobs is to cross themselves repeatedly every time the bus passes a chapel or church—a task that requires full concentration, for there are chapels everywhere, and not one must be missed, even though it may lie on a hillside a half-mile off the road.

We were going to Ierapetra. No sooner had we boarded the bus—Inga and I being forced to ride in separate seats owing to the crowded conditions—then I found myself next to another archetypical figure: the endless talker. I spotted him at once by the gleam in his eye. He was a little man, middle-aged, with a rumpled collar and faded suit. He opened cautiously with a few polite inquiries in archaic English. When he asked my profession, I was foolish enough to admit that I was a writer (perhaps I was puffed up by the recent sale of the story which had made this trip possible). That did it.

'Ah-h-h, that is most interesting, for you see'—he paused as for effect—'I, too, am a writer!'

I hope my expressions of interest and surprise were suitable. I asked what sort of writing he did.

'I have written a great novel. For many years I was at sea, aboard ship, and I used my time to write. Perhaps you could help me to translate it into English and have it published in America.'

'Shouldn't you have it published in Greece first?'

'Oh, no—the Greeks don't read. Also, there is the question of films. If it is published in America, it will attract the notice of Hollywood producers, who will surely wish to make a film from my book.'

'No doubt.'

'If I don't bother you, perhaps you would care to have me relate the story? Very well. Of course to tell it *all* would require many hours, so I will tell only the most important parts. It is entitled "The Beggar's Return". It is about a Cretan seaman, from Ierapetra—which is by chance my own town—who is captured by the Germans after his ship sinks during the war. For years he is a prisoner—I have written many, many chapters about this, but I will pass over them now, for I know you are anxious to hear the story.

'After many years the sailor returns to his town—but now he is a crippled old beggar. As he walks through the fields towards the town he sees a beautiful girl who is weeping. He recognises her as his daughter, who was a little girl when he left but who is now a young lady. She does not recognise him, and he asks her why she is crying. She explains that it is because her stepfather wants her to marry a man she doesn't love—for his money. She is in love with a good but poor man. Her own father, she says, was killed in the war and her mother was remarried to the Mayor. She is thinking of killing herself. The beggar tells her not to despair, and his words cheer her up. He doesn't tell her who he is—But perhaps I am wearying you?' the story-teller anxiously broke off.

No, it's fascinating—please go on,' I assured him, 'Sometimes I may look out at the country we are passing, but I assure you I am listening to every word.' And I was, more or less, even though I don't remember every twist and turn of the tortuous plot that unfolded. The gist of it was that the beggar was recognised by no one—not even his wife—and kept his identity a secret. He lived in a secluded shack outside the town, and was able on his begging trips into the town to keep an eye on his former wife and daughter and the turns in their fortune. I don't remember exactly how the author manoeuvred his characters into that most typically Greek of situations—the Sunday excursion to the country. Anyway, there they were: a busload of town Greeks, including our heroine and the bad rich boy she is supposed to marry *and* somewhere in a back seat, the poor good boy she loves.

'They arrived at a taverna in the country, and all were eating, drinking, singing—a real *glendi,*' continued the writer, 'But the bad young man put into the girl's wine-glass a potion to make her get drunk and ah—forget herself. Later, he takes her for a walk; they come to a dark river and he must lift her up to help her across'—the story-teller's agitation was increasing with every word as he approached some sort of climax in his narrative: sweat poured from his brow, he ran his finger under his shirt-collar, his voice trembled as he announced: 'All of the circumstances were favourable for' (he looked about the bus, lowered his voice) 'excuse the expression—it is necessary—*fornication*!' He gasped and leaned back in his seat, then continued tragically, 'And—there *was* fornication!'

'Ah—the poor girl!' I exclaimed sympathetically.

'But you see,' the author hastened to explain, 'It only happened because she was drugged She was really a *good* girl.'

'Of course. But then what happened?'

'After she recovered from the drug, and realised what had happened, she wanted to kill herself. She runs towards a cliff with the intention of throwing herself over it. But on the way she trips on a rock, falls and breaks her leg'. The author paused to light a cigarette, then went on.

'But also on the excursion, as you may remember, was the man she loved—the *good* man. When he sees her running towards the cliff, he runs after her, but *he falls* and breaks *his* leg, too.'

I interjected, 'You mean they both break their legs?'

'Yes—you know how it is in Crete, rocks everywhere. And they were town people, not used to be out in the country.'

'Yes of course—quite plausible. Please go on.'

'The girl is taken to a hospital. She has to stay there for some weeks while her leg is in a cast. In the next bed lies the young man who loves her. They have opportunity to talk, and she explains what happened with the love potion. He declares that he still loves her, and he forgives her. They decide to get married—but the problem is, they have no money. Her stepfather, the Mayor, does not like this boy, and if she marries him she will lose her dowry. They do not know what to do, and they cry together. There are many of these scenes in the hospital, which I will pass over because there is not time to tell all.

'After they leave the hospital she sees the beggar in the street, and he tells her to come to his little house and to bring her lover. They go there, and the beggar takes up his crutches and shows them that they are hollow inside—they are filled with gold coins! He tells the girl that he is really her father, and they cry and fall in each other's arms.' (A scene straight out of Greek tragedy.)

Our bus was approaching Ierapetra. The little man hurried to finish his tale, the words spilling out one on top of another. 'The beggar gave his daughter all of his money as a dowry so she could be married. They were married and lived happily. The beggar goes to live with them, and has the great joy of seeing his own grandson before he dies.'

'But wait!' I exclaimed, 'What about the beggar's former wife, who married the Mayor? Was she convicted of bigamy, or what? Didn't the beggar go to live with her again?'

The author smiled rather uncomfortably, 'No. You see—he was old.'

The bus was pulling into Ierapetra. 'How long is your book?' I wanted to know.

'About one thousand pages.'

'What—a thousand pages to tell that story?'

'Yes—you see, there are many descriptions, a great deal of history. Something like "Gone With the Wind". If you would like to read it and to help me with the translation, perhaps we could arrange to meet. . .'

'Some other time, I said hastily, 'Sorry, but we have an appointment today. Tomorrow, too.'

*   *   *

When you arrive in Ierapetra you feel you have made a big step towards Africa. There is something hot, dusty, neglected in the air. The stucco houses of the fishermen's quarter lie baking in the sun. Down by the Libyan Sea—the very name of which has an exotic ring to our northern ears—there are shady trees where the big fishing boats lie with their prows facing inland. There is a crumbling Venetian fort on a spit of land. A broad flat highway of a beach runs on for endless miles east and west of town. Inland are great tomato plantations. Somewhere among these coastal sands they dug up the Roman boy—a very fine bronze statue, now to be seen in the museum in Herakleion. It is well that they removed it, for somehow it would have seemed out of place here. In the little municipal museum are more appropriate objects: several impressive Minoan sarcophagi from the district. Of all the relics of many eras to be seen on this dry southern shore, none pulses with more vitality than these painted figures on clay coffins for people who died perhaps four thousand years ago. This art is sophisticated, highly developed; and yet there is a touch of the primitive, in the figures with great solitary staring eyes that start out from every corner of the coffins. The essential continuity of Cretan life is there: the perennial goats suckling their spring kids, watched by the timeless shepherds; th'

59

squirming, fantastic octopuses and other marine creatures that Cretan fishermen haul in every day. Roman, Venetian, Turkish remains have a foreign look: you know they were impositions—but the Minoans were Cretans and their art dances with the freedom and playfulness of self-assured natives.

Leaving the museum, we found ourselves on the beach, where the fishermen were bringing in the morning's catch. They had been lucky: the nets were alive with fish of many forms and colours. There was even a shark, about four feet long. They slit open her belly and out swam eight or ten baby sharks, each about a foot in length. I never thought it possible to feel sympathy for a shark, but one couldn't help feeling sorry for that one. The destruction of living creatures is always a moving and terrible sight; so we felt, but none of the local people appeared to share our over-civilised scruples. The crowd of assembled children cheered when the mother's stomach was cut open, and they harried the babies with sticks and stones. And it is not only sharks that receive such treatment—we have seen gangs of children assist in the slaughter of pigs, goats and lambs, shouting and laughing with delight while watching the animals' death agonies. Africa again: the bringing in of the catch or the hunt, the harrying and killing of wild beasts, the reviling and torture of captured enemies are great occasions, relished by all primitive peoples.

We walked away, along the waterfront street. Suddenly I had an uneasy feeling that the shark was watching me reproachfully. I was right: the mounted head of a shark was staring at me from within a small barber shop. Noting our interest, the barber paused in his work and motioned us to come in. He was the prototype of all barbers, the barber raised to the *nth* degree: smooth, suave, oily, courteous. His wavy black hair glistened with promade; his round belly protruded from his white coat. The neglected customer waited patiently in his chair while the barber, gesturing like an impresario, showed us the contents of his shop. On all the walls were thousands of marine objects: shells of all shapes and sizes, starfish, lobsters, clams, crabs, shark fins, flying fish, the jawbone of a whale. Waving his scissors as though they were a magic wand, the barber flipped an electric switch: instantly the shark's head seemed to spring to life; its tiny eyes turned reddish and baleful; inside its gaping mouth two red lights gleamed between awesome teeth.

Interspersed among the curiosities were photographs of the barber taken at various times of his life—in army uniform, dressed up for his wedding, and so on. In all of them he appeared unnatural, posed; only here, presiding over his sea-cave of a shop, scissors and comb in hand, was he truly in his element. I was sorry that I didn't need a haircut just then; having him work on one would be an experience—like being painted by Picasso or photographed by Steichen.

Leaving the shop, we were approached by a little bald man in white shoes: 'Hello, people—would you like to see where Napoleon slept?' 'Later,' we told the man. He bowed, 'Always at your service. Ask for Costas—everyone knows me.' Grinning like a shark, he padded silently away.

We drifted off into the fishermen's quarter. The tiny cubes of houses were blue or pink or green-washed. Women sat on their doorsteps, peeling enormous artichokes. Here and there a radio blared, or a man snored. The men fished all night, slept all day. If one sneezed in this quarter, all the neighbours knew it. There would be nothing private about the so-called intimate side of marriage here; children would learn the facts of life at first hand. An illicit affair would involve fantastically complicated intrigues, and even then no one would be deceived.

The sun was pounding on our heads. We sought the shade of some acacias in a dusty square near a crumbling mosque. Women were drawing water from an old Turkish fountain. We bought some peaches from a vendor, and took seats at a rickety wooden table. From nowhere the proprietor appeared—every table in Greece has a hidden proprietor somewhere. We said we didn't want anything— just wanted to eat our peaches. He bowed, disappeared, and came back a moment later with a plate and two knives. We peeled the peaches and ate them slowly. A loudspeaker wailed oriental laments, sensual music. The slender minaret, the rounded dome of the mosque now appeared as erotic symbols. Even the peaches seemed erotic; the Turkish preoccupation with fruit—melons, grapes, medlars—was obviously an aspect of their anal eroticism. I became fascinated by the ripe bouncing buttocks of a girl who passed and re-passed our table on her way to the spring. I fancied that she gave an extra wiggle when she drew near us. She couldn't have been over thirteen, but girls, like fruit, ripen early on the south coast. The music rippled and danced, the singer panted and moaned, the heat danced before our eyes in waves. Obviously the music was Turkish, though the words were Greek—it was *buttocky* music.

Pulling ourselves together, we got to our feet. The heat was beating on our backs and we sought shady side streets. We were in the old, run-down quarter of Turkish houses with two stories and ramshackle wooden balconies. Doors hung askew on one hinge, and we caught glimpses of overgrown abandoned courtyards. There was another fragment of a mosque, apparently used as a warehouse. A man on crutches hobbled by—and suddenly the wild story of the beggar's return seemed more credible.

Another man was sitting on the pavement, in the midst of a jumble of wires like a barbed wire entanglement. On a concrete block in front of him were spread neatly a glass of water, two glasses of *raki*, and a little plate of black olives and green beans which he was nonchalantly eating. Just then the head and shoulders of another man appeared through a gaping hole in the pavement at our feet. Slowly he pulled himself out, like a snake emerging from its lair. He helped himself to an olive, smiled at us and offered us a drink. The drinks were brought from a nearby café and we consumed them on the spot. They told us they were telephone men repairing underground lines—as likely a story as any. But then we were ready to believe anything.

The drinks dazed us, and we drifted back to town, past the local branch of the Greek-American Cultural Institute (second storey over a bicycle shop) and on to the main square in the so-called 'modern' part of town. We sat on chairs in the middle of the sidewalk; they belonged to a café which was out of sight around the corner. Just then a voice right behind us said clearly, in perfect English: 'Let's see the football results ... West Ham wins ...' It belonged to a young English tourist. He was reading from the air mail edition of an English newspaper, and speaking to a Cretan who looked as though he didn't understand a word of English and had never seen a football match. Well might the English cling to their air mail editions and football scores, as a drowning man clings to his log —otherwise they might drown in such a sea of surrealism as this.

The rest of the day passed in a red glare. We bathed in the sea, which was like a warm tub. . . we ate and drank too much. . . we slept in the shade of a caique drawn up on the sand. We put off looking for a room until early evening when the sun had set and the worst of the heat had passed. By then the town had filled with excursionists from Salonika who had arrived in several chartered buses. We learned too late that there was not a single room to be had in the whole town. With night coming on we wandered from one desolate corner to another. Finally we had to face the fact that we would have to sleep out on the beach.

And just then Costas appeared—the little man with the shark's smile who had offered to show us Napoleon's house. He resembled some oriental genie or gnome, with his tanned bald pate gleaming under the electric street lamp, his back hunched, still wearing the same faded tennis shoes. Speaking American English, he explained that he is a sort of tourist welcomer and general factotum for foreigners. It was a point of honour with him to take care of all travellers—not a very strenuous job, as there were few tourists. Except when the excursion buses from Salonika arrived. We explained our problem to him. Unfortunately, there would be no rooms available that night in town—of that he was sure. But perhaps the Bishop could put us up. He motioned to us to follow, and set off at a sort of lope along the waterfront. We wondered whether he was actually going to knock on the door of the Bishop's Palace—but by then we didn't care: we were bone-weary and ready to flop down anywhere.

Out of the darkness loomed a huge concrete block of a house, like a prison or the headquarters of the secret service, with barbed wire strung around it. It was, according to our friend, a new building for housing delegations of priests and seminarians. . . perhaps they would have a bed. He went off to a neighbouring building to ask the Bishop, and we sank down on the front steps. I think we dozed. . . I don't know how much time passed before Costas came back. With him were two young seminarians. 'The Bishop says he will be honoured to have you as guests—no payment will be required. These young gentlemen will show you to your room. I wish you good-night and pleasant dreams.' We detained him long enough to press a small gratuity into his hand, and then he faded away into the night—undoubtedly the god of strangers in disguise.

Winds of Crete

7

Festival in Shangri-La

Crete is sometimes referred to by other Greeks as 'the sixth continent'. (Sixth? I should have thought seventh at least—but it is typically Greek to demote Australia, by implication, to the status of a mere island, while elevating their own Crete to continental rank.) However, the point is well taken, for within the boundaries of this long, narrow island one can find the variety of vegetation, scenery and climate that would be expected of a much larger land mass.

For the long-term resident, the continental qualities of Crete offer means of escape when one scene becomes too monotonous or a certain type of weather too oppressive. We felt this need by late summer when rising Sirius ushered in the Dog Days. Bound to our hot seashore, backed by country now as bare and brown as a desert, we no longer found pleasure or stimulation in sun and sea. The town came to life only after sunset, when people would sit outdoors at little tables along the waterfront, drinking glass after glass of cold water and panting for a breath of cool breeze. The arrival of the northwesterly winds known as *meltemia* in mid-July improved matters, but still the feeling of monotony could not be dissipated. A trip inland, to the cool mountains, seemed to be the antidote. We knew that somewhere up there, among the hidden folds of Mount Dikte, was a high plateau blessed with a salubrious climate. So we had been told. It sounded irresistible, so we packed our rucksack and boarded a bus.

The bus was even more crowded than usual, as many people were travelling up to the Lassithi Plateau for the great *panegyri* of the Beheading of Saint John the Baptist at the end of August. The mountain roads were bumpy, dusty and interminable. The qualities of a yogi or stoic had to be developed for such travel, if they were not already present. But after the bus had climbed upward around a few hairpin turns, we began to feel more alive. The air became cooler, more refreshing. We ignored the terrifying gorges that yawned on either side. Nor did we mind the snail's pace and the frequent stops at villages where ever more passengers piled aboard, until they were

64

sitting three and four abreast and standing in the aisles and leaning out the windows and finally even were perched on the luggage racks on top of the bus. No matter—we were absorbed in the new-found pleasure of just breathing that mountain air.

At last, nearly five hours after starting out, the old machine ground up the last grade, and there, spread out far and wide below us, was the green plateau. The patchwork pattern of fieldsand orchards contrasted sharply with the barren scree of the surrounding mountains. But it was the windmills that really amazed us. Everywhere, in every corner of the ten-mile-wide expanse, the white sails were turning in the breeze, pumping water from cisterns to gardens. I don't know who counted them, or why (a lost bet, perhaps?), but there are said to be more than 10,000 of them—or more than ten times the number of mills remaining in Holland, and surely the greatest concentration of windmills in the world. Coming upon all of this so suddenly, after the long drive through the gaunt mountains, was like stumbling into Shangri-La.

The plateau lies some 3,000 feet above the sea, at the foot of Mount Dikte which towers another 4,000 feet or so to the southeast. Around the rim of the plain, half-hidden among the foothills are eighteen villages; the people live in them and commute, as it were, to their fields which are scattered far and wide over the tableland. The modern road nearly circles the plateau, linking the communities with one another and with the outside world by way of the eastern approach from Neapolis (the one we had come on) and from the west with Herakleion. Until the late 1930s there were no roads at all, and access to the plateau was only by tortuous mule paths. Isolated in their mountain fastness, the Lassithians developed a character of their own and acquired a reputation for resisting invaders matched only by that of the famous and warlike Sphakians of western Crete. They proved so troublesome to the Venetians that the occupying power found it necessary to clear everyone out of the plateau; but in a hundred years or so they were all back, and tradition has it that the Turks managed to penetrate their stronghold only once.

Our bus was slowly making its way around the plain, stopping at every village. We stayed aboard for the whole tour, as our destination, Psychro ('ice-cold'—that sounded promising) was one of the last stops on the bus line.

On this high plateau, with mountains all around, one truly felt as though one were in the depths of a continent, with no smell or sign of the sea. The climate had changed completely in the course of a few miles and a few hours. Gone were the almost sub-tropical growths of the coasts of Crete: orange groves, tomato and banana plantations had been replaced by orchards that would have been at home in a far more northerly latitude. Psychro lies amidst enticing glades of oak, chestnut and poplar. Apple orchards abound, and potatoes are grown on the plain. Peasants were harvesting the last of the wheat as we arrived—a full two months later than those of the lowlands. Water was everywhere: it gushed forth from a copious spring on the village square of Psychro, and journeyed in little rills and runnels here and there across the plain among the ever-turning sails of the mills. The oriental somnolence, the erotic haze of the seacoast were gone; the people seemed alert, hard-working. We stepped off the bus and stretched our aching legs, enchanted by this cool paradise—the sort of paradise the Arabs or the Persians would have dreamed of, and praised in song and verse. We wandered into a grove with trees full of fat red apples; and Inga, with her feminine instinct for symbolic re-enactments, plucked one and handed it to me. 'We'll have to pay for this,' I warned, as I bit into the sweet, juicy fruit. 'Don't be silly,' she replied, 'Eat and enjoy it while you can.'

Many a tiny community reaps reflected glory from a native son who has gone forth and made his name in the world. Thus with Psychro; for none other than Zeus himself, the Father of the Gods, was born in a cave just above the village.* The place has been a goal for countless pilgrims throughout the centuries. The Minoans venerated the cave, for it was here that their King Minos received his Law Code direct from the supreme deity. Nowadays the pilgrims are tourists, from whom the local people make a little money by acting as guides and renting out donkeys. With typical peasant wisdom, they declined an offer by the government to build a road nearly up to the cave, for they feared that cars and buses would drive right through the village without buying anything or requiring any of their services. †

We engaged a lad as a guide and set out on the twenty-minute walk to the cavern's mouth. We mounted upward through a thick growth of scrub oaks and shrubs, until a great black orifice appeared, guarded by a wild fig tree—the ancient symbol of fertility.

---

*This honour has been claimed for several other caves, notably the one on Mount Ida in central Crete where large numbers of post-Minoan cult objects have been found, but the one at Psychro would seem to be the most likely site.

† The government later built the road anyway.

Festival in Shangri-La

The loud buzzing of thousands of bees reminded us of the ancient legend of the nine Curetes who guarded the infant Zeus on the mountainside: they were the first to discover honey and to gather sheep into flocks, and they also invented swords and a wild war-dance.

The cave looked dark and uninviting, but we were equipped with candles and a flashlight. We scrambled down a steep and slippery incline into a vast, damp chamber. From the roof hung giant stalactites, and from the floor stalagmites thrust upward in an effort to meet them. Slipping through a narrow opening to the left of a pool of water, we found ourselves in the inner sanctum, the birth-chamber of the King of the Gods. A small flattened area to one side, surrounded by beautiful and fantastic formations of rosy-pink rock, was said to be the actual site of the birth. It was here that the British archaeologist Hogarth found, in 1900, many hundreds of votive offerings—knives, miniature double axes, women's ornaments—that had been placed there by Minoan worshippers some three or four thousand years ago. I could readily understand why this place was considered sacred, for it was one of the most impressive caves that I have ever explored, though by no means the largest. The birth chamber itself was almost cosy—if a cave can ever be so described. We felt a little sorry to leave it. As we climbed up the damp pathway and emerged into the warm, dry air of the mountainside, Inga remarked, 'Well, how's that for one of your Symbolic Re-enactments?'

We were staying in the Tourist Pavilion, which turned out to be an ordinary village house, reached by following a cobbled lane. From its terrace there was a good view of the plain and of the peak of Dikte, high up in the southeast where it caught the last rays of the setting sun that night. For a long time we stood on the terrace and drank the deliciously cool air and listened to the silence. The plateau was warm during the day, but the minute the sun disappeared it became chilly. For the first time in months, we slept under blankets.

Tried to sleep. I awoke towards midnight with my face burning and swollen. Wondering if I were ill, I lit the kerosene lamp. I found a reddish-brown, flat bug on my pillow; crushed it, and blood spewed out. Thinking that it was the only one, I went back to bed—but within half an hour I had killed six more by flashlight. They seemed to be coming out of the adjoining woodwork. I had never encountered anything like them before, and didn't know what they were—though I had my suspicions. Reluctantly, I woke Inga, who was sleeping in the bed by the window.

'I seem to have some sort of bugs,' I said, 'Do you suppose they could be bedbugs?'

She looked at one and shook her head. 'No—bedbugs are much smaller.'

I went back to bed. 'Well, nothing to worry about then, I guess.'

Within ten minutes I was up again.

'Whatever you call them they're biting hell out of me. Let's move into the room across the hall.'

Luckily, the room was empty. No more bugs that night. The next morning we told the woman of the house about them, and she assaulted the wall vigorously with an archaic flit gun. Apparently it worked, for the young Englishman who occupied that room a day or two later made no complaints.

But our troubles weren't over. Inga woke towards morning complaining of stomach cramps and diarrhoea. This was a bad place to suffer from such an ailment, for the toilet was outside, through the yard and down past the stable where the animals were quartered. She had plucked the apples of paradise, and now she must pay for it: thus might her illness have been explained. In reality, however, her sin had been more prosaic though no less deadly: just before leaving Ayios Nikolaos she had eaten an ice cream bought from a decidedly grubby street vendor. Fortunately, we had some Entero-Vioforma tablets with us (the most effective remedy). Even so, she had to stay in her room the next day, and could eat only rusks and camomile tea, and rice with olive oil and lemon (the Cretan panacea for all interior ills). The family that ran the inn were most solicitous, and provided large quantities of tea and sympathy—while I, feeling rather guilty, went off and climbed Mount Dikte.

The next day was August 29th, the day of the Beheading of John the Baptist. Large numbers of people had camped out the night before around the little church of St John in the centre of the plateau. It was an all-night party, with much drinking and singing and little sleeping. All work had stopped on the eve of the festival; the farmers had been hurrying to get through the wheat harvest in time for this event. The women had cut the wheat with hand sickles; then they had threshed it on circular stone floors by driving oxen harnessed to flat sledges round and round; and finally they had sifted wheat from chaff by tossing it high in the air with wooden threshing forks. We had witnessed the last of the threshing on the day of our arrival. Now the year's hardest work was over—and a celebration was in order.

Early on the morning of the 29th the entire plateau seemed to be in movement as the villagers converged on the church from every corner. Thousands of them came riding on their mules and donkeys, kicking up long avenues of dust. The animals were tethered to windmills in the vicinity of the church; all of the fields for half a mile around became a vast parking lot for them. The raucous braying of several hundred asses added to the general din. People who didn't come with animals came afoot or in beat-up buses that rattled over the dusty roads. Apparently every bus in eastern Crete had been pressed into service for the occasion.

Although religious services were going on inside the church, no one except old women seemed to pay any attention to them. The others would light a brief candle and then join the noisy crowd that kept moving restlessly about. The occasion seemed to be primarily social rather than religious. For some, too, it provided a marvellous commercial opportunity. Itinerant pedlars had set up shop outside the church precincts and were doing a roaring trade in combs, mirrors and trinkets of all sorts. Others hawked watermelons, grapes and warm soft drinks. Impromptu coffee-shops had been established out in the fields, and thick Turkish coffee was brewing over wood fires for the old men who sat on wooden benches, sipping and talking endlessly.

A number of loudspeakers set on poles carried the droning intonations of the priests to the unheeding multitude. Only an extra large splash of colour or noise could catch the attention of this milling mass. Such was the dramatic arrival of the Bishop of Neapolis outside the church, in a long black car, with horn honking and dust flying. Surrounded by flunkeys and retainers, he made his grand appearance, clad in golden robes and dark sun-glasses.

Another little climax of excitement occurred with the appearance of a brass band from Sitia. They piled out of the bus, all decked out in white uniforms with gold braid, and started playing immediately adding their brass-blaring and drum-thumping to the general uproar. People ran towards them from all directions, as though they had never seen a brass band before. Quite possibly they hadn't.

In the midst of it all a small party of English tourists arrived by taxi. They seemed to have strayed from the path of tourism where everything is arranged; the anarchy and spontaneity of a Cretan festival was not at all what they had in mind. Finally one of the ladies approached me and asked, 'Excuse me, but can you tell us when the folkloric dancing will commence? At the tourist office in Herakleion they assured us there would be costumed folk dances.'

'I don't think there will be anything organised,' I told her
'Anyway, they wouldn't dance here because this is the religious par
of it. But if you go to any of the coffee-shops in the villages thi
afternoon, you are sure to see plenty of spontaneous, unorganisec
dancing.'

She thanked me rather distantly and returned to her party, from
whence came loud expressions of disappointment. Soon they got ir
their hired car and drove away, having hardly bothered to glance a'
the activities around them.

I don't know what the tourists would have made of the dancing tha'
started in the coffee-houses that afternoon and went on inter-
mittently for the three days of the festival. Sometimes—about once
an hour on the average—there was a dance worth seeing, when some
vigorous young men would do a lively *pentozali* or *pedikto*, the
ancient leaping dance of eastern Crete which, according to some
theories, derives from the war dance invented by the Curetes. Most
of the time, however, it was a colossal bore: there would be a ragged
circle with the dancers loosely linked by handkerchiefs in their
hands, some of them not even dancing but just shuffling around,
waving to friends, smoking cigarettes, while they waited for their
turn to lead the *syrto*. This dance is graceful enough when properly
performed, but it hardly ever is. It is not in the Cretan character to
take a modest part in a circle of dancers, following the movements of
the leader; each one is consumed with impatience and boredom until
he can take the lead and indulge in a bravado display of jumping and
heel-slapping. Costumes? There were some shepherds in boots and
army breeches—but I hardly think that is the sort of costumes the
tourists had in mind. Old men still wear 'costumes'—but old men
hardly ever dance.

Inga and I sat and watched it awhile, but finally we had to leave
because so many people were forcing drinks and food on us. At that
relatively early time of our stay on Crete, we had not yet devised any
of the 'defences against hospitality' without which the ordeal of
being a guest becomes unbearable. The famous hospitality is purely
a ritual, with the hapless guest cast in the role of sacrificial victim; his
wishes and needs are not considered. If he tries to reject his enforced
role, he risks giving offence. But there are various little tricks he may
employ to mitigate his ordeal; for instance, taking a mere sip from
the many glasses of strong drink he is offered will usually satisfy the
demands of the situation. Likewise with food: except in unusual
circumstances, one needn't always eat everything that is shoved at

one—that would be physically impossible. A few mouthfuls, eaten with a show of relish, will usually make the hostess happy.

One of the best defences against hospitality is a room of one's own, to retire to and recover—that we already had in Psychro. There were many later occasions when we were lodged as guests in some peasant house when we longed for such a refuge. Often the only thing one can do is to get out in the country for a long walk.

That's what we did that night. It was evening and the plateau was cool. The stars were out, and the peak of Dikte was etched against the Milky Way. The shrill music of the lyre followed us along the winding road. The Cretans were dancing, as they always have, for themselves and not for others. They do it only when they feel the spirit or *kefi*. There would be no 'folkloric dancing' at Lassithi that year. We hoped there never would be.

Inga was taking the bus back to Ayios Nikolaos. I decided to hike up into the hills. In this we were following the pattern set for us by the islanders: the men, the shepherds, had come down from the mountains for the festival, and now they were returning to their heights, leaving their womenfolk in the valley until the next reunion. Inga actually had the company of several village women on the bus—they were going down to do some shopping and to visit relatives in Ayios Nikolaos—and she told me later that she had enjoyed thoroughly the feeling they exuded of having *their* place, *their* activities, apart from those of the men. They—and Inga shared this feeling—had no desire to take part in masculine affairs. 'I feel very close to these women,' Inga said after this trip, 'Their lives are hard, and they are very tough, but they laugh all the time—and they make me laugh too. I learn from them all the time, and I'm not sorry that I can't go with you to the mountains—I have my own adventures down here with the village wives and the old crones.'

My trail led up into the hills to the east of the plateau, and beyond them I came upon yet another, higher, plateau called Katharo. It lies some four thousand feet above the sea and is the exclusive preserve of the Kritsa people, who grow grapes and potatoes and wheat there, and spend several months each year in their stone-built summer houses. Shepherds, too, use the plateau as a base for grazing their flocks on the heights of Mount Dikte that rise directly above.

At the head of the great ravine at the western end of the plain I met a tall shepherd: dark, with a drooping moustache, he looked like a Mexican Indian and greeted me with the aloof dignity that would be

71

expected of one. He wore a dark brown, ankle length cloak of goat hair against the chill of the high altitude; on his back he carried a fine *sakouli* or woven knapsack all in deep red except for two bold black stripes down the middle. Farther on there were women working in the fields; they were more colourful, with their blue, red or brown dresses, their black head coverings and beige boots. I had the feeling that I was in a totally remote and unspoiled place—a valley in Central Asia, perhaps—where traditional life goes on untouched by modernism.

There is a fine forest of oak beyond the plateau, on the eastern slopes of Dikte. As I walked down through it, following the old cobbled path instead of the newer gravel road, a gentle rain began to fall—the first I'd seen in months. The woods were lovely in the rain, redolent with the smell of ferns and mosses. It was an enchanted forest, and I met not a soul during the entire hike through it. On the far side I came out high above Kritsa, with the sun coming out from the clouds behind me. Across the reach of open country a perfect rainbow arched its back like a cat stretching. Beneath it lay Merabello Bay and the lower foothills. For the first time in my life I thought I would be able to walk right under a rainbow; and I nearly did—it was the closest I had ever come to it.

Some weeks later we again heard the insistent message of a Cretan lyre, and it affected the course of our lives on the island. It was away in Sitia, the easternmost town of Crete and a rather un-Cretan sort of place though pleasant enough, built around its little harbour, with steep streets running up to the derelict Venetian fortress on a hill. But here were no tall, bearded mountaineers, no boots and breeches. An almost Italian air of *dolce vita* had replaced the Cretan swagger. The Italians rather than the Germans occupied Sitia during the last war, but the influence goes much farther back than that, to the time when Venice was the occupying power. Many Venetian names are still heard. (The Cornaros family is still there—perhaps descendants of that famous Vincento Cornaros, author of the long epic poem, *Erotocritos*, which has become a Cretan classic.) The stern and unyielding morality that prevails through the rest of Crete has been watered down here, to the point (shocking!) where boys and girls are allowed to dance together and even to go out on 'dates'. It is also whispered that many married women have their lovers, who are tolerated by the husbands, in the Italian style.

And yet here in this un-Cretan place we heard the best playing of the lyre, that most Cretan of all instruments, the very voice of Crete. Long before we ever went to Sitia we had heard of Ioannis

Dermitzakis, the famous lyre player and composer of *mantinades*. There was a little shop just off the main square of Ayios Nikolaos that specialised in Cretan records, and every afternoon between 5 and 6 they used to play a number of selections over their loudspeaker. We would arrange our errands so that we could pass that way, and then we would linger and listen, leaning against a wall or sitting down at a table outside a *kafeneion* (it being one of the amenities of this country that you can sit at any café table and stay there as long as you like without ordering a thing). And we would notice other listeners, too—especially among the older men in from the villages. And later we learned that most of the records played in those afternoon sessions were by Dermitzakis of Sitia.

And now here we were in Sitia, walking into the little drygoods emporium with its assortment of wares ranging from huge pink brassieres to plastic cups and artificial roses and toy guns. The bulky, bespectacled proprietor rose from his desk behind the door to greet us; we asked if he was Dermitzakis the lyre player, and for reply he reached behind the desk, pulled out a lyre, and commenced to play on the spot.

Dermitzakis was playing the lyre, and all else was forgotten. Business stopped, customers and clerks alike dropped what they were doing and stood in silence or tapped their feet and hummed to themselves. The bow danced across the strings, the little bells bobbled, the insinuating music rose up in little whirlpools; round and round it went, like a tornado gathering in intensity and then dying away, and like a tornado sweeping all before it, into itsvortex. Some foreigners hate the lyre, others find it a bore. It sounds distinctly oriental, yet with a liveliness and volatility that is anything but oriental. This must be the music that the ancients listened to, that accompanied their Dionysian revels and their Eleusinian processions. The instrument itself is akin to a medieval rebeck rather than to the ancient lyre whose name is still bears; but the spirit of the music is wholly Cretan. I am hypnotised by it, as I am by the landscape of Crete, and ideally the two should be taken together, for I know of no instrument so suited to its country as lyre is to Crete. I, a foreigner, could never begin to describe what it means, what it has meant, to Cretans; I would sentimentalise where there is no sentimentality. Perhaps I should confine myself to physiological effects; I never hear a lyre without cold chills playing up and down my spine; my heart beats faster; my breathing becomes more rapid; my feet move irresistibly to the rhythm. Wild atavistic images flood my brain; I am seized by indescribable impulses. Words are totally

superfluous: the music itself tells all; and what it doesn't say, the
landscape does. One writer only has ever managed to get it down on
paper: who else but Nikos Kazantzakis? When this Cretan master
writes of the lyre, you seem to hear it in the background. Cretan
forms and faces rise up: old shaggy men, black-shrouded women,
young arrogant palikars—all dead, but all alive in the dancing notes.
In *Freedom or Death,* perhaps his greatest novel, certainly his
greatest evocation of his native island, Kazantzakis describes the
death of Captain Sefakas, an oak of a man, 100 years old, with many
sons and grandsons. He is dying, and he calls for his friends to come
and pay him court and to drink and eat, and he orders a lyrist to
play. He reclines under a lemon tree on his terrace and his heart rises
with emotion when he hears the lyre; he can hardly stand it any
longer, but the player goes on and on: all of Crete and her struggles is
there, in the music. Finally Captain Sefakas dies, and they leave him
out there in the courtyard all night with a gentle rain falling on his
body. It is one of the great scenes of fiction, and it evokes the spirit of
Crete incomparably.

Dermitzakis is certainly a great lyre player, yet he is an eastern
Cretan, with perhaps a touch of the Italian in his artist's makeup; it
is no accident that he is even better as a guitar and lute player.
Cretans of the west, from the essential Crete in its mountainous
heart, do not really care for his playing; they have their own players
and their own style, which they prefer. And so, paradoxically, here
in the far tame east of the island, listening to the lyre made us think
of the west, of semi-legendary places we had read about or heard
mentioned in songs: of lawless Sphakia, of the White Mountains and
of their foothills, the *Riza* or roots, from whence sprang the soulful
rizitika ballads with their unspeakable longing for freedom. When
we left Sitia it was with a new and firm resolve: to seek out the roots
of Crete, to burrow into them and live there.

.   .   .   .   .

Back in Ayios Nikolaos, the booster spirit had gone wild. Several
ministers of the Greek government had arrived to lay the corner-
stone of a new beach-bungalow resort, to be called the 'Minos
Beach'. The flags were out all over town; everyone was excited, even
the local communist, who told us, 'Now at last we shall have
Progress!'

'Now at last, said we, 'it is really time to find a village.'

8

Looking for a Village

On an island with over half a million inhabitants, four-fifths of whom live in villages, one would think that it would be fairly easy to find a suitable village to live in. It was not so for us, perhaps because of our special requirements: First, we wanted to live near the sea— that eliminated most of the villages, which had been placed inland for protection against pirates. Then, we wanted a beautiful, or at least attractive, location—and that eliminated a good deal more. It should be quiet, yet not too isolated, for we would have to obtain some of our supplies from a town. And, last but far from least, a house of some sort should be available; in many villages that we liked, there were simply no houses to be had.

We preferred to live in western Crete, within reach of the White Mountains and Sphakia, but if we found a sufficiently charming place elsewhere on the island we would not hesitate in taking it. Therefore, as soon as we had saved up a little money from my stories, we set out for western Crete to look around. But we had no fixed itinerary, and were in no hurry: the search for a village offered an excellent pretext for a meandering look at our adopted island. I have always thought that, although the shortest distance between two points may be a straight line, that is not the best way of travelling between them. When I have to go from one place to another, the first thing I do is to consult a map and plan the most roundabout journey I can devise.

Midwinter in Crete—a clear day, not a cloud showing, the mountains all snowy and the Erin-green grass already mottled with the first violet anemones. Knapsacks on our backs—a picnic lunch and a bottle of wine—free and light-hearted! To be united with the one you love, and going travelling together—does any pleasure on earth exceed this?

Some leaves from my journal of that trip.

. . . The long-awaited halcyon days have come, and so we seize the chance to go village-hunting. Missed the bus this morning and had to hitch-hike—more fun anyway.

Winds of Crete

The American base outside Herakleion: of all the odd impositions foisted on Crete from abroad, this is the strangest, an enclave of Americanism surrounded by the raw life of this island. They live in trailers, have their own television, drive about in their huge cars. But they're out of place, and they know it—they even have a lost look about them. We got a ride with two of them, in a battered old car. The driver, a red-headed boy from the Middle West, has been in Crete two months; the other, a southerner, has been here a year or so and will be going home soon. We ask how they like it, if they have travelled about. They haven't been anywhere, are bored with Crete—'We have everything we need right on the Base.' What, for instance? I ask.

'Well,' says the redhead, 'they have club nights all week. Monday, ten-cent mixed drinks; Tuesday, beer for a nickel; Wednesday, free movies; Friday, TV snacks'—and so on. What about Thursday? 'Oh that's a free night—nuthin' to do then.'

Just then there is an explosion and the car swerves. We've had a blowout. Cursing, they get out and search the trunk for a jack. No jack. They'll have to flag another GI and borrow one. They do, and the veteran of the year on Crete crawls under the car—'Hot dam, man, ah sure will be glad to git back to civilisation!' This within a few miles of Knossos. We leave them to their troubles and walk on to Herakleion.

We went to look for the grave of Nikos Kazantzakis on the Venetian wall above the town. Somehow we went astray and wound up in the town cemetery—where he was not allowed burial. Two priests are sitting outside the chapel. Some devil inspires me to ask them where we'll find the grave of Kazantzakis. Their friendly smiles turn to cold stares. One of them finally answers, 'That is a name we do not speak aloud here'—and spits.

I am irresistibly reminded of an experience I had in Ireland, when I rashly asked a schoolmaster in a country town in the west if James Joyce had gained greater acceptance in recent years. He, too, answered with icy coldness: 'We don't even mention him.'

Ireland and Crete, Joyce and Kazantzakis—there are a number of superficial similarities: both writers came from islands with a tradition of revolt against oppressors; both broke with their church, at great personal cost; both wrote long masterpieces on the Ulysses theme; lived most of their lives abroad; achieved foreign recognition long before they were accepted in their homelands. Ireland: home of story-telling, hard drinking, lively dances, lies—likewise Crete.

Ireland, which seems like a Mediterranean isle that somehow got detached from its roots and drifted north, coming to rest beside the alien shores of Britain; Crete, southernmost part of Europe, yet with much of northern austerity in its rocky mountains and fjord-like bays.

These were my perhaps half-baked reflections as I stood by the tomb of Kazantzakis (we found it finally, on the Martinengo Bastion, overlooking the white city below). One can't help thinking of Ireland now because the country is so amazingly green. Mount Ida looms all white and far away to the southwest; nearer at hand lies Iouktas, a perfect profile of reclining Zeus—the ancient Cretans thought he was buried there, but this scandalised the other Greeks who said Zeus couldn't die.

We find the inscription (in demotic Greek, to which the author was faithful to the last):

> I hope for nothing
> I fear nothing
> I am free.

And then we descend into the narrow streets of the city, our heads full of passages from Kazantzakis's *Freedom or Death* which brings this town incomparably to life as it was in Turkish times.

We think of him again in our little hotel, which is an old Turkish house with rickety wooden balconies and sagging stairways, built round a courtyard with a hibiscus tree in the middle. The proprietress looks like a reincarnation of Madame Hortense, the aging 'Bouboulina' of *Zorba the Greek*. A very demure, petite, dark-eyed chambermaid shows us to our room and makes it ready, moving swiftly and silently.During the night I go out to the toilet, which is on the next floor, and meet the chambermaid who is coming up the stairs with a man. They go into the room above us, and unmistakable activities occur . . . and recur . . . until the small hours. Next morning the maid comes into our room with hot water for coffee, as demure, as chaste as ever, with downcast eyes. She is probably earning her dowry thus, so we tip her as well as we can.

*   *   *

We revisit Knossos, as we always do when passing through Herakleion. Once again I'm impressed by the feminine atmosphere of the place. Women everywhere—the famous wall paintings consist almost entirely of females. The birds and dolphins and flowers look *cute*—just as women would see them. There is one memorable fresco in which hundreds of women sit—perhaps the audience at a public entertainment—and they're all talking at once!

These women of Knossos went bare-breasted—an unmistakable indication of female ascendancy, for when men decide what women shall wear, they invariably choose to cover them from head to toe: witness the veiled women of Arab lands or, for that matter, the *modern* Cretan peasant women, who are subject to rigid male authority and who still cover their heads and faces and wear drab shapeless dresses most of the time. Whenever females themselves are allowed to choose their own dress, they expose the maximum amount of flesh; the bikini may have been a male invention, but it was the women who started leaving the tops off. In the far south of Mexico I once visited one of the few remaining matriarchies in the world, that of Tehauntepec: they bathed naked and unashamed in the river, and wore long tresses like the Minoans.

We wander about the ruins, which we have pretty much to ourselves this midwinter morning, and once having started this train of thought, there is no end to it. The famous plumbing, for instance, which so excites the American tourists—especially the female tourists—isn't that, too, a sign of female dominance? One thing the ladies always care about is good plumbing; America is a prime example, or France with its ubiquitous bidets.

Was Sir Arthur Evans aware, as he conducted his laborious excavations, that he was laying bare a queen's palace whose whole ambience, layout and spirit is feminine? Probably not, for there is no written history from Knossos that he could have read—just all those pictures of women talking and preening themselves. When Michael Ventris cracked Linear B the archaeological world waited eagerly to hear what those mysterious inscriptions on the Knossos tablets had to tell. Sad to say, there were no histories, no poems, no stirring stories of great events. Nothing but *lists*: endless catalogues of pots and pans, quantities of supplies stored in pantries, etc., etc. Any husband who has puzzled over his wife's complicated shopping inventories and her confused efforts at keeping a budget will recognise the pattern at once. If men had ruled at Knossos, they would have left us epics; but this was a ladies' kingdom, and so all we have are old shopping lists.

Finally, the layout of the palace itself. This was the original labyrinth, a 'complicated irregular structure with many passages hard to find way through or about without guidance, maze; intricate or tortuous arrangement . . . entangled state of affairs'—thus the Concise Oxford Dictionary has it. Could there be a better definition of the female mind than that? No wonder Theseus was lost without the help of Ariadne and her ball of thread—lost as countless men have been lost since, in the tangled maze of that enticing mystery, Woman. This ancient labyrinth which Sir Arthur dug up in all innocence, is nothing more nor less than a veritable map of the female mind.

True to our meandering programme, we are going south instead of proceeding directly west along the main north coast road. There are some villages on the south coast we'd like to inspect, and on the way we can see Phaestos and Gortyn.

South from Herakleion by bus, and we're in the rolling country of great vineyards—the eparchy or province of Malevisi, which produces our favourite Cretan wine, milder and drier than the sharp, strong wines of Sitia and Kissamo.* The green and fertile landscape, with its white farmhouses, reminds me of Andalusia. But Crete is all change, and soon we are up on the bare brown hills and it's more like Mexico. Then a spectacular descent to the Messara, the traditional breadbasket of Crete and the largest plain on the island, extending some twenty-five miles from the base of Mount Dikte to the Libyan Sea. The vast fields of wheat are tender and green now, ripening in the winter sun.

We get off at Gortyn, once the capital of Roman Crete, now half-buried among olive groves. There is a Basilica dedicated to Saint Titus, the first Bishop of Crete, who was appointed by Saint Paul to convert the Cretans from their evil ways. In his letter to Titus, Paul quotes the Cretan poet Epimenides who had accused his fellow islanders of being 'liars, evil beasts, slow bellies', and then gives detailed instructions for turning the rowdy Cretans into model Boy Scouts. There are some who would say that Titus failed; however, the fragment of his church is still in use, and his name is honoured.

We come to the remains of an older structure, the Roman Odeon. Beside it, evidence of an earlier attempt to make the Cretans behave:

*One would think that this wine of Malevisi is the same as the 'malvoisie' that once enjoyed European renown; but all of the reference works that I have consulted say that malvoisie is the same as malmsey and that both derive from Monembasia in the Peloponnesus.

the famous Law Code, dating from about 500 B.C. It is in a form of archaic Greek, carved in stone in 'ox plough' script; that is, the eye travels from right to left and left to right, as a field is ploughed. This form of writing would seem to be readily comprehensible to the peasant mind. The laws themselves deal with everyday, even rustic, matters such as occupy the modern Cretans: adultery, divorce, dowries, land distribution, and the like.

The silence is shattered by the atonal screeching of a sort of bagpipe; the owner of an old mill just above the site is greeting us by playing that curious instrument, the *askoumadoura* or goatskin bag with small reed pipes inserted.* On Crete we never encountered it anywhere but on the foothills and slopes of Mount Ida and here in the Messara.

This musical mill-owner is a type found often in Greece and Crete, the man who attaches himself to some ancient site and remains there until he becomes part of it, like the olive trees that sprout among the ruins. He doesn't seem to expect money—all he wants is company and some attention. He is delighted when we take an interest in the operation of his mill—which to us is indeed fascinating, with its great millstones grinding wheat into flour, the smell of flour everywhere, the flour-coated cat, fat from the mice that infest the place. The wife and children come out, and they offer us drinks and a snack. They must see thousands of tourists (though not at this season), yet the warmth of their welcome hasn't faded. The gregarious capacities of Greeks are apparently unlimited: 'the more the merrier' could be their national motto—or *oli mazi,* 'all together'. 'Togetherness', a word used by D.H Lawrence in a favourable connotation (he didn't think there was enough of it in the modern world) that has acquired a spurious ring because of its adoption as an advertising slogan by a slick magazine in America—here at least it is a reality, not just an idea or a catchword.

. . . .

Along the dusty road we are overtaken by a caravan of cars, with horns honking and people leaning out of the windows and shouting. It's the political campaign—Greek elections are not far off, and the

*In his book, *Climax in Crete* (Faber, 1946), Dr Theodore Stephanides refers to this instrument as a *gaida* and advances the interesting theory that it may have been the primitive ancestor of the Scottish bagpipe, brought to Britain by the Thracian legion on garrison duty along the Roman wall.

candidates are out meeting the people at the grass roots. None of them offers us a lift—nor could they, for every car is jam-packed.

Suddenly, from the opposite direction, appears another caravan of cars: the rival party. A medieval jousting tournament, fought with cars and horns, begins right on the road; the object seems to be to drive each other into the ditch. Each party is cheered on by its own supporters, riding in buses and on the backs of old trucks in the rear of the caravans. They're all yelling and gesticulating at once, but it seems to be all in fun, for many are grinning and laughing.

The dust is so thick that we have to retreat far up a hillside. It's like a smoke-screen along the road through the Messara where the political caravans have passed. Finally the air clears of dirt and noise, and we hike on in peace. But we have an uneasy feeling that we'll meet these noisy campaigners again.

And sure enough, we do, in the country town of Mires a little farther along. It's market day, and the place is filled with thousands of peasants in from the neighbouring villages. They have tethered their donkeys and mules in a huge 'parking lot' and now they're out, happily inspecting the merchandise that is spread out in front of stalls along the main street—looking into horse's mouths, buying boots and chickens and everything else under the sun. In the midst of it all the political campaign is going on. They have set up a loudspeaker on a balcony overlooking the main square, and a hoarse-voiced, red-faced, black-suited political hack is promising them the sky and the moon. Nobody pays much attention.

Now the politicians are descending into the crowd, shaking hands, talking to people. Mendacity and self-seeking are writ large over their swarthy countenances; they look like small-time party hacks in a gangster-ridden borough of New York or Chicago.

One of them is talking to an old man: 'You like to go to church, don't you?'

'Yes, of course.'

'Well, if the communists take over, there won't be any more churches.'

The old man looks worried and impressed. One vote.

Another politician, to a shepherd: 'You get a good price now for your cheese?'

'Yes, very good.'

'Well, you know the Others will take it away from you.'

'But they say we'll get even more.' The shepherd scratches his head doubtfully. A waverer.

Winds of Crete

Nothing complicated about issues here: everything is either black or white—good or bad—Us or Them. It's all decided in the end on the basis of personal allegiances. Ideology really means nothing; if a politician's father baptized your uncle, then you continue to vote for his party.

A man comes up and greets us in American. 'Hallo, folks, I been three years Salt Lake City Utah good place America plenty money here no good people dorty they no wash...'—this monologue could keep up indefinitely, so I interrupt to ask what kind of work he does.

'Doctor,' he replies, turning momentarily laconic, and opens a woven string bag to show his foul-looking panaceas in tin cans and wrapped in old newspapers. 'You got earache? I squeeze onion juice in it, make you well right away.' I had been absent-mindedly rubbing my ear, and now I hastily drop my hand and assure him there's nothing wrong with me.

'Any time you feeling sick, just come to me—I fix you right up.' We flee.

Farther into the Messara, at Phaestos, we meet another Greek who has attached himself to a site— the famous Alexander of Henry Miller's *Colossus of Maroussi*. A small, dark, humble man who insists on showing us around the site, although we really can't afford a guide. We tell him so, but he says he'll come along anyway. The setting, with the whole Messara valley spread below us, Mount Dikte rising at the far end, and the massif of Mount Ida hovering to the west, renders us speechless; it would be nice if it had the same effect on Alexander. He keeps up a non-stop spiel, much of which is utter nonsense. We are going through the foundations of a handsome, spacious palace, well and strongly built by a highly civilised race some 2,000 years before Christ. We pause here and there to muse over some corner of masonry, or to gaze over the view; but Alexander hurries us on. 'Look this way, please, people—very, very old stairs.' We look, just to humour him. Finally we can't stand it any more, we just have to break away, to a small grove of pines where we can sit awhile in peace. Poor Alexander, he is off by himself, uncomprehending and sulky. The one thing no Greek can understand is why anyone would want to be left alone. But with the sun setting beyond the Libyan Sea, and a near-full moon rising in the east above Dikte, we simply can't listen to that standardised tourist spiel. Later we make amends, and have drinks with him on the terrace of the tourist pavilion. He shows us a postcard from his idol, Henry Miller, and tells us he gets a letter from him every week, and that he is coming to see him this year. A simple, lovable man, touched once in his life by fame, and living on it ever since.

Next day we're trudging across the Messara, heading for Lentas on the other side of the Asterousia Mountains, where we might find a place suitable for living. Not much chance of a ride here, but a woman comes along on a donkey, and insists on dismounting and giving Inga her place. Inga loves to ride on donkeys, and tells the woman so, adding that she will miss them when she goes back to Sweden. The woman is amazed: 'What—you don't have donkeys in Sweden? Then must you always walk?' I butt in and say they have horses instead, and the woman says, 'Ah, that's better—Sweden must be a rich place.' I don't know what century she is living in, but it isn't the twentieth, and we don't want to be the first to corrupt her innocence.

We finally get to Lentas, in a truck that is going down to this remote south coast community to pick up tomatoes, which are grown here the year round. Also, says the driver, this spot is so warm that swallows winter here. At first glance we think we might like to join the swallows, for Lentas is lovely: a bay sheltered by two promontories, a tiny village right on the beach, and bare brown mountains above. The Libyan Sea stretches away to the south, with a distant ship bound east for Suez on the horizon. The western promontory resembles a crouching lion, hence the ancient name *Leben* (derived from a Phoenician-Semitic word). This was a spa in ancient times, and the water is still renowned for its healing qualities—good for the stomach, says our truck driver. •

We wander about the fields above the village, and find the remains of the Temple of Asclepius, god of health. A small white church stands inside the temple precincts, surrounded by the bases of the ancient columns; a common thing in Greece, but not always so obvious as here. A little way off, we find the remains of the Temple of Zeus, with a charming mosaic of a prancing sea-horse.

Everywhere we walk, people call to us and give us tomatoes which they pick right from their fields. Soon we're so loaded we don't know what to do with all the fruit. We sit down and start eating it on the spot; each of us consumes about a dozen tomatoes, one after the other. Ripe, sweet, juicy—a meal in itself.

Lentas appeals to us enormously, but we doubt whether we could live here—it's too isolated, and there wouldn't be food available for much of the year (we suspect that tomatoes might pall eventually). And, at the moment, no house is free. But it's a marvellous place for a sojourn, and we're keeping it in mind. Of all the places we have seen so far in Crete, we would like most to return here.

We camp out on the beach, rolled up snug in our Swedish eiderdowns. The night is calm and clear. Before dawn we are startled awake by distant dull blasts that sound like some impending invasion. Out on the moonlit sea we discern the outline of a small boat, and then we realise what it is: they are fishing with dynamite. This practice, though dangerous to men and wasteful of fish, and strictly forbidden, is none the less widespread around all the coasts of Crete.* This may have something to do with the fact that fish are scarcer and more expensive in Crete than you would expect on an island in the Mediterranean.

Next day we hike the coast road (more like a mule path than a highway) to Kali Limenes, which turns out to be much farther east than we had thought. If we hadn't got a lift part way with another tomato truck, we would have been walking all night.

Kali Limenes is the 'Fair Havens' mentioned in Saint Paul's account of his voyage to Rome (Acts:27). Paul advised the Romans with whom he was travelling that it would be best to spend the winter at Fair Havens (he was a terribly presumptuous prisoner, passing out unsolicited advice to right and left, and always quick to cry 'I told you so' when they had ignored it and things went wrong). But the ship's master thought it would be better to sail along the south coast to Phenice (now Loutro, in Sphakia) and winter in the better harbour there. Accordingly, 'And when the south wind blew softly . . . they sailed close by Crete.' But out of the blue came 'a tempestuous wind, called Euroclydon' (probably a northeaster), and they were blown out to sea, beyond the island of Clauda (now Gavdos). The storm lasted several days, and Paul had the exquisite satisfaction of lecturing them all: 'Sirs, ye should have hearkened unto me, and not have loosed from Crete . . .', etc. Eventually they were shipwrecked on Malta. This must be one of the first recorded instances of the suddenness and treachery of the winds of Crete.

The name of Fair Havens today is belied by a shipwrecked tugboat lying askew west of the village. The village itself isn't very

---

*The strictness of the law may be self-defeating in this case; according to the Rockefeller Foundation report, *Crete: A Case Study of an Underdeveloped Area* (Princeton, 1953). 'The penalties for dynamiting were so severe that gendarmes were not anxious to catch any person in the act; consequently it went on unabated.'

fair, either—the contrast with Lentas is striking. It reminds me of some God-forsaken banana port in Central America; even the fishermen lounging under the acacias outside the sole *kafeneion* have the evil-eyed indolence of Mexican bandits. Perhaps they are merely tired after a night of dynamite fishing—a practice in which they undoubtedly indulge, for hardly a one of them has ten fingers intact: missing thumbs, forefingers, whole hands testify to the hazards of their clandestine trade. Like most of the Cretans who *look* like rascals, they are friendly enough, with a sort of child-like innocence that belies their rough exterior. Some of them offer us a ride in their boat around to Matala, and we are happy to accept, for it saves us a strenuous walk overland. We are glad to get away from this end-of-the-world place before the rot sets in: I have visions of myself as the white man gone to seed in some tropical hell-hole, lounging about at midday, bleary-eyed, still in pyjamas and with a coffee cup full of gin. We'll cross that village off our list.

Matala has been a port, and quite likely a resort, since Minoan times. It's still a resort, though not of the glossy well-advertised kind. Cretans come here in summer and either occupy small houses or live in the innumerable caves that have been dug in the hard-packed earth of the cliffs above the harbour. Some of the caves are veritable apartments, with several rooms, fireplaces, and proper doors and windows. They have been occupied at intervals for thousands of years. Soon there will be alternative accommodation: a tourist pavilion is being built. As a place to live in, Matala doesn't appeal to us, but it's interesting to walk through the caves and to inspect the pools by the sea hewn out of the rock. When you look out to sea you are startled by a vision of snowy mountains on the horizon—you wouldn't expect anything there but open sea, but owing to the curve of the island and the angle of this bay, what you see are the White Mountains of western Crete. We took a long look at them, and decided we had better head straight for them; we would try to find a village within reach of them. Mountains and sea we wanted: the sea is everywhere—but there are no mountains like these snowy sentinels of western Crete.

In the end we simply picked it off the map.

We went back over the central spine of Crete, by way of Ayia Galini to Rethymnon and the north coast, and there we paused for breath and to reconsider our plans. We opened up the big map of Crete, and west of Rethymnon, where a broad bay cuts deep into the coast at the edge of the mountains, our fingers came to rest and we said: 'There—that would be the best location.' There was a tiny village marked Georgioupolis. Not a very romantic-sounding name, but the ancient town nearby, which once had given its name to the bay itself, was better: Amphimalla. What would it actually look like? We were getting impatient now, and couldn't bother with hitch-hiking, so we took a bus. The view from the top of the hill west of town, looking back over the weathered domes and minarets of Rethymnon towards Mount Ida, was very fine; but we were straining our eyes in the opposite direction, towards the west.

The White Mountains loomed closer: a jagged country with shaggy booted shepherds (we seemed to hear an imaginary lyre playing the *pentozali*). We felt that at long last we were penetrating into the real Crete. It was as though we had been required to serve an apprenticeship first, to prepare ourselves for the experience of meeting life in the raw, without rationalisation, without coverup of any kind. The months of introduction, the time in Ayios Nikolaos, had stripped away some of the veils of illusion that we had brought with us from the north. Now we were ready for a sterner test: the test of living in a village in this harsh part of Crete. Time would decide whether we could accept the lessons which such a landscape, such a people might have to tell us about human nature, about ourselves: but we were all afire to make the attempt, to be tried by this new experience.

The bus topped the last hill and then commenced the long descent into the plain of Dramia, at the end of which lay Georgioupolis, our map-chosen village. On our right hand a wide white beach stretched away for many miles; at its western end the cliffs of Cape Drepanon rose abruptly, and at the base of the cape, amidst a grove of towering eucalyptus trees, was the village.

The bus drops us in front of a coffee-shop on the village square. A group of men are playing cards under a tree. They bid us welcome and order drinks. Their manner is more aloof than we have been accustomed to in the east—friendly, but with a decent masculine reserve. We learn that several of them are Sphakians who maintain a cheese-making establishment here during the winter when the flocks are down from the mountains. Sheep, children and cards seem to be their main interests in life. One of them, Georgios, is constantly playing with his little boy. He demands to know why we have no children—'It only takes nine months!'

'He didn't waste one minute!' booms a voice in American English. We turn, and see a great bald bronze-domed man rolling into view.

'Welcome! I am Xenophon!' He eases down and starts telling about his life in the mines of Utah and his landlord in San Francisco. But at heart he is a Cretan—of a Sphakian family—and he has been back for many years.

We ask about houses. 'Plenty houses here—you like that one over there?' He points a thick finger at a flat-roofed house a bit away from the square. It's perfect but it has an unfinished look about it. 'Never mind—we go talk with landlady, she fix it up for you.'

Kyria Paraskivi, the landlady, is small, wizened, sallow, all in black—the village 'wise-woman', according to Xenophon, and obviously a bit of a witch. We look at the house and it's just right: two rooms and a large kitchen, a covered terrace, a view of the mountains. But no floors, no windows, no toilet. However, she says she will fix it up immediately if we want it.

The bargaining session: she asks 400 drachmas a month, we counter with 200. In the end it is settled at 250 which is perhaps 50 more than a local would pay; but we are well-pleased and so, apparently, is everyone else. She will start the work at once and the house should be ready in two weeks; she will write to us and let us know.

What we like about this village are the trees—the great eucalyptus grove, planted by Prince George, High Commissioner of the first autonomous Crete back in 1898. And the little river of deep, clear, swift-flowing spring water running down from the mountains. And the superb wide sandy beach. And the rough, proud, friendly people.

In Ayios Nikolaos a few days later our friend 'Doc', hearing of the village we have chosen, is horrified: 'It has the worst climate in all of Crete—damp and cold. Before the war it had more malaria than any other place. If you don't die while you're there, you'll die later of something that you caught while you were there!' An ominous warning, which we blithely ignore, going ahead happily with our plans for moving.

But we did take one precaution. Inga had not had a heart examination for over a year and a half. 'Doc' had a friend who was a cardiologist in Herakleion, and he sent Inga to this man, who arranged for X-rays and an electrocardiogram. She sent these reports to her doctors in Sweden, who reported back in due time that, as far as they could tell, there was no change in her condition, and that she was free to stay on in Crete. I suspect that those doctors in their shining modern Swedish hospital had no inkling of what life in a Cretan village is like.

9

The Eucalyptus Grove

We had found the house in January, and the landlady had said it would be ready in two weeks, but we had been in Crete long enough to know that we had to take several grains of salt with that statement. We simply relaxed for the winter, and I made a couple of journeys to the village to see how the work was coming. First the doors were installed, and then a window at a time; then the kitchen floor; in late February the kitchen sink went in. By mid-March they had finally got around to digging a cesspool for an outside toilet. At the beginning of April we received another communication written in the labyrinthine scrawl of Kyria Paraskivi: 'Most Honoured Sir— The house is ready. We are waiting for you. Please come at once.' She had used nearly the same words in January, when the house was far from ready, but we took her at her word this time, judging that even by Cretan standards, she had had enough time.

We moved on the twenty-third of April, Saint George's Day—appropriate for two reasons: it was the name day of our new village, and it is the day when shepherds move their flocks up into the hills. We had been wondering how we would transport our beds and tables and chairs and the gas stove and our shelves of books, but at the last minute the problem was solved by a piece of luck: a Swedish artist with whom we had become friendly offered to move us in his station wagon, as he wanted to have a look at the other end of Crete. We said good-bye to all our friends in town, and listened to their dire warnings. (Doc's last words were: 'You'll be back soon!'). Their hypersensitive local pride seemed to have been offended by our decision to move away; and no explanations about our wanting to get to know the rest of Crete seemed to reach them.

We decided to take our cat, Pushkin, along with us. Moving a cat is really a cruel thing, for they are deeply conservative creatures and hate all change; and, though it may hurt our human vanity to have to admit it, they are more attached to places than to people. Rather than pull poor Pushkin out by the roots from his native place, it would have been better to leave him with the Levendis family; but in this, as in most matters where humans deal with animals, we were thinking more of ourselves than of him: we liked him and wanted to keep him with us.

For the last two days of packing he had regarded our activities with deep suspicion; and now, on the morning of departure, he was plunged in apprehensive melancholy. However, he docilely allowed Inga to carry him out to the car. The trouble began when the engine was started and we drove off. He yowled like a cornered wild cat, and circled the interior of the station wagon at high speed, clawing at windows in a desperate attempt to escape. After about fifteen minutes of this he calmed down into that pathetic resignation of trapped beasts, and spent the rest of the ninety-mile journey in Inga's lap.

We tranversed the by-now-familiar turns, climbs, valleys and ravines of the north coast road in about four hours. When we drove on to the eucalyptus-shaded square of Georgioupolis, half the population turned out to greet us and to help us unload. The house itself still had a rather raw and unfinished look about it, but at least there were floors, doors and windows, and the interior had been whitewashed. The landlady's son-in-law made a sudden appearance laden with boards, hammer and nails: it seems they had forgotten to put a door on the toilet. His background hammering punctuated the yammer of many voices. Pushkin, frightened to death, was consigned to an empty room, where he cowered in a corner.

With such a gang of helpers our household goods were unloaded at record speed, and then the villagers all disappeared at once, like extras in a stage play who make too obvious an exit. Our friend, too, was anxious to leave, as he wished to get back home before dark. We were alone in our new house, and our life in a Cretan village had begun.

From the very beginning we were more involved with our neighbours than we ever had been in the town. Cretans live close-packed, and they have no concept of privacy; in fact, there is no word in modern Greek that corresponds to our 'privacy'. The closest approximation is *monaxia,* but that really means 'loneliness' and it is something the Greeks dislike and fear. Of our house in the village, they said, 'It is a good house, but it has *monaxia'*—for it was detached, a little away from the rest of the village, with a yard and fence of its own.

Monaxia was hardly a problem for us. Our house, though separate, was not far from the square, and there were other houses within a few hundred feet. Our back terrace enjoyed considerable privacy, and it was delightful to sit there on summer afternoons, gazing at Tripali, one of the lesser peaks of the White Mountains, picturesquely framed by the leaves of one of our fig trees. However, if one of us took up a book to read it was likely that one of the villagers, coming and going on nearby paths, would see us and feel obliged to come over and keep us company—for to them reading is the last refuge of boredom, and they simply couldn't imagine what a torment it was, at times when one was immersed in a fascinating book, to have to tear oneself away from it and listen to half an hour of local gossip. Inga suffered more from this than I did, for it was usually the women who came over to pass the time—the men's place was in the coffee-house—and I could always retire discreetly to an inner room. They meant well enough; their aim was to assist us in the never-ending and wearisome job of passing the time. Again and again they would ask, 'But how do you pass your time?' We had no fields to look after, no sheep, no children—what in the world did we do all day?

What did we do, indeed? It was a question that came up sometimes in the letters of friends in England or America or Sweden, who should have known better. We rose with the sun, like the villagers (and what a delight it was to awaken in the freshness of dawn, and open one's eyes in the cool, white, high-ceilinged room—to start another day in Crete!). We would have breakfast on the terrace, and then go about our 'morning chores'. I had to carry water from the nearest tap, which was about fifty yards from the house; we stored it in our kitchen, in a huge *pithos* resembling the ancient Minoan ones that were found at Knossos. This piped water came down from the village of Mathe, a mile above Georgioupolis in the foot-hills, where there were copious springs, and it was good water. But later in the summer the Mathe people, who were constantly squabbling with our villagers over such petty matters as animal grazing rights and land boundaries, decided that they no longer wanted to share their water, and secretly turned off the pipeline. Our villagers appealed to the police, and the water was turned on again—but only for a short time. There was no way to stop the upper villagers from turning off the water at night, and so we had to accept the situation, and take our water from a large open well in low ground about five minutes' walk from our house. Water-carrying is women's work in Crete, and the fact that I took on this job instead of Inga aroused much comment. Their explanation of this strange phenomenon, as we later learned, was that I did it only because I was very much in love.

The Eucalyptus Grove

While I carried water, Inga would go out in search of some food for lunch. There were few grocery supplies available in such a tiny village—only a few tins of sardines and corned beef on the dusty shelves of the coffee-houses—but, fortunately, fresh fish were plentiful in this season, and there were adequate vegetables, eggs, potatoes and so on to be had from various neighbours. Canea, the nearest big town, lay some twenty-five miles away to the west; we found it necessary to go there by bus at least once a month on a shopping expedition. Then there was Leonidas, a local jack-of-all-trades who operated a decrepit motorcycle with a sort of cart attached behind; he went often to Canea, and for a few drachmas would pick up anything one ordered from the market—usually he would forget it the first time, but there was always *avrio,* literally 'tomorrow' but more accurately 'in the near future'.

Going for fish in the early morning was a very pleasant task, and sometimes I went along with Inga. We would sit on the terrace of Nikos' taverna above the riverbank until the chug-chug-chug of the engines told us the boats were coming in. They came up the river and tied up under the great trees lining the bank. A few people would go down to see what had been caught, and the bronzed, barefoot fishermen would untangle the fish from the nets, weigh them and sell them on the spot. The fish that weren't sold at once were sent on the morning bus to the market in Canea, where they sold readily, as Georgioupolis fish were considered the best in Crete. We thought these fish were so tasty because of the cold water from the springs that entered the sea here, but Nikos, the fat tavern-keeper, had another explanation: 'It's from the olive trees farther up the river. Oil seeps into the water from the roots, and that goes out to sea and gives the fish their flavour.' When we laughed at this, he became slightly offended—he hadn't been joking.

About once a week we had a chance to buy fresh meat. Nearly every Saturday morning Georgios, the Sphakian cheesemaker whose 'factory' was on the square just behind our house, would slaughter a sheep or a kid or, occasionally, a pig. These were public occasions, attended by a large gang of barefoot children. The killing took place out in the open, in a corner of the square, and the whole thing was plainly visible from our corner window, though we tried not to look. We couldn't avoid hearing the cries of the dying beasts, or the shrill shouts and laughter of the excited children. Georgios would then calmly hang up the animal from a branch of a tree, and proceed to skin it. He was a large, swarthy man in boots and breeches and a dirty apron, stained where he had wiped his bloody hands. He would stick a large knife between his teeth while he scooped out the entrails with his hands, and laid them to one side; nothing would be thrown away, and some village woman would clean the intestines and stuff them with odds and ends, and they would make a tasty dish to be relished by the unsqueamish Cretans. For us, however, it took a strong stomach to walk over, after this, and buy a piece of meat for the day's dinner.

Georgios also supplied us with milk and cheese. He bought the milk from shepherds who grazed their flocks on the plain of Dramia, and made it into cheese with the help of his Sphakian partner and one or two assistants. They sold it in Canea and Athens for very good prices. Cheese-making is a mountaineer's occupation, and these displaced Sphakians stood out in sharp contrast with the lowlanders. They were big fellows, well over six feet tall, and they never spoke in less than a shout; it was amusing to listen to their rude jokes, delivered in the sing-song dialect of their mountain district.

After awhile we discovered that Georgios had been charging us a little too much for the milk, that in fact he overcharged everyone when he saw a chance to, and so we started buying direct from one of our neighbours, a little shepherd named Nikoli. He brought the milk to our house in a bucket, and sometimes we would have to go looking for him when milking had been delayed or forgotten. Nikoli was completely shiftless and irresponsible, and he cared little about the sheep, for they were not his own; he was grazing them on contract for the well-to-do owner. His family was among the poorest in the village. All of them—mother, father, two daughters and a son —occupied one small room with no windows at the back of someone else's house. Nikoli's great weakness was gambling; any cash he could lay hands on went immediately into the hands of some card-sharper in Canea. He was in debt and in trouble with the authorities because he constantly allowed the sheep to drift on to other people's land; but none of this seemed to worry him—he was already at the bottom, and had nowhere else to go. We paid for the milk in advance, a week at a time, and after awhile we learned to try to give the money to his wife, if we wanted it to do some good, for if Nikoli got it, invariably it would go into his expensive vice. Sometimes he would come and ask us for a loan, but he was ashamed to do this— even the lowest of the Cretans never quite abandon their *philotimo* or personal honour and pride—and would always try to justify it by recounting tales (largely imaginary, we suspected) of his heroic exploits during the war when he was up in the mountains with the *andartes* (guerrillas). All of which was totally unnecessary, for we always gave him whatever he asked for without question; and he never failed to repay it—in milk.

The search for food, and the carrying of water and emptying of garbage (it was just thrown out in the fields around the village) were our basic daily chores. After they were done, Inga would concentrate on studying Greek or on her reading, and I would retire to my workroom to earn some money so that we could stay on in Crete. Dickens said, 'Life is given to us solely on the condition that we boldly defend it to the last'—and for the time being, I had hit on an effective way of defending our life in Crete and fending off the dreaded return to northern shores: I was writing little articles for newspapers about all the places I had visited long before on my travels about Europe. I was earning from \$25 to \$50 for each of these pieces, and that was quite a goodly sum by Cretan village standards: two such sales a month, and we had enough to live on; more, and we could bank a little. Occasionally some distant friend would commiserate with me by letter from America or England on my being 'forced' to do 'hack work', but I didn't feel that way about it at all—on the contrary, I felt like offering my sympathy to those who had to stay where they were. I regarded it as honest labour, like making chairs or painting houses, and I had certain standards of craftsmanship; the stories had no literary pretensions whatsoever, but they had to be in clear, simple English, and I was scrupulous about getting the facts right—after all, they were intended as a service to readers. Thus we earned our fish and bread and wine.

Towards noon on most days we would stroll down to the sea, along a narrow marshy path through neck-high forests of sea-grass, and then we would swim out slowly into the clear sea and turn and tread water, gazing at the white village half-hidden among the eucalyptus trees, and beyond the green foot-hills rising abruptly to the still-snowflecked peaks of the White Mountains. The whole tableau was improbably harmonious, with the dramatic climax of the peaks in precisely the right spot for picturesque effect. Then on the broad empty strip of sand that stretched away to the east for miles, we would run or stroll or sit and read or go to sleep. Most of the time we had it all to ourselves, for very few of the villagers ventured into the sea, even on the hottest days. The attitude of most Cretans towards the sea is medieval: it is an object of fear and distrust and superstition, to be avoided as much as possible. Our neighbours were much concerned about our (to them) excessive sea-bathing, and we were warned many times of the dangers we were exposing ourselves to, and of how we might be 'weakened' by too much swimming. Their general attitude was neatly expressed by a grizzled old shepherd who told us, 'I go in the sea once a year, in July—and I always catch a cold from it!'

Only in the dead heat of midsummer, in July and August, would a few of the local people dare to bathe. It was amusing to watch them. The women in their black baggy underslips (few had bathing suits) would step gingerly into the water—which had about the temperature of a warm bath—and then leap back, screaming 'Oh, it's like ice!' Then they would flop down in a foot or two of water— they dared not go in deeper—and splash about, and roll in the sand, and emerge all clotted with wet sand. The instant they were out, in the sun, they covered their heads and shoulders with towels and coats—for they dreaded the sun almost as much as they did the sea. The men were little better; few could swim a stroke—if a man could dog-paddle a few paces he was regarded as an excellent swimmer. It was rather disillusioning, too, to see some fine figure of a man, tall and dark and booted, strip himself of his regalia and reveal a white pasty body, and then go awkwardly splashing into the water like some young girl. The mountains were their element, and they did not show up to good advantage elsewhere.

One day the greatest folk hero of the area came to our beach. He was a man, from a nearby village—thick set, middle-aged, with a bristly moustache—and he was a hero because he had fathered sixteen children, of whom no less than fourteen were sons! Even in Crete, where large families are the rule, this was extraordinary, and he enjoyed unprecedented prestige, adulation and envy. On this day he arrived at the seaside with some half a dozen of his boys. He sat down heavily on a sand dune and commenced to pull off his high boots. The boys, meanwhile, stripped quickly and ran into the sea; two or three of them were already in the water even before he had got the first boot off. By the time he had removed his socks and started to struggle with his thick woollen breeches, the whole crowd of boys was frolicking in the water. Followed slowly his heavy undervest (the Cretan men always wear them, even in the middle of the summer), and then he donned a baggy woollen bathing suit of the sort worn in the 1920s, with a white belt and buckle. But still some vestiges of his dignity as a father-hero clung to him, as he stepped slowly into the sea, dipped to his waist, and then after three minutes went ashore again, and repeated the whole process in reverse. Again booted and trousered like a Cretan, he signalled to his lads and they obediently ran ashore and dressed; and the whole procession left the way it had come, disappearing through the tall grass. It was the only time I ever saw them there.

Could these be the descendants of the ancient Greeks who, naked and proud, exercised and sunbathed in their gymnasia: the Greeks who held that a man who could neither swim nor read belonged to the lowest class of citizens? The black weight of centuries of Pauline Christian body-hatred intervened; the Middle Ages like a dark curtain stood between them and the ancients. Nowadays, cool Scandinavians from the northern forests are more truly pagan than the people who inhabit the Mediterranean itself—for which all honour to them!

It was the ancient spirit that still inspired me. The achievement of balance, order, harmony—the Golden Mean, the reconciliation of body, mind and spirit—this had been my struggle for years, and it had led me here, to the shores of the sea where the idea had originated. Perhaps both of us shared an element of pagan sensuality —but if so, not in the usual sense, which implies indulgence, but in a simple and even austere way. Like the Cretans, we were connoisseurs of a glass of water, a breath of air: ascetic epicureans who demanded nothing but the best of the basic elements—and little more. A Cretan village was one of the few places on earth where such simple and difficult demands could have been met. And here, for some few dazzling months, while our fortune held, we enjoyed a perfectly balanced life. Later, swept up by what Hardy called 'the harrowing contingencies of human experience, the unexpectedness of things', we would look back on this golden period with wistful longing. It was not easily or quickly achieved, nor once lost, readily regained.

*   *   *

Our life was almost too perfect. The dish would have been too bland, it would have lacked for salt, had it not been for the people. The life of Cretan peasants may appear idyllic to first-time visitors enchanted by the hospitality and the apparent simplicity, but the rawness lurks just beneath the surface. They were indeed kind to us; there was a steady stream of women bearing plates of food, fresh-baked bread, or bottles of wine to our door; and there was a veritable plague of children who would knock gently, and then shyly hand us a bouquet of sweet-smelling wild flowers—sometimes, touchingly, no more than a few daisies and some wisps of weed. But children's motives, like those of their elders, are mixed; and those offerings were no doubt partly motivated by a desire for the sweets that we sometimes offered them. What a bundle of contradictions is human nature! And Cretans, being arch-human, embodied these contradictory elements in striking ways. The very same woman who could bring us ten fresh eggs and a bottle of wine out of sheer generosity could, later in the day, cheat us out of two or three drachmas when we bought vegetables from her corner shop.

The Turks (and they should know!) had a saying: 'If you give a Cretan your finger, he will grab your hand—and rip off your arm.' Quite true; that's the Cretans as we knew them, to a T. But it is equally true that a Cretan inspired by generosity is capable of ripping off his own arm and handing it to you. Ferocity and generosity co-exist in the breasts of these bewildering and paradoxical people.

There is a strong streak of malice in the Cretan peasant make-up. They relish openly the misfortunes of others, and seek to enhance their own reputations by constantly denigrating others. Gossip ruled the village, and fear of neighbours' comments stalked every house. And not only their words were to be feared: the Cretan is like a scorpion, he has a sting in his tail, and can lash out with it in strange and unexpected ways.

Kyria Anna, the fat, good-natured wife of Nikos the tavern-keeper, suffered from a variety of ailments. She was delighted when she got word from Canea that a bottle of rare and expensive medicine, not available in Greece, had been brought to her by a relative returning from America. As she was unable to go to Canea immediately, she asked a neighbour to pick it up for her. But on the morning that he went to Canea, this neighbour got into an argument over some trivial matter with Anna's husband, Nikos; and he took out his spite on poor Anna—by throwing her medicine in the river.

There was an industrious family that had laboured long and hard to plant and tend a field of vines, the sort that grow higher than a man's head, and yield the sweetest and juiciest of grapes. While this was going on, they got into a quarrel with another family. The young men of this other family went into the vineyard one dark night with axes and, in a hard night's work cut down every one of the precious vines. But Crete *is* changing; just a few years ago, this sort of thing would have flared inevitably into acts of violence and bloodshed (in certain mountain areas, it still would); but this time, the case went to court where it dragged on for a long time before the offenders were made to pay up.

These family quarrels often go far back, to some real or imaginary slight of long ago, the memory of which has been kept alive and rancorous while the moment of revenge was patiently awaited.

The Eucalyptus Grove

Every village is a labyrinth of such feuds and antagonisms, in which the innocent stranger is as helpless as Theseus without his ball of thread. As time passed and we heard more and more stories—first one side's version and then the other—it was possible to trace some of these antipathies at least part way back to their origins. For instance, the case just cited, of the ruined vineyard, had its origin in a situation that is always highly inflammable: family pride and the honour of the women. One of the brothers who owned the vineyard had made love, some time before, to a village girl who became pregnant. There was no certainty that he was to blame because it was known that she had been with other men, and so he refused to marry her. It was the outraged brothers of the girl who chopped down the vines. That's progress, Cretan-style—a few years ago they would have killed, first the girl, and then the man who had wronged her.

The man who had dishonoured the girl married another village woman, had a child by her and then went off to work in Germany. This young woman, Maria, a dressmaker, became quite friendly with Inga and told her of all her troubles. She was miserably unhappy because she had been in love with another young man, Stavros, but had not been able to marry him because his family objected; instead, her own family had arranged this match with a man she disliked. Stavros left the village, became a merchant marine officer, and made many trips abroad. He returned for a visit during our first summer in the village—a handsome, intelligent fellow of twenty-nine who spoke good English. Poor Maria, still as much in love with him as ever, was beside herself; yet she didn't dare speak to him, nor even look at him, in the certain knowledge that her neighbours would at once write to her husband in Germany about it. She was a prisoner of gossip and the opinions of others, trapped in the village, getting old before her time, hating her child and her life, and with no possibility of leaving. When I asked the young man how he felt about it, he shrugged philosophically, 'Perhaps my parents knew best. They are older and wiser, and could see things more clearly'. It was a typically Greek statement: these passionate people have a profound distrust of passion, and in a patriarchal and traditionalist society, the young habitually defer to the decisions of their elders.

But not always, I am happy to say, for there is a way, sanctioned by long tradition, for passion to win through: the time-honoured Cretan custom of marriage by abduction. A young man sees a girl he likes; he has no patience for the endless family negotiations over dowry, the formalities of engagement and the ordeal of the wedding;

97

and with one grand gesture he cuts through all of that—he steals the girl. We heard many such stories, for the practice seems still to be as active as ever. There was a plump, rather bowlegged woman named Crystalenia who told Inga her story. When she was sixteen years old, she had been off in the fields by the sea, picking *horta* with another girl. A village boy, also sixteen—and barefooted, she emphasized that—came up to them with a knife in his hand. He ordered the other girl to run away, and she did—though she had the presence of mind to come back for her basket after running a few paces empty-handed. The plucky lad told the girl that unless she came with him, he would cut off her head and throw it in the sea—and she, terrified, took him at his word. He took her off to a cave in the mountains high above the village. After a few days they returned to the village and were duly married, though not without considerable quarrelling between the two families: the boy's parents thought the girl's father didn't offer a big enough dowry! Fortunately, no blood feud started, and they settled down to a happy married life. We often saw them together, on their way to the fields: Andreas, the husband, thickset, heavily-moustached, riding on a donkey while Crystalenia walked happily behind.

Inga asked this woman whether she hadn't given the boy some encouragement, and Crystalenia admitted, with some coyness, that she had, indeed, 'given him the eye' as she sat in the window of her house while he passed by. This recalls the remarks of Herodotus on the ancient Persian attitude towards woman-stealing: 'Abducting young women, in their opinion, is not, indeed, a lawful act; but it is stupid after the event to make a fuss about it. The only sensible thing is to take no notice; for it is obvious that no young woman allows herself to be abducted if she does not wish to be.' The Greeks, however, took such matters more seriously and invaded Asia 'merely on account of a girl from Sparta.'*

They are still apt to take such affairs quite seriously , and more than one blood feud has resulted from an abduction, especially in the more lawless and remote areas such as Sphakia and, to a lesser extent, the slopes of Mount Ida. It was in the latter region that the most famous abduction of recent times occurred, in 1951, an affair that made international news and nearly caused a civil war in Crete. The girl was named Tassoula, and by all accounts she was fair to look upon. She was the daughter of a famous wartime guerrilla

* Herodotus, *Histories,* Book One, translated by Aubrey de Selincourt (Penguin Classics).

leader from Herakleion. A young man from the mountain village of Anoyia fell in love with her and, assisted by a comrade, succeeded in kidnapping her. The young man, who had served with the *andartes* under his sweetheart's father, knew Mount Ida very well, and he took her to a cave that had been used during the war as a hideout. He cleverly chose a cave that was so well-known (it had been used to hide Major-General Kreipe, the German Commandant in Crete, who had been kidnapped by partisans and English agents and spirited away by boat to Egypt) that his pursuers wouldn't even bother to look in it—the principle used by the purloiner of the letter in Poe's story. The girl's enraged father and a large body of followers swarmed up to Anoyia and threatened to burn the village again (the Germans had burned it in retaliation for the Kreipe kidnapping) if Tassoula weren't returned. But the villagers—a tough lot—were ready to resist, and the threat was not carried out. They combed the slopes of the mountain, but failed to look in the most obvious place. The episode had political ramifications because the party of the girl's father were Venizelists (Liberals), whereas the boy's family were Royalists—always an inflammable confrontation in Greece. The couple spent some two weeks in the cave and, according to the popular version of the story—it has now entered the realm of folklore—he never touched her, and offered to allow her to leave any time she wished. But she wavered, and eventually they managed to get off the mountain and away to Athens, where they set up housekeeping. But this Cretan version of *Romeo and Juliet* had, alas, a modern sequel: it ended in the divorce court.

The earliest and most famous of all Cretan abductions was the mythological one of the maiden Europa by Zeus disguised as a bull. But there is also historical evidence that the custom of abduction has roots deep in the Cretan past. The Hellenistic geographer Strabo (64 B.C.-19 A.D.) had this to say about the Cretans: 'They have a peculiar custom in regard to love affairs, for they win the objects of their love, not by persuasion, but by abduction . . .'* But it immediately becomes apparent that Strabo is writing solely about *homosexual* love affairs, in which an older man carries off a boy to some country hideaway; and further, that these affairs were conducted with the tacit consent of the boy to be abducted and of his friends and family. They would be informed in advance when the abduction would take place, and they would offer no resistance, or

* *Geography of Strabo* (Loeb Classical Library), Vol V, Book X, English translation by H. L. Jones.

only token resistance. After the idyll in the country the lover would
return the boy to the town and present him with lavish gifts, some of
which were also rigidly prescribed by tradition and custom. The boy
would then enjoy great prestige in the community, for, as Strabo
tells us, it was actually disgraceful for a well-born lad *not* to obtain a
lover. It would seem as though this highly elaborate and ritualised
procedure was a sophisticated—and perverted—version of a still
more ancient tradition, to which the *modern* heterosexual
abductions, with their honeymoons in caves and the danger of
ensuing feuds, bear a closer resemblance.

The Cretans relish all such tales of abduction and rape—especially
the women, whose conversation is definitely on the bawdy side, and
who are ever ready to cackle lecherously over some story of sexual
misdemeanors. They delighted in telling Inga these stories, perhaps
to test her and see what her reaction would be. They also demanded
to know the English and Swedish words for the sexual parts, and
shouted out these words over the village square amid screams of
laughter. One word in particular delighted these lecherous
crones—the Swedish word for the female sex organ, which sounds
almost exactly like the name of the Greek goat cheese, *feta*. The
whole village took this up, and for many days, while the fad lasted
we couldn't go into a coffee-shop or into Georgio's cheese-shop
without being asked slyly if we would like some good *feta* today
The *Greek* word for the same organ can be a pitfall for the unwary
foreigner, for its pronunciation is perilously close to the feminine
form of 'alone', *moni*—if you lengthen the 'o' a bit, so that it sounds
like 'moony', you've got it. One of the village girls who was taking a
course in English at the Gymnasium in Vamos got into trouble with
her father over this word. The English word 'moon' had come up in
her lessons, and in reading the lesson over and over again,, she
repeated this word but made it sound like 'moony'. (It is common
for Greeks trying to learn English to add a vowel sound at the end of
a word, as most Greek words end this way.) Her father, overhearing
this repetition of what sounded to him like a very dirty word
demanded, 'What sort of things are they teaching you in that school
You must stop this filth at once!'—and he took away her book. The
contretemps was smoothed over only by Inga's intervention, but
even after hearing her patient explanation that 'moon' in English
means only the harmless *fengari,* he appeared very doubtful.

Always a good source of local lore was our landlady, Kyria
Paraskivi, or 'Madame Friday' as we dubbed her (*Paraskivi* is the

word for Friday in Greek). Small, bent, gnarled like a gnome, sallow-faced (she probably had malaria for years, like everyone else who lived in the village before DDT spraying eliminated this menace to health), she was always in widow's weeds for her husband, who had died long ago. Sharp black eyes gleamed craftily out of the seamed yellow face; she had a reputation for being *poneri* which could mean clever, but also tricky. Probably she had to be tricky in order to survive, during the hard years of the German occupation and the civil war, all alone, with two children to bring up and keep out of harm's way. The hardships of widowhood were increased because she had daughters; sons could have worked, brought in money to the household, whereas daughters represent a fearful strain on the economy of a poor family, for they must be provided with dowries. The elder daughter had been married off to a good-natured but rather pathetic man named Panayiotis. His great virtue as a son-in-law was that he had not been in a position to command much of a dowry. As a result of some childhood illness, he didn't seem 'quite right': he was thin, and knock-kneed, and he stammered. All of his brothers and sisters had emigrated to America, and the parents had followed them. The sole member of the once-large family left in the village was Panayiotis. He lived now in the little house by the sea, together with Madame Friday and her daughter, and their little girl, and he held no more authority in this miniature matriarchy than might have been expected. They all lived on the proceeds of their meagre olive groves and vines and peanut fields. Panayiotis used to appear at festivals and other public occasions, rigged out in a white coat and an ice-cream vendor's hat, both several sizes too large for him, and tried to peddle peanuts. Trying to sell peanuts in this district where practically everyone had large fields of them on the plain of Dramia was a ludicrous and pathetic operation, like selling ice to Eskimos, and I never once saw him make a sale. I suppose they had no other product to offer.

Madame Friday's other daughter had emigrated to Montreal, where she had found employment in a factory. (In Montreal there is a regular colony of people from this corner of Crete, including some seventy from the tiny village of Mathe alone.) This daughter had been engaged before leaving for the New World, but the fellow had summarily left her and married another girl—with a larger dowry, probably. The plan was that the girl would stay long enough in Canada to earn a handsome dowry, and then return to the village and wait for an offer. She had sent home the money that had been used to build our house, and it had been built slowly, when the payments arrived, a wall or two at a time, almost stone by stone. It would, of course, form a principal part of her dowry. They were very glad to rent us the house, for it represented the first return on the investment.

The thought of that girl, back from the world, sitting on the terrace of her house, doing her interminable knitting, and waiting for some man to be attracted not to her but to her dowry, compelled one to realise that there were indeed grave faults with the social system of this country. Yet the system seemed to be accepted by everyone; seldom, if ever, did we hear a word of criticism of it. Secretly we hoped the girl would have sense enough not to return, but to stay in the New World, whatever its hardships might be. Madame Friday, however, was hoping against hope that the girl *would* return; she talked of it constantly, and her secret dread was that the daughter would marry and never come back.

Madame Friday was highly regarded as a 'practical doctor' and midwife. Once, when a child developed a badly swollen neck gland, she was called in and prescribed a poultice of mashed raisins. She also made a paste of eggs, garlic and one or two other ingredients, and rubbed it on the patient's head in the shape of a cross, murmuring certain ritual phrases which were efficacious, only when the moon was dark. The child survived all this, no doubt owing as much to its natural resistance against remedies as well as disease. Faith, too, probably played a big part in these cures, for there was no doubt that the people put more trust in them than in most modern medicines. (I say 'most' medicines, because certain ones had caught on, had become almost fads: penicillin was the latest, and as it was freely available without prescription from any pharmacy in Canea, it was being given for everything from colds to measles. A lot of this business went to Madame Friday, for she had the only needle and syringe in the village.) Just to be on the safe side, most people would combine the newer treatments with the older or 'practical' remedies. For instance, after giving a child who had mumps a shot of penicillin, the healer would put the mystic *pentalpha* sign on both cheeks in blue ink—a five-pointed star with a line across each point, so that it looked like five A's, or alphas, around a circle. This sign was regarded more highly than the injections—and with some justification, for it is doubtful whether penicillin is of any use at all against mumps.

Later, when we had a touch of 'grippe', Madame Friday was around us with all sorts of advice and remedies. 'The grippe wants *tsikoudia,'** she croaked. By which she meant, not only that we should drink the fiery stuff (which would have been pleasant enough), but that we should rub our necks and chests and backs vigorously with it, and then cover up with warm clothing. Not a bad idea, actually. She also prescribed the classic *ventouses*, or cupping-glasses, and insisted on applying them herself to Inga (I flatly refused this, as I did most of her remedies). The procedure was thus: several thick tumblers were laid out in a row by the patient's bedside; wads of cotton were soaked in alcohol and wound on sticks; matches were at hand. The patient was made to lie with her upper back exposed. Then, with the hocus-pocus of a conjurer about to perform a trick, the old lady lighted the torches one by one and heated the glasses with them. The piping hot glasses were applied immediately to the victim's exposed back. Inga's yelps and screams filled the house, mingled with laughter, for the whole business *was* funny. Madame Friday, a grim witch all in black, slightly scandalised because we laughed, kept grimly at it until Inga's back was thoroughly red and tender, then piled the covers on, gave her a shot of *tsikoudia*, and mumbled one of her incantations. Next day the patient was well again.

* * *

Our nearest neighbours were Papa Leonidas, the village priest, and his wife and four small children. Greek Orthodox priests are allowed to marry and have families, but by so doing they renounce all possibility of ascending the hierarchy, for bishops must be celibate. Wives in Crete, merging themselves completely in the lives of their men, often abandon not only their family names, but also their Christian names; thus the wife of Papa Leonidas was known to everyone simply as 'Papadia' or 'Mrs Priest.' (This custom is carried so far that wives often become known forever by the feminine form of their husbands' *nick-names*: for example, the wife of a man nick-named 'Fasoulaki' or 'Little Bean' became known to one and all as 'Fasoulina', and she kept this name even long after the death of her husband.) Inga and Papadia became fast friends; often we enjoyed the company of the children, who were in and out of our yard all day.

---

* In western Crete, *raki,* is called *tsikoudia,* and so I shall refer to it by that name from now on. The word comes from *tsikouda,* the pulp of grapes left after they have been trodden for wine, from which the strong drink is then distilled.

Our favourite was the youngest, a wistful, surprisingly fair-haired lad named Nikos. The oldest girl was seven, and there was another boy of six and a girl of five. Children came along at the rate of one every year or two; another was on the way. Their house was tiny; they all slept in the same room. The wife did most of the cooking outdoors over an open fire, even on rainy days when she would hold an umbrella with one hand while she stirred the pot with the other. This despite the fact that she had a perfectly good gas stove inside! Probably she had grown up with outdoor cooking over brushwood fires, and kept to it by force of habit. Certainly they were not poor: the priest, who was the son of a famous *pallikari* leader from Vamos, the provincial capital of Apokoronas, had inherited extensive vineyards; and his wife brought a dowry of 60,000 drachmas to the household. They had a large radio, that symbol of peasant affluence, and the children were always well-dressed and well-fed—in striking contrast with many of the poorer children of the village. Papadia was a wonderful cook, as we well knew, for she was forever sending over plates of *dolmades* (stuffed vine leaves) and other tasty dishes.

Yet, despite their relative affluence, Papadia had few clothes, and hardly ever went anywhere. Most of the time, indeed, she was either pregnant or nursing. All day she worked about the house and in the yard. Her husband, whose priestly duties could hardly be said to constitute a crushing burden of work, spent most of his time in the coffeehouses, talking with the men; seldom did he lift a finger to help his wife, even with the heavier tasks. I say this not as a personal criticism of him, for it is the pattern followed in most Cretan homes: he was merely behaving like everyone else. By all rights this woman ought to have been discontented with her lot, for she was in precisely the situation that so many modern woman find hateful. She was not discontented; on the contrary she was one of the happiest women I have ever seen. It was a pleasure to be near her and to feel the glow of joy and pride that she radiated. Her body may have been toil-worn, but her face bore the unmistakable lineaments of satisfaction and contentment. I wouldn't claim that all Cretan women are like her, for we met many who were unhappy—often because of bad match-making. But she was not at all unusual and in the course of our travels in Crete we met enough of her sort to see clearly that it *is* possible for a woman to find real happiness in the fulfilment of her traditional role.

But even Crete is becoming slowly more 'modern'—that is, machines are being brought in, little by little, to do the work that men and women have always done with their hands; and with a little more money and an increase in leisure time, people are developing restless desires for more 'things': motor-bikes, transistor radios, new clothes. We witnessed the advent of some of these new things in our village.

At the start of the warm weather in May the priest bought a large Italian-made refrigerator; naturally, it created quite a sensation, for it was the only refrigerator in the village. The people promptly nicknamed it *to pharos*—the lighthouse—and at first we didn't see the connection, until Papadia opened the door and showed us: 'See, the light blinks on—then you close the door and it goes off. Just like the *pharos* on Cape Drepanon.'

This purchase certainly made sense. The priest's house, unlike ours and several others in the village, was wired for electricity, and the community was fortunate in having electric power available because of the proximity of a small generating station a short distance up the river. Why not take advantage of an opportunity to make life easier for a busy mother? But such is the force of old habits, that they found little use for the new machine. They still bought fresh meat on slaughter days, and cooked it and ate it immediately; likewise with fish; and the milk they sometimes got from the cheese factory was never chilled, but heated and drunk with sugar in the Greek style. What was there to put in the gleaming new refrigerator? Any Greek would know: a pitcher of water and a bowl of fruit. Hardly anything else. The cold water was greatly appreciated by everyone, but it scarcely seemed to justify the expense. The machine was always turned up high and never defrosted. Great ice crystals formed all over the inside; when the door was opened, one peered into an ice-cave complete, with stalagmites and stalactites. In the midst of it all, a half-frozen pitcher of water. All night long the machine was grinding and humming, but apparently this soothed rather than annoyed the family of six who shared the one room with the icy monster. We told the priest that it would be possible to turn the thing down, but he showed no interest whatever; he wanted ice and plenty of it. From a purely selfish point of view, it was convenient for us, as they allowed us to keep meat and fish and milk in it—in fact welcomed a chance to get more use out of it.

The icy idyll ended abruptly when the first electricity bill came in. Suddenly the priest realised that he had been paying heavily for those glasses of cold water. Off went the refrigerator, and it sat there, unplugged and silent, a lighthouse without a light, for the rest of the summer. At last, however, it became more generally useful—as a storage cupboard for utensils in the overcrowded little house. As a status symbol (its primary purpose, anyway, we suspected) its value was not impaired, for it could be turned on for special occasions such as festivals or name days, and cold water provided for a houseful of appreciative guests.

Better than any refrigerator is an orange grove, or a melon patch, or a fig tree. Georgillis, another of our neighbours, had all of these, plus a large flock of sheep—and he shared the products freely with us. The orange grove was right next to our house, and he repeatedly urged us to go there any time we liked, and to pick all the fruit we wanted. Often we walked across the fields to his house to buy vegetables, but these transactions could not have been at all profitable for him because for every drachma's worth of produce he sold us he felt obliged to give away something worth twice as much. His Cretan *philotimo* would not allow him to profit from strangers.

Georgillis was a mountaineer; he had moved down from his native village in the hills because of some 'family matters' (*oikoyeniaka*) which is the euphemistic Cretan expression for their notorious blood feuds. He had a goat-beard and often smelled of billy-goat, because the house where he lived with his wife and son was also the home of several goats and other creatures. Georgillis had been a guerrilla fighter in the mountains during the war and his wife always referred to him, respectfully, as 'the *pallikari*'. She was almost more of a *pallikari* than he was. Swathed from head to foot in permanent black for the sons she had lost in wars and feuds, she went out in the fields and did heavy work, and tended the flocks like any shepherd. She could throw rocks at errant sheep with the deadly accuracy of a young man—though she must have been well over sixty. Rumour had it that she had avenged the sons killed in feuds herself, and that she always carried a pistol hidden in her dress. For some reason we always called her 'Thea' or 'Auntie', though to most of the villagers she was known simply as 'Georgillina', the wife of Georgillis. She had seven sons and six of them had died violent deaths. The one who remained, Ioannis, was in his early twenties, and they seemed to have brought him up in the family tradition of reckless independence. Shortly after our arrival in the village, he was taken off to jail because he had pastured his flocks on someone else's land. The court had offered him a choice of paying a fine, the equivalent of about sixty dollars, or of imprisonment for thirty days. He chose jail— or perhaps the family chose it for him, not wishing to pay out such a lump sum. He returned looking thinner and paler, but not at all daunted. Jail seems to hold no social stigma whatever among the Cretans; if anything, it is something to boast and joke about.

Georgillis was a big talker, even for a Cretan, and a hard drinker, even for a Cretan, and an ingenious liar, even for a Cretan—but we liked him. There was nothing pretentious about him, and the talk, the drink and the lies were all in fun, part of the game of life.

Every morning Mr Xenophon Grillos made his magnificent entrance into the sea. With slow and stately dignity he would march his 264 pounds across the sand into the shallows. He would then swim, using some archaic and long-forgotten stroke, and while thus splashing and snorting, he resembled a great brown whale with a bald head. Then he would paddle along at a leisurely pace, booming out the Orthodox Liturgy in a tremendous bass that drifted far over the water to the sand dunes where we lay. Although very human and intensely alive, Xenophon seemed already to have assumed mythological proportions. He was one of the great characters, larger than life, that this country creates: Greece's greatest product and her finest contribution to the world.

When he spoke, it was in the language of hyperbole; to a stranger, it might have sounded like inordinate boasting, but such talk is the rule in Crete, where a man who doesn't boast may have his manhood come under suspicion. He loved to regale the assembled coffee-house loungers with passages from the *Odyssey* and the *Iliad,* and with moral aphorisms and tales, usually of trickery and cunning, from ancient times. Above all, he admired the Spartans. (Foreigners who tend to think of ancient Greece almost solely in terms of Athens are often surprised to discover the esteem in which Sparta is held by many modern Greeks. This is all the more natural in Crete, whose ancient customs were quite similar to those of Sparta.)

'I am Spartiac man!' he would often repeat to me, in his American English which was surprisingly good, considering that he had spent but six years in America, and had been back in Greece for fifty years. 'When I was a boy, I used to sleep on hard floor, summer and winter, with only one blanket. I used to run up mountains, like wild goat. Now I am strong man, seventy-four years old, still I go in sea every day, summer and winter. I no eat meat, no drink coffee. Fresh meat got too many proteins. Wine got too many proteins. I live from fruits, fishes. Squeeze dozen oranges every day, drink the gravy! Maybe I will be like my father, he lived to be 114 and then died from an accident.'

It was all familiar: his Spartan habits, his dietary notions, his ambition to live to 100—yet somehow it never became boring. He could have told more interesting tales, had he chosen to, for he had lived through the San Fransisco earthquake and fire, had worked in the mines of Utah, had returned to Greece to fight in the Balkan Wars, and later, during the Second World War when he was an official in the Canea customs house, had passed secret information about German movements to the British agents operating in the mountains. But invariably he passed over the more dramatic adventures of his life, and talked about everyday things. I could never get him to tell about the San Francisco earthquake; he preferred to talk about the man who ran the boarding house where he lived, and how he had wanted Xenophon to marry his daughter.

He belonged to the extensive and powerful Grillos clan, who had moved down from Sphakia to Apokoronas and had become so notorious for their activities, legitimate and otherwise, that they became the subject of a proverb: 'If it weren't for the Grilloi (which also means crickets in Greek) and the south wind, Apokoronas would be a perfect place to live.' He had sons, daughters, grandchildren and great-grandchildren scattered about Greece. He was a famous figure throughout the Canea district, renowned for, among other things, feats of physical strength. It was unusual for a man of this background to choose to live in a village instead of Canea or Athens; but he loved the fruits, flowers, sunshine, sea-bathing and coffee-house conversations of the village. He dressed as he lived, simply and comfortably: sandals, khakis, huge undershirt stretched over barrel chest. Every day he walked up to his vineyard on a hilltop and lay naked in the sun. His bald dome was tanned a permanent deep bronze; he exuded health and child-like joy.

The dubious amenities, of village life were not for his wife, however. She was a big, raw-boned woman who seemed as strong-willed as Xenophon, and that is saying a lot. She insisted on spending the winters in Athens, with her children; Xenophon refused to budge from the village, and so was left to keep house for himself. Their battle of wills was fought to a draw, but she lost the contest for public opinion—her independent action earned the opprobium of all the villagers, for in Crete the man is always assumed to be right, and woe betide any woman who is bold enough to challenge her lord and master. Now in summer the wife was back, but she faced virtual ostracism from her neighbours, and she and her husband exchanged no words, even while occupying the same house, even while she was cooking and serving his meals. Eventually the situation thawed somewhat; verbal intercourse, at least, was resumed.

Xenophon had his revenge by telling this story to the general approval of everyone in the coffee-house, that ultimate forum of village life: 'Woman is a piece of the devil. When God had made Adam, he said to himself, "Ah, poor fellow, he'll be lonely—I'll make a woman to keep him company." While Adam slept, the Lord sent the archangel to take his rib to make a woman. The archangel did this, and then he started back with it. Along the road he met the Devil, who stopped him and asked, "What bone is that you have there? Can I look at it?"—and then he grabbed it and ran off. The archangel chased the Devil all over the country, and round and round the mountain, but he couldn't catch him. Finally the Devil ran into a narrow deep cave, too narrow for the archangel to follow, but the tip of his tail was sticking out. The archangel got hold of the tail, and he pulled and pulled, and suddenly the end of it broke off in his hand. So the archangel looked at it, and he thought, 'Well, what can I do? It's getting late and I have to get back to Heaven. I'll never get that bone back from the Devil. I'll just take this along and give it to Him instead." He did, and the Lord didn't know the difference, and made woman from it. So you see, when you catch hold of a woman, you better look out, because you have got the Devil by the tail.' Late in May our little village had a royal visitor. Inga and I were in the house, going about our usual tasks, when a breathless child ran up and said we were wanted on the square. Unaware that we were being summoned to a royal audience, we went as we were: in old clothes and sandals.

Under the great trees chairs had been set up and a party of visitors was being entertained. Their cars were parked nearby, and the whole village population had gathered around. Xenophon, in the forefront, was extolling the virtues of the place. Doubtless he had told them about us, the only foreigners living here, and we had been summoned out of curiosity.

The leading figure of the entourage was Princess Marie of Greece, widow of Prince George, whose name is known to all Cretans. He is best remembered for that historic day of December 21, 1898, when he landed at Suda Bay as High Commissioner for the Great Powers and proclaimed the autonomy of Crete, and centuries of bondage fell away. That moment is vividly described in Kazantzakis's *Zorba the Greek* (translated by Carl Wildman, Simon and Schuster, New York): . . . 'Have you ever seen a whole people gone mad because they've seen their liberty?. . . If I live a thousand years, . . . what I saw that day I'll never forget! And if each of us could choose his paradise . . . I'd say to the Almighty: 'Lord, let my paradise be a Crete decked with myrtle and flags and let the minute when Prince George set foot on Cretan soil last for centuries!''

Prince George remained as High Commissioner for some eight years, and introduced some reforms and improvements, but became involved in a power struggle with the rising figure, Eleftherios Venizelos, who considered his methods autocratic. He was forced to leave after the Revolution of 1905. During this period and until Crete finally gained union with Greece in 1913, the island had its own flag, coinage and postage stamps. The capital was at Canea.

Although a princess of Greece and of Denmark, and aunt of the late King Paul, the Duke of Edinburgh and Princess Marina, Duchess of Kent, Princess Marie had overcome all these handicaps —and they *were* handicaps—to pursue a scientific career and to achieve international distinction in her own right, and under her own maiden name of Marie Bonaparte. After consulting Sigmund Freud as a patient in 1925, she had trained under him as a practitioner and teacher of psychoanalysis, and had done much original work in this field. She maintained a lifelong, close friendship with Freud and was largely responsible for getting him safely away from Vienna to England in 1938, when she raised the large sum demanded by the Nazis for his exit visa.

Now here was this great lady, sitting in our village square and inviting us to join her. Though over eighty, and rather fragile-appearing, she had alert, clear eyes and a very definite, almost haughty manner of speech and gesture. She looked the very picture of an aged aristocratic lady, from her grey hair and clearly defined features to the tips of her long white fingers. It would have been fascinating to speak with her about her friendship with Freud and her opinions on various psychoanalytical matters, but with a crowd of villagers all around, and the community president attempting an awkward speech, it was hardly possible. Instead we exchanged rather banal pleasantries about the village and answered her questions, for she was curious to know how we managed for food here, and how we happened to choose this place, and so on. We were high in our praises of the people and the place (Xenophon looking very pleased at hearing his beloved fruits and fishes extolled to royal strangers). We conversed in English, and she addressed the Cretans in, surprisingly, rather halting Greek (a woman said afterwards to Inga that she spoke Greek 'as you do'—not exactly a compliment to either of them).

110

The Eucalyptus Grove

The princess told us that she had come to this village for two reasons: because it was named for her husband (Georgioupolis= Georgetown), and because she wanted to see the eucalyptus trees that he had planted long ago. This was a sort of pilgrimage in his memory—as, indeed, her whole tour of Crete must have been. She had been swimming earlier in the day at Galatas, west of Canea, and spoke glowingly of the benefits of sea bathing. We agreed with her, and started to tell about *our* lovely beach—but one of the ladies-in-waiting hastily motioned to us to desist, and in an undertone explained, 'Please don't tell her about beaches—she'll insist on having another swim!'

A shy little girl came up with a bouquet of wild flowers. The princess bade us all farewell, and the party went off to look at the original eucalyptus tree. The royal audience, alfresco, had ended. I doubt very much whether most of the villagers had any idea who she was. That evening, one of our neighbour women informed us that she was 'the old English queen'.

Some months later we were greatly saddened to read of the death of Marie Bonaparte; but it was good to reflect that she had had that last pilgrimage to Crete, and that the eucalyptus grove of Georgioupolis had given her such obvious pleasure.

10

Wedding in the Amari

Now we were in the heart of western Crete, with vast reaches of mountains, whole provinces, hundreds of villages inviting exploration. Crete, with its infinite variety and its astonishing changes within a few miles, never becomes boring but leads one ever onwards, deeper into its labyrinth. Until I knew every spring, every footpath, every village and ravine, I would never tire of this island. With Georgioupolis as our base, we set out on a series of excursions and explorations in the Canea and Rethymnon prefectures.

The first of these many trips occurred only a few days after we had moved. Easter came around again, our second in Crete—how fast that year had passed! And we wanted to get away, up somewhere in the hills. Someone suggested Spili, a large village in the Rethymnon district to the east of us (that should have warned us away: recommended places seldom live up to expectations). We took the bus along the north coast road to Rethymnon, where we had to wait a few hours for the afternoon bus to Spili. Those few hours were quite enough, for despite the rakish charm of some of the older streets running down towards the harbour, the town as a whole struck us as dreary and depressing; and we were subjected to a battery of not particularly friendly stares of even greater intensity than one usually encounters in Crete. A pack of unruly schoolboys followed us about, and mothers called to their children to 'come and look at the strangers'. We acquired a sudden new sympathy for the animals in zoos that have no refuge from vulgar curiosity.

The up-country was better, with its olive grounds and its open views towards distant mountains. The little villages along the road looked neat, with well-kept houses festooned with flowerpots. The Rethymnon district is supposed to be one of the most 'civilised' in all Crete, and it has produced a number of writers and university professors. The novelist, Pandelis Prevelakis, a good friend of Kazantzakis and a talent in his own right, is a native of this province, and his little masterpiece of a novel, *The Sun of Death,* is set in a Rethymnon village.

Spili, one of the largest of these roadside communities, was attractive, too, but it had been marred somewhat by the construction of a hideous big church just across the road from the inn where we found a room. One would think that Crete is already sufficiently supplied with churches, and that money and labour might well be diverted from further church-building towards something more useful, such as schools and hospitals; yet every village aspires to have one of these gimcrack monstrosities—old churches, weathered into harmony with their surroundings, will not do. The trouble with Spili was that the main road from Rethymnon to the south coast port of Ayia Galini had brought it prosperity, and it was developing a 'country town' atmosphere. However, it was Good Friday, and here we were.

We went to church in the evening, and again we were disappointed: no lovely processions around the village, only around that ugly churchyard. Cretan festivals are pretty much of a lottery: the visitor hoping for the beautiful or the traditional observance is as likely to be disappointed as not. However, none of the local people shared our attitude; they were all excited because a Bishop had come. He conducted the services himself—an enormous, big-bellied, purple-faced man with long white beard and hair meticulously combed. His puffy red hands gripped his golden staff as he beat it on the floor in time with the Liturgy, which he bawled in a fog-horn voice. Midway through it he had to compete with a donkey, braying in the road outside; but the donkey was no match for him. His title of *despotis* suited him very well, for he was indeed a despotic figure. Everyone in the church was absolutely terrified of him. I couldn't help thinking of the contrast he would have made alongside one of the pallid 'new theologians', timidly debating 'our image of God'. There was no doubt in *his* mind about the image of God—He would be a figure very much like himself: fat, imposing and tyrannical. Actually, I think the Bishop *was* a kind of God to many of the villagers. Our peasant woman innkeeper was tremendously impressed by him, and bestowed on him the highest praise: 'He is a good man—very rich'. He would have been a fool or a saint if he hadn't been rich, considering that Bishoprics in the Orthodox Church at that time were being auctioned off to the highest bidders. Inga's comment was more astringent: 'He embodies everything that Luther fought against'.

The prospect of listening to the despotic braying all through Easter unnerved us, and so we hired a donkey and a guide the next day, and set out over the hills to the Amari Valley where, away from the main roads, we might hope for a gentle Easter. Our donkey-driver, a lean and leathery man who looked as though he knew every foot of these hills, set a fast pace with Inga following side-saddle on the beast, and me struggling along in the rear of the procession—an arrangement that was to become quite familiar to us during our journeys through roadless areas of western Crete. We climbed upward for a while and then levelled off on a plateau where fields of ripening wheat rippled in the west wind. I had to turn continually to drink in the sight, behind us to the west, of range upon range of blue mountains, with green valleys in between, and white villages on the lower flanks; while high above, like clouds, the snowy summits of the White Mountains floated. Inga enjoyed it all naturally from her position atop the donkey. Under a great carob tree in the centre of the plain we stopped and refreshed ourselves at a spring of clear water. And then we pressed on until the country to the east opened out: Mount Ida looming surprisingly close, just across the deep Amari Valley that yawned like a chasm far below us. At the point where the trail began to descend, the donkey-man left us and we went on by ourselves.

As we descended to Yerakari, the highest of the Amari villages, the scenery seemed almost Alpine, with lush green meadows and tall oaks and firs. The village sits at about 2,500 feet and gets much snow in winter; its vegetation and fruits are quite northern—apples, potatoes and cherries, for which it is famous. The present village is new, the old one having been burned by the Germans in reprisal against the people, who sheltered many English agents and fugitives all during the war.

We wandered into the square, and found ourselves among mountaineers: men in boots and breeches, with the indefinable *esprit* of mountain people, and their blend of friendliness and almost shy reticence. Looking at them, one thought of Wordsworth's lines: "Thou wear'st upon thy forehead clear/The freedom of a Mountaineer:/A face with gladness overspread!' We liked them far better than the Cretans of the lowlands, of the towns and the roadside villages. They all greeted us warmly, and when we ordered drinks from the kafeneion, half a dozen of them vied for the honour of paying for us. No stranger is allowed to pay for his own drinks in a Cretan mountain village. Yerakari had a sort of inn with a room to let, and soon we were comfortably settled in it, resting from our long walk.

* * *

Wedding in the Amari

They resurrected Christ that night, and afterwards, in the churchyard, they burned Judas in a colossal bonfire. While we were observing the spectacle of the excited children running about in the flickering firelight, dodging firecrackers cast at random among the crowd, a woman addressed us in overflowing English. Within minutes she was expounding on 'the Greek Soul'. From there the talk turned to the war, and the lady explained that she had learned her English when the British had helped her to escape to Egypt at the age of sixteen. She introduced herself—Sophie Xekalou was her name—and her husband the village schoolmaster, who was standing nearby quietly puffing on his pipe, in remarkable contrast to his effusive wife. They invited us to have Easter dinner with them the next day, and sometime after midnight we all said 'chronya polla' for the last time and trooped home. Not many people managed to get their Easter candles home that night, for the winds up here on the flank of Mount Kedros blew too quickly.

The next day, in Sophie's charming house, over an excellent dinner, we heard a great deal more about the war, which had affected the Amari Valley directly, for this was the main 'spy route' for British agents moving from one end of German-occupied Crete to the other. Sophie and her husband, like most people we met in this part of Crete, had a passionate admiration for the English. As an impressionable girl in wartime Cairo, she had watched a British military parade and thought it 'the most beautiful thing she had ever seen'. She still remembered the war songs and the jokes. While she spoke of all this, her two sons absorbed it all silently; the mother seemed to dominate the household, yet the father exercised a kind of silent authority, too—he seemed to regard his wife's bubbling enthusiasms with a tolerant, slightly amused affection. As Sophie continued to speak of her interests and talents, such as singing (she had been urged to study voice abroad, but instead had married and come to this village) and drawing, and of her girlhood in Herakleion, I suddenly became aware that, as so often happens in Crete today, I was in the presence of a familiar nineteenth-century type: the town woman of good bourgeois family, with some talent and artistic inclinations, who goes to live in the provinces and then feels 'buried' (Sophie's own word for how she felt). She seemed to have stepped right out of the pages of some Russian or French novel. Her high ideals and fine manners were in sharp contrast to the rude peasants of Yerakari, and I suspected that, despite her love of old Cretan customs, songs and handicrafts, she was rather isolated among these people; she admitted to having but one friend in the village.

Yet she shared with her husband the typical liberals' desire to help
educate the people, to improve their lot through books and learning
They spoke in strong terms of the need for reforms in Greece. The
yearning for a better future, and their faith in education and
progress, were quite characteristic of nineteenth century optimism
untainted by twentieth century despair and cynicism.

Towards the end of the evening the husband and wife joined in
singing Cretan songs; both of them had unusually fine voices. With
intense emotion they sang the familiar old *rizitiko* ballad, that begins
'When will the sky be clear, when will the spring appear?' It originated
in the roots of the White Mountains during the long centuries of
Venetian and Turkish oppression, but it has been taken over as a
sort of anthem by the Venizelist liberals of western Crete. The singer
of the ballad plans to take up his gun in the spring, and kill the
enemies of his country—rather a blood-thirsty dream, but the song
is beautiful and approaches in depth of feeling the folk songs of
Russia. We have heard it countless times, yet never was it sung with
more moving intensity than that night in Yerakari. All of the longing
for a better future, for reforms and education and enlightenment
that characterise the more intelligent people of the Greek provinces
went into that song. It rang in our ears long after we had said our
good-nights and left the house, to make our way through the dark
lanes to our inn.

Two roads lead down from Yerakari: one heads generally northward, towards the head of the main Amari Valley, and the other
dips in an easterly direction around the flank of Mount Kedros
eventually joining the main road down the Amari at a lower point.
Our plan was to stay high up, and after some time to catch a bus back
to Rethymnon from one of the villages at the upper end of the valley
but first we wanted to have a look at this rather out-of-the-way
corner, so we set out for a stroll, intending to return to Yerakari by
midday. The dirt road wound among the oaks and firs, and soon we
came to a semi-ruined Byzantine church, Ayios Ioannis, where we
examined some frescoes by an artist who seemed to delight in
painting tortured neurasthenic faces reminiscent of those by Edvard
Munch: surprising to say the least, in such a setting as this. The
Byzantines, seemingly so utterly remote from everything modern
must have shared at least one thing with twentieth century man: the
frustrations and neuroses of all-encompassing bureaucracy. Those
worried saints on the walls of Ayios Ioannis might just as well have
been American civil servants called upon by the Un-American

ctivities Committee to explain their political and sexual pecca-
illoes.

But, just as the topography of Crete changes completely and un-
xpectedly during a journey of a few miles, so with the human land-
cape. At Sophie's house the night before, we had been in the world
f nineteenth century provincial liberals; in the chapel of Ayios
bannis, we were in Byzantium, with surprising echoes of modern
mes; and now, as we wandered into the narrow lanes of the tiny
illage of Kardaki, we were on the verge of the Age of Heroes. In a
ourtyard of a house we saw several *pallikaria* sitting about, drinking
nd talking and being waited on by their womenfolk; they hailed us
nd called us over for a drink. The drink was the most potent
ikoudia, and I had no sooner downed one glass at a manful gulp
an another was pressed upon me—that, it seemed, was their
ormal pace of drinking. It was all part of the display of masculinity
at goes with the *pallikari* cult in which all Cretan mountaineers
articipate. The original *pallikaria* were medieval foot soldiers ac-
ompanying mounted knights; but the term is in general use today to
enote any brave and manly fellow—or any fellow who *looks*
ifficiently fearless.

The master of the house, we soon learned, was the biggest and
oisiest *pallikari* of all, a man named Sotirios Monachoyios who was
s friendly and boisterous as a Great Dane puppy. The three or four
ther men who lounged about—all in their full regalia of boots,
reeches, headkerchiefs and so on—were wartime comrades who
ad assisted the British agents who had passed this way. While they
iterrupted one another to regale us with blood-curdling war stories,
otirios rummaged through old cardboard boxes covered with dust,
roducing in turn a list of all the English and New Zealander soldiers
ho had passed down the Amari chain of villages during the war, a
tter of praise by a leading British agent, and finally the *pièce de
ésistance,* a citation in Greek from a high-ranking English general;
ne of the others read it aloud, with occasional corrections by
otirios, who had it by heart. There was no doubt about it, he was
ie real thing: a genuine, certified Hero, and proud of it. I was im-
iensely impressed, but Inga's attention wandered; she murmured to
ie. 'Have you noticed his mother?' I hadn't: she was an incon-
picuous bent figure in black, with a pointed nose on which rested a
attered pair of spectacles; but the most outstanding thing about her
as the look of tired resignation on her face. 'It must be difficult to
ave a hero in the house all the time,' said Inga, voicing the universal
pinion of women.

Winds of Crete

After consuming half a dozen *tsikoudia* in quick succession, together with some food which I gulped down without even noticing
what it was, our hosts announced that they would take us to see a
Byzantine chapel that was 'better than Ayios Ioannis'. It was a
boisterous procession that staggered through the lanes, singing
loudly. One of the heroes showed us two bullets which, he declared,
he was saving to shoot into the ceiling at the *glendi* (merry-making)
they would have that night. Sotirios extracted a pistol from his belt
and waved it in the air, shouting 'Boom-boom'. I couldn't help
feeling relieved that we wouldn't be there when the shooting started,
for in their present condition they might well aim at the ceiling and
hit the floor—and it was unlikely that their marksmanship would
have improved by nightfall.

Before reaching the white chapel, they respectfully straightened
up, rewound their *sarikia,* and assumed an air of stiff restraint and
sobriety. Standing under an imposing fresco of Christ Pantocrator,
Sotirios solemnly informed us that this church was very, very old—
pre-Christian in fact.

Inga moistened her hand and rubbed away the waxy film that
covered one of the faces on the wall; immediately the colours and
features came to life. Our companions, enchanted by this, offered
enthusiastic assistance; one of them ran out and returned with a
large bucket of water, and they all set to work, moistening their
handkerchiefs, rubbing the walls and slopping water all over. They
were well on their way to cleaning the whole church; and to avoid
that disaster, we tactfully indicated our desire to leave.

On the way back to the village, by a different path, they showed us
the spot where the Germans shot several villagers in reprisal for the
help that had been given the English. Nearby there was a small
monument and under it a crypt containing the skulls and bones of
the slaughtered ones—a reminder that the *pallikaria* had been a
necessary part of Cretan life, and that it is only recently they have
become redundant.

We stopped for a final *tsikoudia* outside another house with some
relatives of Sotirios. One of them, an ancient crone in black with one
front tooth left, fell instantly in love with my red beard, and the
whole time we were there she had one arm around my shoulders and
with her other hand kept stroking my beard. 'Ah, if I were younger!'
she croaked. This was the only Cretan woman who had ever said she
liked my beard. A last, bone-breaking handshake from each of the
heroes, and we were on our way back to Yerakari; but halfway there

we collapsed in a meadow under some stately oaks, to recover at leisure from the after-effects of heroic hospitality.

We would have rested much longer, had we known what was in store for us. As it was, we went back to Yerakari, picked up our knapsacks, and set out to walk around the head of the Amari. By the time we reached the crossroads at the top of the valley, the spring sun was high in the sky and we were dusty and tired, so we sat down on some rocks by the roadside to rest.

We had been sitting thus for about five minutes when the notes of a lyre reached us on the clear air of the heights, and soon afterwards we saw some sort of procession approaching along the road from the nearest village. As it drew nearer, we could see that it was a wedding party led by two musicians, a lyre and a lute player. They were followed by a young man, doubtless the bridegroom, escorted by a troop of friends and relatives. There must have been some thirty or forty people in the party, all dressed up in their Sunday best, and all of their eyes were on us, two bedraggled tramps sitting at the roadside. Is there any other country where sweaty strangers would be picked up off the road and invited as guests of honour to a wedding? But here in Crete it was inevitable; we had known it the moment we saw the party coming.

A tall young man in a dark suit detached himself from the crowd and spoke to us in American, 'Hello, my friends—will you come along to our wedding?' Vainly we sought for excuses: our tiredness, our inappropriate attire, our knapsacks. It was no use—we were once again the prisoners of hospitality. They wouldn't even allow us to carry our own luggage; our new-found friend, who called himself 'John' instead of 'Ioannis' because he had been to America while working on a merchant ship, shouldered both of the sacks himself. He was from the village of Apostoli, and it was his brother who was being married. They were on their way to claim the bride.

We left the road and started down a steep stony path. The women in the party stopped, sat down on rocks, and opened the brown paper sacks they were all carrying. They took out high-heeled shoes and put them on in place of their low walking shoes. After that, they teetered and slipped over the stones like mules on a wet pavement. Fortunately, it was not far to the house of the bride's family.

The bride's father and mother were at the gate to greet all the new arrivals. Inside, on the airy terraces under grape arbours, a large party was already assembled. We were all given a glass of *tsikoudia* and a special wedding cookie as we passed into the yard. Inga and I were shown to chairs on the upper terrace. The musicians began to play Cretan dances, and immediately a circle formed. 'John', sitting next to us, asked if we wouldn't rather hear a cha-cha or tango (his idea of the latest modern dances). He said he had been a champion Cretan dancer, but that when he was in America he had come to prefer the newer dances. Also, he expressed regrets that they could not offer us whiskey, which he claimed he preferred to *tsikoudia*. I had the impression that he was basically a good fellow, bright and handsome, of sound peasant stock, but that he had been slightly corrupted by a touch of the American poison; Greece is full of such miserable specimens. However, we finally convinced him that we liked Cretan dances and Cretan drinks better; and he got up and joined the circle and gave a memorable *Chaniotikos* complete with high leaps and thigh-slapping—a performance worthy of a former champion.

We were taken to an inner room to see the bride. There she sat, arrayed for the sacrifice: encased in yards and yards of tulle and lace, red-faced and embarrassed. She was a rather winsome lass for whom we felt instant sympathy in her present plight. In an adjoining room her dowry was laid out for the admiration of all: not only the hand-woven things on which the prospective bride had spent all her spare time for years, but also, in places where they were sure to be seen and commented on, the factory-made stockings and panties and brassières and plastic handbags that had been bought in Rethymnon. Out among the men, the bridegroom looked miserable in his own way, all dressed up in a white shirt and suit and tie, while his whole appearance and bearing cried out for boots, breeches and *sariki*.

The guests were being taken in relays into a large room downstairs. Eventually our turn came, and we sat down to a long table with some thirty others. The harried family of the bride were feeding the entire village that day, and good food it was, too: roast lamb, choice cheese, salad, good wine. But many of the guests partook sparingly, saving room for the second feast later in the day, at the bridegroom's house.

In due time, everyone having eaten and drunk, the entire crowd of several hundred people trooped down the lane to the little church. As many as could, crowded inside; the rest hung about outside. Inga and I were given a place near the ruddy-faced, white-bearded, twinkly-eyed old priest. He looked like an archaic magus in his flowing robes, about to perform his sacred rituals. But there was no solemnity in the atmosphere, just warmth and good humour, even gaiety. Laughter and small talk never ceased; at times one could scarcely hear the priest because of the incessant background chatter. The bride became tearful at the climactic moment when the *stephania,* the little white crowns, linked by a ribbon, were placed on the heads of the couple by the priest and then, exchanged three times by the *koumbaros* or best man. But a *koumbaros* is much more than a best man; he will be the protector of the new family and his relation to it is as strong as a blood tie in the eyes of the Orthodox Church. He will stand god-father to at least the first child, and if possible will give some financial assistance to it through the years. The strength of the *koumbaros* relationship has been fading somewhat in Crete in recent years, but it is still a very important one. The importance of ritual in the lives of peasants cannot be overestimated, and we have heard it said many times that a couple is not 'really married' until these crowns have been exchanged. A common word for the wedding itself, *stephanoma,* takes its name from the crowning, as does the verb, *stephanono,* to marry.

Now the couple were considered to be united forever, and the good spirits of the crowd positively bubbled over as the old priest joined hands with the bride and groom and performed the ancient 'Isaiah Dance' around the altar. Then all of us got a handful of walnuts mixed with honey—obvious procreative symbols—and the priest had a large drink of wine (echoes of the wedding at Cana). One of the guests, a large red-faced fellow, loudly demanded a drink of wine, too, and the priest gaily handed over a glass, spilling wine on the heads of people as it was passed from hand to hand. The man drank it all down at one gulp, and wiped his mouth on his sleeve; the onlookers said 'Bravo, bravo!' After that there was a great deal of confusion, a rush for the door, and much kissing and handshaking of the bride and groom.

Outside, on the wide terrace of the churchyard, high above the Amari Valley, with Mount Ida hovering over it all like a great guardian angel, the wedding dance was performed. The bride and groom first danced together, once and then twice around the circle; then the two fathers took their turns and danced with the bride; and then one by one all of the male relatives on both sides stepped up, grasped the girl's white handkerchief, and led her round and round. As each man finished his dance, he would throw some money on the ground for the newlyweds; by the end of the dance, more than a thousand drachmas had been collected. The dancing must have gone on for nearly an hour, yet throughout it all the bride maintained her poise, whirling and stepping lightly in her voluminous skirts, in a kind of trance perhaps induced by her new state and by the feeling of joy and relief that the actual ceremony was over.

Then at last the bride and groom mounted handsome mules, decorated with fine woven saddle blankets, and started out for their new home. There was a stop at the bride's house, where her suitcase was loaded on to the husband's mule; and the crowd all trooped into the house and seized items of her dowry to carry to the new home. Inga carried a large pillow; I had a red, yellow and green woven blanket. The couple rode ahead, on up the hill, and the rest of us streamed along behind.

The neighbouring village of Apostoli was the destination. Here we arrived at a large house with spacious terraces: a huge partiarchal establishment dominated by the figure of the bridegroom's father, a well-to-do peasant, big, brawny and hearty, clumping about in high black boots, seeing to it that all the guests were well cared for. In a long, low, whitewashed room, under huge handhewn roof beams of smoke-darkened cypress wood, everyone sat on chairs and on the long benches that lined the walls, while the floorboards creaked and groaned under the stamping feet of dancers, and the lyre and lute players churned up beads of sweat on their brows by their frenzied music-making. And now the real feasting began. Again in relays, the guests were invited into another room where long tables were laid for fifty diners at a time. The women of the household brought on course after course: two meat dishes, potatoes and macaroni, *mizithropites* or cream cheese cakes, fruit and wine. Everything was of the finest quality in this prosperous house; the wine, especially, ranked as the best we had tasted in Crete, equal indeed to the first-rank products of French vineyards. 'This is what they drank at Cana!' said one of our tablemates, a grinning old man who was gorging himself on meat and drink. Macaroni and potatoes he spurned: 'Why should I eat such things here?' he said candidly, 'I get macaroni every day—here I eat meat!' And forthwith he helped himself to more.

The air was full of talk and laughter and singing. 'Songs of the board' were in order—beautiful old *rizitika* ballads reserved for weddings and similar occasions. And they sang plaintive or satirical or bawdy couplets, *mantinades*, ending always with the refrain, '*Aman! Aman!*' which is Turkish for 'Mercy!' Some of these they composed on the spot for the occasion, including two in our honour. Even John, the young brother of the groom, shed entirely his false mantle of modernism, and sang *mantinades* and danced Cretan style with the others. The party lasted, by time-honoured custom, all night; but we gave out long before the others, and retired to the guest room of our host's house, to a blessed privacy and rest that the bride and groom were no doubt longing for. Owls and night-hawks, accustomed to their nocturnal flights above a sleep-muffled village, must have been sorely puzzled and alarmed, for there were shouts, voices raised in song, the high-pitched sound of the lyre, the clink of many glasses and, some time past midnight, volley after volley of rifle shots resounding off the hillsides in pure joy.

11

In the White Mountains

Mountains and sea: great upheavals of earth and rock, and moving expanses of water—these are the twin necessities of my spirit. An astrologer would probably say that this need followed naturally for me, born in January under the sign of Capricorn, a goat with a fish tail—and likewise for Inga, an Aquarian or water-bearer who just missed being a Capricorn by one day. Whatever the explanation, we both felt this magic pull of water and rock, and we agreed that man's physical environment is of the utmost importance to his spiritual happiness. In Crete one is never out of sight of mountains, nor far enough from the sea not to feel it in the air, even though it may not be in view. We consciously sought them during our years on the island. The first requirements of any new house we moved to were not whether it had water or electricity or any such inessential mundane things—but whether mountains were framed in the windows, and the sea in our back yard.

In western Crete what held us, what fascinated us and never palled, was the constant presence of the White Mountains. They are called 'white' not so much because of the snow that covers them for some six months of every year, but because of the peculiar dazzling whiteness of their naked rock summits during snowless periods. They have always had their name—*Levka Ori*—even in ancient times. They aren't spectacularly high, by Alpine or Andean standards; the highest peak is a little over eight thousand feet, slightly lower than Mount Ida in central Crete.* (Some shepherds of my acquaintance once sought to remedy this deficiency, and make 'the *Levka Ori* as high as *Psiloriti*'—as Ida is called—by piling up huge stones on the summit. This was a characteristically Cretan gesture in its quixotic display of frantic energy for a mystic ideal—challenging nature for the sake of the honour of one's own place.) But in this range that

---

* It seems typical of the confusion, mystery and controversy surrounding all things Cretan, that no two reference books seem to agree on the altitudes of mountains on the island. I have taken the safer course, and given approximate figures.

forms roughly a great triangle there are more than twenty peaks over six thousand feet in height and, rising sheer from the sea as it does on the south coast, the range gives an impression of grandeur that can only be called—do I dare to make such a comparison?— Himalayan. I have never seen the Himalayas from the northern hills of India— that is one of my still unfulfilled dreams of travel—but I have pondered long over many pictures of them, and more recently I was told by a man who had actually just been to India, and who stopped off in Crete on his way home, that the resemblance between the two ranges was astonishing. The White Mountains have the Himalayan quality of changing appearance from one hour, even from one minute, to the next. Veiled in mists, viewed over the labyrinthine foot-hills on the north side that are known as the *Riza,* or **root,** they appeared awesome and remote. In summer, bare and scorched, they presented—to my eyes—a friendlier aspect, for now I could hope to go there, to walk over them. For of course I could not resist the challenge of these alluring summits—nothing for it but that I must go there, and the sooner the better.

We both went, which was even better. Inga could not hope to climb to the upper heights, but there was one trip that we could do together: down the Samaria Gorge. This deep canyon in the midst of the highest peaks of the White Mountains extends for some twelve miles from the plateau of Omalo down to the Libyan Sea. We had dreamed of making this trip before we ever came to Crete, having read fabulous stories of the gorge. Therefore, the trip was certain of success, for nothing in life gives as much satisfaction as the actual living of old dreams.

The Omalo, unlike the plateau of Lassithi which it somewhat resembles, harbours no permanent community. In winter when it is snowbound the summer shepherds who inhabit the stone huts around its perimeter migrate to their villages lower down. They were all in residence when we arrived, and we heard the musical sound of sheep-bells and the harsher noise of shepherds' fierce yelling as they rounded up the animals for the evening milking. At the solitary kafeneion in the centre of the plain we obtained a rude and delicious meal of yogurt and dark bread made from Omalo wheat. We spent the night in a rough but cosy stone hut which the proprietor offered us.

Sunrise, and we were out, walking along a narrow rutted road over the plain towards a distant wall of grey rock, the mountain called Gigilos, where we knew the gorge began. Here in the bottom of this oval saucer amid encircling hills, one did not sense fully that one was in the heart of the mountains. That awareness came with breathtaking suddenness when we climbed the rim of the saucer, and everything—road, plain, the very solid ground under our feet—simply vanished, and below us the chasm opened, infinitely deeper, wider and grander than anything we had been led to expect. They say that this is 'the biggest gorge in Europe', but that sounds tepid: here at the brink of Samaria the comparisons that leap to the mind are on a greater scale—one thinks of Yosemite and the Grand Canyon itself.

A deep breath, a backward glance at the level plateau, and then the plunge. The trail zig-zagged steeply, amid wind-gnarled cypresses that jutted at odd angles from the rocky slopes. We were climbing down the Xiloscalo, or 'ladder', the path that dips three thousand feet from the Omalo to the bottom of the upper gorge. The overhanging mass of Gigilo's grey cliffs tilted threateningly overhead, and off to the right, towards the west, was the knife-edged saddle that marked the border between the eparchies of Sphakia and Selino —country that I was later to know by heart after several high-altitude outings. We were now in Sphakia, the mountain-walled stronghold of southwestern Crete where wildness—of men, animals, and nature —turns at bay and snarls at encroaching civilization. It was wildness that we wanted, that we had wanted from the beginning.

Our pace was leisurely, as the spirit of the place demanded. We had hours, days, weeks ahead of us—there were no time limits at all to this excursion. We felt that haste would have been a kind of violation. We had rucksacks, sleeping bags, food, and in the bottom of the ravine was a stream of pure, cold water. When we reached the stream we were tired and hot from the steep climb down (downhill walking being often more difficult than uphill) and so we found a sheltered spot in a glade of cypresses, where a waterfall sparkled into a rock pool, and undressed and bathed naked in the wondrously reviving water. Then we lay on smooth round boulders in the warm sun, and coupled as casually and freely as two birds or beasts. Birds, water, trees: there *are* paradises on earth. Our true needs are dazzling in their simplicity.

Neither of us found the gorge terrifying, as some writers have described it. Certainly the gorge is haunted: everywhere in it one feels the presence of the old nature deities—nereids, satyrs, nymphs —but they are on the whole benevolent spirits.

Above all it is Britomartis of the hunt to whom this gorge is consecrated. She was a Cretan goddess, or perhaps merely a protégé of Artemis—it is not quite clear which—to whom the cypresses in the heart of the gorge were supposedly dedicated. Now a tiny chapel of Ayios Nikolaos stands there, doubtless on the exact site of the ancient temple. It is dwarfed by the tremendous cypresses, the final grove of what was once a forest that covered all of Crete. These are not the trim pencil-thin cypresses of Tuscan landscapes but their shaggier cousins, the *cypress horizontalis,* with wide-spread branches, trunks several feet in girth, towering a hundred and fifty feet and more in height—the tree to which the Cretans refer when they wish to praise a fine man, saying that he is as tall (or as strong) as a cypress. They had been spared by the woodcutters who for thousands of years had stripped the forests of Crete, first for the pillars of Minoan palaces, then for masts and timbers for the ships of Rome and Venice—spared partly because of the inaccessibility of the spot, but mainly because temple cypresses always have been, and still are, considered sacred.

We were guests of Britomartis that night—camped out in her grove, on beds of cypress boughs. We lay long and gazed at the stars overhead between the walls of the ravine, and listened to night sounds. When the nearly-full moon rolled over the eastern bastion the gorge and grove filled with yellow light, so bright that, as a test, I got out pencil and notebook and was able to write: 'This has been as nearly perfect as a day can be. What a *joy* life can be! I hope I live to attain wisdom in old age, but if I had to die young, I would die happy now.'

I would have liked nothing better than to live out my days in the midst of all that wild beauty, hunting partridges and wild goats, tending a small garden, chopping wood in winter. Yet the men and women who *had* lived here had left willingly. There had been, in the middle of the ravine, a tiny village, a close community of four or five related households, members of the Viglis clan—renowned feuders, sheep stealers and illegal hunters of ibex. Now the government had moved in and bought their land, with the intention of making the gorge into a sort of natural park. The plan, like so many in Greece, had lain fallow for a long time, but the villagers had been moved out of Samaria itself and down to Ayia Roumeli at the lower end of the gorge. We came upon their village about an hour's walk below the chapel: just a half dozen rude houses—stone walls, sod roofs—and a few poor olive trees struggling for life.

We crossed the stream bed—winter torrents had here carved a deep cleft between rock walls—on a neglected wooden footbridge. Doors hung ajar and empty chairs sat on terraces under mulberry trees laden with rotting fruit. And it was not only fruit that was rotting. A ghastly stench filled the air of the first lane we entered, and suddenly at our feet lay Horror: the decaying carcass of a goat. We retreated hastily, and tried another lane. Here it was more peaceful: nothing but bird-sounds, and an occasional soft, almost imperceptible puff! as another mulberry fell to the ground. We stepped into a house, cautiously climbed a creaking stairway. Everything rough-hewn and hand-carved: chairs, chests, benches. A faded *sakouli* hung on a peg; a mouldy blanket lay on a bench. I opened a chest and got a shock: there lay a rifle and a bandolier of cartridges! Quickly I shut it and involuntarily looked around. Those famous feuders might still be lurking about, and how would they regard this intrusion? We left that house hastily.

But we couldn't resist the mulberries. I found a heavy ladder against a wall and moved it—it took all my strength—to a position where we could climb to a roof terrace directly under the thickest branch. And we stood there and feasted ourselves, gorged like birds on the fruits of paradise. Then, gathering courage, we went inside another house, found a suitable bench, and lay down for a comfortable siesta during the hot hours.

I started awake: had I heard a footstep? Then a door creaked, and there were steps on the stairs. Inga woke too, and we waited with bated breath. The head and shoulders of a young man appeared in the trap door. When he saw us he stopped short, surely as surprised as we were, yet betraying it by no sign. I greeted him: '*Hairetai!* Are we in your house?'

'Yes,' he replied, coming forward and extending his hand, all the while gazing at us most curiously, 'It was my house. Now they've all gone. I've come from Canea today and I'm going to Ayia Roumeli.' All the way from Canea—about forty miles, much of it on foot over the mountains, all of it in one day—and yet he had nothing with him, no food, no jacket, nothing but the light clothes he stood in.

He went on, 'I have been working on a ship. I haven't been back here for over a year. When I went away my family was living in this house.' And he had returned unencumbered with any luggage—and found us.

'Weren't they sorry to leave here?' I asked.

'Why? There's nothing here.'

'But it's beautiful—it's paradise!'

'*Paradise? This?* This is hell!'

He glanced about the room, stepped out on the terrace and casually picked a few mulberries. After a few minutes he turned to leave.

'Shall we have company together to Ayia Roumeli?' he asked.

'We'd like to stay here awhile. Excuse us for using your house.'

He gestured grandly over the empty rooms, 'You're welcome. It's not mine any more—it's yours.'

He went down the stairs, through the lane and over the wooden foot-bridge without ever looking back: a man apparently free of the past. And yet, if that were so, why had he stopped here at all?

* * *

We lingered until late afternoon, enchanted by the ghostly atmosphere and by the wildly romantic setting of this village at the juncture of two forks of the ravine, beneath towering peaks. Yet people had lived here, apparently for centuries, for there had been ancient temples, and in Byzantine times a church had been built and covered with frescoes. It still stands, a little below the village, with strange Arabic faces peering from the peeling walls. Entering these old chapels is rather like walking into a human brain—even the exterior, white, with a single black gaping doorway, resembles a skull. Within are ancient images, put there long ago on wet plaster; half-effaced and altered by time, they lurk there forever—like the archetypical figures of our unconscious mind. A face emerges from the gloom: it is the phototype of the stern father. Then a woman's head, her eyes soft with affection; a child; animals. They have the compulsive power of dream-images.

Below the village all human traces were quickly obliterated. The path petered out among stones, and even the stream vanished underground. The gorge narrowed, the walls became sheer, clouds hovered low, and a light rain began to fall. The misty rain rendered the light on rocks and trees mellow and soft. The cliff-sides were streaked with splashes of red and black, like abstract paintings by a prehistoric master. We heard rocks falling somewhere high overhead; they echoed and re-echoed in the great corridor of cliffs. Ahead were several great rams with curved mythical horns, staring at us with eyes of Pan. Only at this point did we feel a tingle of *Panic* fear in our spines, as though the great god were alive and very close; our senses stiffened at the smell of danger in the air. A little farther on there was more tangible evidence of hazard: large rocks had fallen from a thousand feet above, quite recently, dislodging trees and earth as they plummeted. Perhaps they had been loosened by the hooves of one of the last herds of Cretan ibex that now haunt these heights, having been hunted away from every other part of the island where they once roamed freely.

But soon the gurgling stream reappeared from underground, and there were more trees and even flowers, oleanders. Thus we came to a wide place among the pines where stands the little chapel of Christ, solidly built with a good level floor. We gathered boughs and shrubs, spread a bed, made a fire and had hot bouillon for supper; and then slept soundly in the comfort and security of the little church, while outside the rain let up and a mighty wind blew up through the southern gates of the gorge.

In the morning we idled over breakfast, and waited for the sun to reach into the depths of this narrow cleft. High in the forest on the eastern side a tiny plume of smoke could be seen: some shepherd must have started a fire. Fanned by the south wind, the smoke increased and tiny tongues of flame appeared. Fearing forest fire, which would spread rapidly in this bone-dry season, we hurried for the first time, wishing to get to Ayia Roumeli to report the blaze. Below our campsite the ravine constricted sharply and we passed through 'the Gates', the narrowest part of the gorge. I measured the width with the rangefinder of my camera: just twelve feet. The stream was low enough now to permit us to get through easily, with some jumping from stone to stone, but in other seasons the water rises, sometimes as high as six or ten feet (the marks were clearly visible on the cliffs). In winter the gorge is cut off from the world, hemmed in by torrents at the lower end and snowbound in its upper reaches.

The ravine now widened, and we passed through a veritable forest of oleanders in full blossom, and came thus to the outlying houses of the upper village of Ayia Roumeli. At the 'Paradise' kafeneion the the proprietor, a white-bearded six-footer in boots and breeches, was sitting on a bench in a shady arbour, talking with several men. Someone offered us coffee, and we sat down with them. They were all watching the fire, which had spread alarmingly in the time since we first saw it. The high wind was fanning the flames. One of the men had a pair of field glasses which they took turns using.

'Is anyone doing anything about that fire?' I inquired.

'Bah! It's nothing—it will go out by itself when the wind drops,' said the man with the glasses.

'I could tell the police about it when we go down to the lower village,' I rashly offered.

Several men spoke at once: 'No, no—don't mention it to anybody! If they find out about it, they'll want us all to go up there and put it out.'

'After all, it's not our concern—the government owns that forest now,' said the kafeneion owner.

'That's right—let them put it out,' chimed in another.

They were hoping for one of two things: (1) That the fire would go out of its own accord (in a dry country, with a high wind blowing!) or, (2) That it would get so bad that the authorities would have to send firefighters from Canea. They also spoke vaguely of an airplane that might fly over from Canea and spray water on the flames. Thus the time passed in pleasant, idle talk and speculation.

Inga and I had lunch in the kafeneion, and then the owner showed us an abandoned loft where we could spread our sleeping bags for the essential midday siesta. We slept, awoke and had coffee, strolled about the village; thus passed a leisurely afternoon. The men were still watching the fire.

Ioannis Manoledakis, the kafeneion owner, offered to put us up for the night in his rustic shop. We gladly accepted, for it was a mile's walk to the seaside village, and it was pleasant here among the fire-watchers. Thus we were absolved from a moral dilemma: on the one hand, the voice of conscience telling us to report the fire to the police in the lower village; on the other, our reluctance to interfere in any way with the natural workings of local affairs—especially when it would mean making enemies of a whole village of Sphakians.

That night there was a most spectacular fireworks display high up in the gorge. The wind was doing its work well, and the flames were leaping higher and higher. An acrid smell of smoke reached all the way down to the village. And of course the police at the station down by the sea did eventually find out about it—they were informed by some frightened schoolchildren. They arrived in the evening, out of breath from a fast walk, and very angry.

'Why didn't you tell us?' the young chief demanded of the kafeneion man, 'It was your duty to tell us!'

The old Sphakian exploded: '*Duty*? *I* have no such duty—I have no duties to anybody!' He spoke for all Sphakians, perhaps for all Cretans. Centuries of misrule have inculcated a profound distrust for, and alienation from, all central governments. The government —to *kratos*—is something far away, in which the individual takes no part. There is no such thing as civic responsibility: the only obligations recognised as binding are those of the family—and they are iron-clad. As an adherent of Thoreau's principle of civil disobedience I had a secret sympathy with them; but of course they carried it too far—their disobedience was *un*civil.

There was nothing to be done that night, but early next morning the district police captain, summoned all the way from Hora Sphakion (ten miles down the coast,) arrived in a rage, and rounded up all the men and drafted them as fire-fighters. They had endless excuses; I've never seen such a gang of malingerers. Able-bodied men, bursting with rude animal vigour, pleaded rheumatism, bad feet, all manner of aches and pains. But the captain was in no mood for accepting excuses, and in the end they all had to go—even our host, the extremely reluctant old kafeneion proprietor. (But the wily fox won out: within an hour he was back. 'I didn't get past the chapel,' he explained cheerfully as he came up with long strides, 'Then my bad foot gave out. I went in and lit a candle, and praise God, it's better now!' He winked.)

By midday the men up on the mountain had put out the fire and were back in the village. Their delaying tactics had made the job somewhat easier for them, for by the time they had reached the fire the wind had dropped. Never underestimate the power of procrastination.

I suppose we had a natural sympathy for these dawdlers because of our own tendencies in that direction. We had certainly set some kind of slowness record for progress down the gorge, and now we continued to idle in Ayia Roumeli. Eventually we did get down to the lower village, where we bathed in the glass-clear sea off great smooth rocks, and camped for the night on a bed of soft sand in the ruins of the ancient city of Tarra.

*　　*　　*

The coast from Ayia Roumeli westwards, in the area where the eparchies of Sphakia and Selino meet, is the wildest and steepest in all of Crete. The White Mountains here plunge from their uppermost pinnacles straight into the immense depths of the Libyan Sea in a series of thrusting headlands. There are no roads, and what trails there are, are for mountaineers or mountain goats. Between Ayia Roumeli and Souyia, the first tiny Selino village, there are no settlements for ten or twelve miles. To look at this country from an open boat plying along the coast, you wouldn't think that men had ever lived there. But tucked away in the distant Selino hills and at isolated spots along the shore there had been cities that had made a certain mark in history. Their league, the Confederation of Oreioi (they were mountaineers—the *Levka Ori* men), had been allied with Gortyn and Cyrenaica about 300 B.C., and had taken part in wars as well as trade. We had slept the night on the sandy ruins of Tarra, which had belonged to the League and which had been populated for a thousand years, from the fifth century B.C. to the fifth A.D. when it probably fell to pirates. And the next day we joined the Ayia Roumeliotes in two hazardously overloaded boats for a voyage and a celebration that must have been an exact replica of countless pilgrimages by the sun-worshipping ancients of Tarra. Nowadays, of course, the naked realities of pagan pantheism have been decorously covered with the fig-leaves of Christian piety, but the disguise is extremely thin: the Prophet Elijah, whose day we were supposed to be on our way to celebrate, is called *Elias* in Greek—too much like the word for sun, *Helios,* for mere coincidence. There is not a locality in Greece that hasn't got a hilltop with a chapel dedicated to 'Elias'. His rites are simple and charming, an outdoor nature festival: the people trek to the hilltops where they spend the night in dancing, singing and drinking, and then they all watch the sun rise the next morning while the priests intone their liturgies. The local site for these sites was a hill that rises abruptly above a tiny cove at a place called Trypiti, above five or six miles west of Ayia Roumeli. There is a great cave by the sea just at the outlet of a deep ravine that penetrates into the core of the mountains. It would be a social occasion, for the Seliniotes would come, by boat from Souyia and Paleochora and overland from Koustoyerako and other mountain villages.

The *glendi* had already started in the cave by the time we arrived, the Selino contingent having got there first. There were profuse greetings—everyone from each village seemed to have a cousin or *koumbaros* in the others, and apparently they didn't see one another very often—and then the dancing resumed. The music, which in former years would have been provided by native instrumentalists, now came from a Japanese *pik-up*-time's latest variation on the archaic theme of these festivities. The sportive atmosphere induced by the unique setting must have been the same always. There was a certain amount of teasing among the boys and girls from different communities, who would have had few opportunities to be together. Festivals in the open air doubtless have always had erotic under-tones, but in this case the rigid moral code imposed by Orthodox Christianity would effectively prevent any outbursts of pagan sensuality. The symbolism was there, however; and it became fairly obvious when some boys caught a long black snake and dangled it before the girls. Screams and pandemonium, with an unfortunate result: the serpent landed squarely in the lap of a stout lady from one of the Selino villages. (In fact, as we soon learned, she was not a Cretan at all but a mainland Greek who had married a man from this area; they lived in Athens and had come here for a summer visit.) Her piercing screams sent everyone for cover. As soon as the first shock wave had subsided, she turned the superior scorn of a town Greek full blast on to these peasants:

'Look at me, a woman from *Athens,* sitting in a Cretan cave with a crowd of villagers—and instead of treating me with the proper respect you throw wild animals at me! I shall leave at once!'

She gathered up her things, and rounded up the members of her party; but nature thwarted her, for the wind was rising again, and the Selino boatman declared that it would be dangerous to put out to sea. Eventually she was forced to subside. All of the villagers were extremely polite and conciliatory: they told her how sorry they were and offered her goats' eyeballs and other tasty morsels from their food baskets—all of which merely added to her self-pity. 'Me, an *Athenian,* trapped in a cave with a crowd of shepherds!' And in the end it turned out even worse than she had feared: the sea got rougher still, and the boat was unable to leave that night as planned. The lady announced that under no circumstances would she accompany the villagers up the hill to the chapel; instead, she and her relatives would bed down for a miserable night in the windy cave. When they finally did get away safely (we heard about it later) she declared that it had been the worst experience of her life, and that she would never again return to these savage shores.

The rest of us waited until the sun was low enough to make walking pleasant and then climbed the hill of Prophet Elias at a leisurely pace. They had told us the walk would take 'twenty minutes'—the correct formula with such directions is to multiply by three—and so we arrived at the peak after an hour's climb, just in time to see the sun sink into the vast sea. The setting of this jagged outcrop was, in truth, stupendous: the steep coastline, the Libyan Sea with the island of Gavdos floating on the southern horizon, inland the ravines and peaks of the last corner of the White Mountains where the ibexes still roam freely. The upper part of the trail had taken us over a broad slope carpeted with thyme in full blossom; in the red sunset light its usual violet deepened to purple, and its pungent smell refreshed us. There were noble Aleppo pines in a grove near the summit, and here the Selino villagers had tethered their magnificent mules and removed the rich red-and-black saddle blankets. At the very top, near the little white chapel of the Sun God (alias Elias), a knot of people gathered around a hawk-faced country priest while he intoned the liturgy and spilled incense fumes into the west wind. Afterwards huge chunks of black bread and honey in combs straight from the hives were distributed to all of us. The honey was an eagerly awaited delicacy of the occasion, for the hives were located on the thyme slope and were seldom visited because of their remoteness. It was like the wild nectar that sustained John the Baptist in the wilderness, and it had an invigorating effect on us all, after our steep walk: now we were ready for the long night's vigil.

Bonfires were lit on the lee side of the summit rocks. Food was spread out, demijohns of wine and *tsikoudia* appeared, and all joined in with zest. After the eating there was singing and dancing, this time to the music of a real lute and lyre, for the *pick-up* had belonged to the Athenian lady, and she was a thousand feet below in the cave, lamenting her ill luck. The Seliniotes were free with their food and drink: though their taste ran a little too much toward goats' heads for us, their cheese and wine were of the finest. About nine a cry went up: *To Fengari!* 'The Moon!'—and there it was, rising full and round and surprisingly big, right out of the Libyan Sea. After that the party went on by moonlight, all night; but as for us, we retired into our sleeping bags under the Aleppo pines, and went to sleep to the dull thud-thud of the tethered mules' hooves as they grazed about the site.

We slept like babes, and awoke with a start in grey dawn light. We hastened up the hill just in time to see the sun rise while the priest went through his ritual inside the chapel. *Helios* had had his due from his minions below, and could sail on proudly for another year.

The sun means freedom. It recurs again and again in the *rizitika* ballads from the time when Crete lay oppressed and longed for liberty. In one of these songs an eagle (the Cretan rebel) sits on a high mountain, covered with snow and ice, and begs the sun to rise and melt the bonds of slavery. Freedom is the only ideal that means anything to a Cretan, the only reality he will fight for. The struggle for it is the main theme of that arch-Cretan voice, Nikos Kazantzakis. *Freedom or Death*, his great novel of the almost superhuman deeds of Captain Michalis—a man modelled on his own father—often seems exaggerated to readers in hyper-civilised lands where the will to fight for anything, even freedom, has atrophied. It is not exaggerated, it is a statement in sober truth, but if it is too much for the literal-minded, there is another source: the well-documented history of the Cretan resistance to the German invasion in 1941.

The German army at that time was a machine that was regarded as invincible. It had rolled over country after country, crushing human beings like so many ants beneath the wheels of a tank. The Cretans threw themselves at this machine—and it was the machine that faltered. Hitler launched his pet élite corps, the paratroops, upon Crete. These arrogant young Nazis expected a quick, easy victory. More than that, they expected—due to a failure of Intelligence reports and an inability to understand the psychology of a people whose whole history is a story of unending struggle for freedom—they expected, unbelievable as it sounds, to be welcomed with open arms.

The Cretans—old men and women and children mostly, for the young men were off in Albania fighting the Italians—welcomed the invaders with whatever weapons were at hand: rusty shotguns, knives, axes, sickles, even sticks and stones. They fell upon the hapless troopers and cut them to ribbons whenever they had a chance. Neither the attackers nor the British Commonwealth defenders (New Zealanders and Australians mostly) had ever seen anything like it. Thanks to this unique collaboration of local population and defending army (and despite the ineptitude of most of the British generals) the Germans were held up in their invasion timetable by a week of the fiercest fighting of the war. They suffered their heaviest casualties so far: over fifteen thousand in all, including more than five thousand killed. The shattered paratroopers were never again committed to battle as a complete unit.

After this savage introduction to the Cretan labyrinth the Nazis reacted as might have been expected: with vicious reprisals against the population. The rule was that ten Cretans were to die for every one German killed by civilians. The machine had prevailed—or so it seemed—and village squares were turned into places of execution, and whole communities were destroyed—burnt out and gutted. Yet the Cretans held together in resistance—for this was the only kind of organized community action they could understand, the best-learned lesson from their fierce past. After the overwhelming Nazi air superiority had finally won out, and the British forces had been evacuated by boat from Sphakia, the Cretans—at great risk to themselves—sheltered the numerous stragglers who had not found places in the boats. Later they helped the British agents who infiltrated the occupied island and began to organise espionage and resistance activities.

The wild corner of Selino that had just witnessed the annual propitiation of the sun god, and that we were now entering in the company of a group of villagers and a train of mules bound from Prophet Elias to Koustoyerako, had been an important centre of these resistance activities. Among the pilgrims to the *panegyri* were several members of the Paterakis family, a famous clan of modern palikars who had formed the mainstay of a highly effective guerrilla band. One of their most successful exploits had been the dramatic ambush of a German detachment that was preparing to execute the women and children of Koustoyerako. The machine gun was set up in the village square and the Nazi officer was just giving the signal to fire when the partisan sharpshooters opened up from their hiding-place nearly four hundred metres away. Costis Paterakis fired the first shot and it killed the officer; several other Germans fell at the next volley and the rest ran for their lives. In the confusion all the women and children escaped to the hills. The Germans returned later in force and systematically destroyed the village. The Cretans lived in the mountains after that, using remote sheepfolds as hide-outs.

These deeds are well documented, but to hear the Paterakis brothers talk, one would hardly guess that they had ever occurred: for these men had little of the boastfulness that is typical of so many Cretans. By Greek standards, they were almost laconic. The impression they gave was of sober strength and reliability. Manolis in particular—perhaps the best known of the brothers because of the leading part he had played in the celebrated kidnapping of the German general—was the very image of the sort of man who could pass the 'Monty' test, General Montgomery's criterion of a good man: whether one would be willing to 'go into the jungle with him'. The mountains, not the jungle, were the milieu of this hawk-nosed, eagle-eyed mountaineer; he had been all over Crete, in the Lassithi and Mount Ida regions as well as the White Mountains in his own backyard, and his knowledge of the island surpassed that of any other Cretan I had met.

I was curious to know how these men who had fought and suffered so much during the German occupation regarded the Germans who were now starting to return to the islands as tourists. It was Manolis who answered my question:

'Most of those who come now were too young to be in the war. And even if they had been, what difference would it make? It was war—they were soldiers. True, they did some bad things but at least they didn't rape our women. It was the *Turks* who were the real barbarians.' To hear him talk, one would have thought that the Turks had been here more recently than the Germans.

He went on, 'Some Germans came here to look for the bones of those that were killed in the war. We helped them, because we knew where to look. They were very nice Germans and we gave them hospitality; they stayed in our house. We found many bones and afterwards they took them all the way back to Germany to bury them.

'Now there are more Germans here. They say they are sorry for what happened in the war, and so they have come to do something for us. They are all young people, and very good.'

Further inquiry revealed that the Germans were staying in Livadas, the village below Koustoyerako, and that they were building some sort of house—no one could tell us exactly what kind of house, or for what purpose. Our curiosity was piqued, and we decided to continue on to Livadas immediately, as it was still early in the day, and then return later to Koustoyerako, where we had been invited to stay with the Paterakis family.

Much of Selino unfurled below us as we walked down the path from the eagle's eyrie of Koustoyerako, high on the flanks of the mountains, to the lower village of Livadas. Away to the west stretched range upon range of great rounded hills with terraced slopes and bare tops. It reminded me, improbably, of certain parts of northern Japan's rugged interior through which I had hiked long ago.

We found the Germans, all right: it would have been impossible *not* to find them, in that village. They were just finishing their project: a handsome large house built against a hillside, Cretan in style, yet somehow more solid-looking than most local structures, showing more evidence of careful workmanship. A carpenter, dressed in the 'Black Respectability' garb of the north German guilds—bell-bottomed trousers, black vest and wide-brimmed hat—was putting some finishing touches on doors and windows, while a mason in dirty lederhosen was laying stones along the foot of the stairway. A tall blond young man came up to us and, speaking excellent English, said that he had already heard from the villagers that we were coming, and offered to show us around.

'Here,' said our guide (whose name was Hans), with an expansive gesture, 'is the large main room, where they can have lectures and community meetings. Here is a room where the district doctor can examine people when he comes on his rounds. This is a recreation room, for the youth of the village.'

'How did you happen to choose this corner of Crete for such a project?' I wanted to know.

'Well, you know our organisation is attempting to atone for some of the crimes committed by the Nazis. Of course we realise that true atonement may be impossible, but we feel that some gesture must be made. We have done projects in Norway, Holland and other countries. We wanted to do something in Crete because the people here suffered so much. We heard about this village from a Cretan who is a professor in a German university. Our project, this community house, is to be not only for Livadas but for the other three villages of this area. And over in Kandanos some other members of our group are putting in waterpipes that were badly needed.'

'Haven't you had any trouble with the people in the other villages? Wouldn't they be jealous because you chose Livadas to build in?'

'Yes, we have had that problem, and many others—you cannot imagine! It is not that they blame us because of the war—on the contrary, they all assure us that that is all forgotten. But they cannot understand that we are working for nothing, that we are a private organisation with limited resources. They think we are employed by the German government and that we are *obligated* to do this work for them—therefore they feel free to make the most impossible demands! For instance, the priest , who helped us with some translating and other small matters at the beginning, presented us with a fantastic bill for his services. And we found that the community was divided into two factions, each of which wanted the house built in its part of the village. We compromised by putting it in the middle, but even then there was trouble: we had to cut down an olive tree that was owned by an old woman, and in order to pay for this each person was to be assessed forty drachmas. They complained much about this, and some still haven't paid.'

Hans sighed, and lit a cigarette. We were standing on the terrace looking out over a valley full of olive groves. 'But that was only the beginning. The real trouble came with the other villages. They could not understand that we were building a community centre for all of them. They thought we were building a tourist hotel, and that the Cretan professor in Germany had bribed us to do the project in his village! It was all too fantastic—we tried and tried to explain, but it was like talking to children. No tourists for hundreds of miles, and they all want tourist hotels—it's too much!'

'The worst came one day when our leader went down there'—he pointed to a little village far down in the valley—'to Moni, on some errand. Suddenly he was surrounded by an angry crowd of people—it was like a riot—all shouting and demanding to know why we had chosen Livadas and not *their* village for our project. They were demanding that we give them electricity as a compensation. None of the villages here have electricity, and such a project was quite beyond the resources of our group. But our leader offered instead to give them furniture—desks and chairs—for the school, which he had heard were needed. That made them really angry! "No," they shouted, "electricity or nothing." It was very bad for a few minutes, until finally our leader was rescued by the mayor of this village. After that we received warnings—it was not safe for us to go there. And some of them got up a petition to the Bishop, complaining about us—perhaps that is why he didn't come to the opening ceremony we had for the new house last week, though he had always been friendly and promised us his support. It has been a very confusing time. But now the work is nearly finished, and I think at last we *have* made them understand the purpose of our coming here, and what the community house is for.'

Several villagers had come up the steps, and now Hans introduced one of them to us as the mayor, or 'president' of the community. He shook hands cordially and invited us to come to his kafeneion for drinks. As Inga strolled ahead with Hans, he laid hold of my arm conspiratorially and lowered his voice, 'They say you are a writer,' he began, 'So maybe you could make some propaganda in your country so that tourists will know about our new hotel. Our village has many *efkolies'*—conveniences! here of all places—'Look at the view!'—he gestured grandly, and here he had a point: the view, extending over ten or fifteen miles of hills, *was* superb. Then he theatrically inhaled several deep breaths, and beat his chest with his fist: 'Smell the air! Like medicine. Good for rheumatism, asthma—for everything! They'll come here by the thousands when they hear about it.'

'But Hans told me,' I began cautiously, 'that it is not a hotel, but a . . .' I groped for words, finding it difficult to express 'community centre' in Greek, 'That it's for everybody, for all the villages to use.'

His face reddened and he raised his voice, 'They have no need for such a place! Haven't they got their own kafeneions? That is where people can meet. This house is for *our* village, and we're going to make a hotel of it!'

Hans had overheard the last part, and he began explaining patiently, for what must have been the hundredth time, 'No, no—it's a house for all the villages. For meetings, for lectures. . . .'

We reached the kafeneion and sat down. The Germans were all there, having drinks after their session of hard work. They were very gay and noisy and flushed with the exaltation of the fellowship of work and what they had accomplished together. They all spoke Greek surprisingly well, and they exchanged jokes with the Cretans in the local dialect. They had a great deal of energy to spare, and two of them started a sort of clapping game with one another's hands, while some others burst into song. The Cretans stirred uneasily . . . what dormant memories might this be reviving? Were the sons who came to atone so very different, after all, from the fathers who had come to conquer? Suddenly the Cretans, too, began to sing: rather quietly, even shyly, at first, and then louder and stronger. It was one of the old *rizitika* ballads about freedom. The Germans responded by singing even louder, and it became a sort of contest, all in fun with much laughing and yet, underneath, something else . . .

We left them sitting there, the two groups, each with its dream: the German dream of atonement through work, the Cretan dream of freedom—freedom from everything and everybody, even—*especially*—those who came to do them good. As we walked back to Koustoyerako we turned for a last look at the handsome result of the German's hard work: the best-built structure in that part of Crete, and a monument to the complexities of the Cretan labyrinth that have defeated so many intruders, those who came with good intentions no less than those who came to do evil.

But these complexities faded when we returned to Koustoyerako, to the simple, austere and warmly hospitable Paterakis household where we were guests. Everything in that house was functional and homely: no piece of furniture, and no individual, was redundant. There was no pretence about anything. Guns hung on the walls, not for show, but because that was the handiest place for them. We ate slabs of cheese from the family sheep fold, with a bowl of honey from the local hives to dip it in; later there was a succulent stew made from a hare one of the brothers had shot—whether in or out of season, we neither knew nor cared. Early in the evening we retired to a bed of quilts laid on the terrace; they had wanted us to sleep indoors but we had insisted—for to sleep out under a sky full of stars in a White Mountain village is one of life's luminous adventures. In nearly every way this visit resembled dozens of others we had made to Cretan villages, yet the pleasure of them never dimmed. To be so far from the mundane life of towns, with no thoughts of time (neither of us carried a timepiece—we went by the sun), no need to hurry, no mail to bring disquieting news, to let the days glide by: it was escapism, pure and simple, and all the more enjoyable when one admitted it frankly, and banished all guilt about it.

But even on these most leisurely of excursions a day would come when we would feel an urge to return to *our* village, to catch our breath and assimilate a multitude of impressions. For Inga, that time had arrived, and so before sunrise the next morning she walked, in company with some village women, down to the road in the valley far below, where the bus from Souyia passed (a recent innovation—until the last year there had been no road to these parts). Then the long ride over the mountains to the world—to the hot lowlands of the north coast, back to Canea and Georgioupolis.

For my part, I could not resist the lure of the *Madara* or upper reaches of the White Mountains. Manolis had mentioned that he would be going up to the sheepfold of Achlada, and I leaped at his offer to take me along if I wished. We started before dawn to take advantage of the coolest time of day. Up and up we went, following a rocky stream bed into forested regions where the pristine air was pure tonic for the lungs. After a couple of hours of hard climbing we passed the tree-lined and emerged at Achlada, where the fold stood in a dry and lonely gully below some rounded peaks. During the war the Germans had blasted it out as a penalty for the guerrilla activity that had centred around it. Lately a new cheese-making hut had been built, and there we joined the shepherds at their morning meal of yoghurt and black bread soaked in water. There was another guest present, a Sphakian from a remote fold high on Gigilos, far across a vast ravine, who had walked over as casually as a housewife visiting her neighbour—merely to borrow a little yogurt so that he could start a new batch. Most of the talk was of highly technical matters involving sheep and goats, grazing and cheese-making and the fluctuations of the market in Canea.

My instinct was to go on and on, over one ridge after another, higher into the peak area. After we had rested, Manolis accompanied me for some distance, an ideal—and necessary—guide in this region of immense rockslides and precipitous chasms. Sure-footed as a mountain goat, with a gun on his arm and a dog at his feet—now he was in his element, functioning at the peak of his powers. To go with him on such a trek was a rare privilege. He told me that he had once had a chance to go to New Zealand with his family—to follow the great stream of emigrating Greeks—but that he had preferred to remain, despite the poverty and hardship. He was not talkative or eloquent, but when he sat on a rock high above a canyon and said, 'How could I leave? I grew up in these mountains.'—I understood that here at last was a wise man.

I left him there on his rock, and went on alone into the stony wilderness of the Selino-Sphakia border saddle that we had seen from the other side many days before, when we had started down the Samaria Gorge. Manolis was greatly concerned that I shouldn't lose the way, and he waved and shouted directions until he was just a tiny black speck on a distant steep slope. Now I felt that I, too, was in my element, and I surged forward joyously towards the peak of Gigilos. From its summit I surveyed an immense panorama of all the country we had traversed in the last few days: the Omalo, the Gorge, the highest peaks of the *Levka Ori* across the mile-deep chasm to the east. Then I made my way down to the Gigilos sheepfold by nightfall, and again enjoyed shepherds' hospitality over the common yoghurt pot and the pungent thyme fire. There were only three of them, two men and a boy—Ayia Roumeliotes far from home, which was a good eight hours' hard hiking from here.

From their hut one could see, miles below, the hill of Prophet Elias where we had recently celebrated the ancient rites of the sun. I pointed to it, and told them I had been there.

'Yes,' said the oldest man, 'We saw the lights—big bonfires—and we knew there were many people.'

It added a new dimension to my memory of that night out: the image of those three shepherds, high on their lonely pinnacle, wistfully watching the festive bonfires several thousand feet below.

*   *   *

My turn came, too, to return to the dusty plains; but I came back to the Madara, again and again, to drink deep of its pristine springs Linoselli, Lagonero, Zarani: renowned names among mountain men, waters that quench the thirst and heal the spirit—and to stand on its upper peaks: Pachnes, Grias Soros, Trocharis—and survey all of western Crete with the eagle's proprietary gaze. Up on the naked basaltic rock, in a confusing maze of craters and pits and pot-holes, and mighty cracks, and deserts of lava dust, one felt that one was touring the moon's surface without ever leaving old earth. I am sure that the moon really is very much like the upper reaches of the Madara, which would make an ideal training ground for astronauts —only I am glad that the space exploiters have never made the discovery. Men will foul the moon's surface, as they have much of the earth's—but may the *Levka Ori* be spared!

Winds of Crete

And there was infinite variety up there above the treeline. There were patterns and shapes—cones, angles, masses—that would have delighted a sculptor. Some of the mountains looked like sprawling prehistoric beasts, or huge elephants with wrinkled black hides. Terrifying expanses of solid rock, reflecting the sun's rays into one's eyes in sharp splinters of light, and fields of razorsharp stones that cut the best boots to ribbons, would give way suddenly to alpine meadows of green grass and thick growths of *malotira*, a native herb that is good for making tea, and equally useful for making a soft fragrant bed to sleep on. There was always plenty of small game—partridges and hares in profusion—and had I cared to use a gun I could have lived off the country; but I did not feel that I had any right to deprive them of their joyous lives—though, hypocritically, I never turned down a shepherd's offer of a plate of rabbit stew!

The shepherds' hospitality was always the same: they never failed to offer one a bed on the stone benches of their huts, and to share what food they had with any stranger. I shall never forget one night in a hut so high up that the air was ice-cold, even during a midsummer heat wave. I was hiking from Anopolis in Sphakia to Therisso in the *Riza*—a week's trek over the highest peaks—and I was bone-tired. I came upon this hut just at sunset, and found a fierce figure in front of me: a shaggy Sphakian with a huge white beard and a surly expression, with a sub-machine-gun at the ready over one shoulder. For once I wondered how I might be received, but I need not have feared—for he showed all the solicitude of a woman about my tiredness and cold, and gave me a thick white cloak to wrap myself in. Then he built a fire in the hut, and there by the flickering flames he roasted great chunks of sheep that he had slaughtered just that day, and passed them with quiet ceremoniousness to me and his two young sons.

I learned that the sub-machine-gun was for self-defence in feuds, and that someone (he blamed Theriossiotes from the north) had recently stolen all his goats—a severe economic blow to such a poor family. Much later, when I returned to Sphakia, I heard the sad sequel to this: he had quarrelled in a kafeneion with two men from a rival family—about animals, as usual—and he had pulled out his pistol and shot one of them dead on the spot, and would have killed the other had he not been forcibly restrained. He went to jail for twenty years—virtually a life sentence for a man so old— and his boys were forced to leave Crete for fear of reprisals.

That is the violent side of mountain life in Crete, and one can no more ignore it than one can ignore the harsh facts of nature: how creatures prey on one another, and live much of their lives in fear. Life up there is strong, gamey meat—yet far more nourishing than the insipid fare of the towns below. And there is joy there, too— the savage joy of shepherds expressed in the resounding volleys of shots which they sometimes discharge for no purpose other than to give vent to their high spirits (to be greeted in this way on departure or arrival is to feel honoured in a way that the empty platitudes of polite society can never match). There, is joy also in the animal world: no one could doubt it who had ever sat entranced on a high peak and watched great eagles sailing and soaring on vagrant wind-streams. Superb and unassailable in their incomparable power and range, they enjoy a freedom that all other creatures must envy. I thought then, and still do, that if I were to be reincarnated in any animal form, and had a choice, I would rather be an eagle than anything else. A *Cretan* eagle.

12

The Archaic Face

I am not one of those who subscribe to the belief that 'appearances are deceiving'. On the contrary, I firmly believe that appearances—specifically faces—have a story for all to read. Breughel and Hogarth knew this; so did Goya. Those who go wrong in their judgments of others, based on faces, have usually erred in their reading. The evidence of faces can be like the prophecies of the oracle at Delphi: true, but notoriously difficult to interpret. This much, however, should be obvious to all with eyes: that the faces of people in modern cities speak plainly of some inner malaise; that modern men no longer have their male certainty; that modern women are a maze of frustrations and anxieties.

In Crete, one of the first things we noticed was that many faces are different—they seem to come from another world. But even here one sees plenty of modern faces, especially in the towns. And then one day, unexpected, unheralded , one sees a face that is like a mask out of a classic tragedy: a face etched so full of awareness and suffering as to take one's breath away. This is an experience that all travellers in Greece have had. The revelatory face usually belongs to some humble soul: a fisherman, perhaps, or his wife or son, or a lonely shepherd high up on a mountainside. Startling it is, while going about one's daily round, to encounter the face of Electra, or suffering Oedipus, or perhaps a satyr or (delightful surprise!) a nymph. And thus one day we looked out our front window in the village, and beheld a true Homeric king strolling down the road under the eucalyptus trees. He was elderly but erect and tall, with a spring in his step. His white beard was trimmed all round in that peculiar Cretan cut, reminiscent of the beards of archaic statues and figurines. He wore with regal nonchalance the full Cretan regalia of high black boots and dark blue breeches, intricately embroidered crossed vest, mulberry-coloured sash, blue cloak richly lined in red; the whole surmounted by the black, fringed *sariki* worn jauntily over his forehead. This costume is essentially manly: sober, dignified, with the restraint and sobriety of dark blue, yet with a touch of dash and swagger in the cut of the cloak and the angle of the head-dress, and the boots—an incomparable blend of style and practicality. It is to the credit of the Cretan mountaineers that they stick to their boots and breeches; they look down on the townspeople in their low shoes and tight suits, referring to them contemptuously as *macripantalonades* or 'long-trouser-wearers'.

And there could be no doubt about it, this man was a mountaineer: specifically, a *Sphakian* mountaineer. He stood out among the lowlanders, an eagle among crows. Later in the day we met him—introduced by Xenophon—and learned that his name was Manolis Polentas and that he came from the high plateau of Askyphou. He was down here for a visit to relatives who had their temporary home on the plain of Dramia. Meeting him was not disappointing. His handshake, firm and strong and dry, was unforgettable, and so was the way he gazed at you with clear blue eyes out of his seamed face. He was a 'kingly' man in the best sense of the word: a natural aristocrat, head of a large family, possessor of great flocks of sheep; a grandfather and great-grandfather, progenitor and patriarch—an exemplar of manhood out of some remote past, miraculously walking through our century.

He was one of the first Sphakians we met, and one of the finest though by no means unique. Their mountainous stronghold soared before our eyes—we saw it every day when we looked out our windows or when we strolled in the square—and now with renewed interest we prepared to go there, to seek out the archaic face of this harsh and forbidding land.

* * *

Travel, if it is really to mean something, should take us not only over the surface of the earth at the present time, like skaters on the thin ice of today, but should take us back, should allow us to meet in person the men and women of other centuries. Mental attitudes and outlook, ways of perceiving reality, have changed far more than we can be aware of; one way to break through to new awareness is to get to know the natives of countries still in the pre-technological period. There can be no greater fallacy than to say that 'people are the same everywhere'. Thank God they are not—at least not yet, though the worldwide spread of technology may be obliterating the differences. Crete in general today is a society in transition, but in the remoter reaches of Sphakia the transition has barely begun—the archaic modes still prevail, and that constitutes the uniqueness and fascination of the region. The price of a ticket into this enclave of the archaic is discomfort, for comfort is a modern concept, practically unheard of in societies like that of Sphakia.

Today there are roads to Sphakia, where until quite recently there were none. It is possible to go by bus all the way over the mountains by way of Askyphou and then down a series of breathtaking hairpin turns to Hora Sphakion, capital of the province, on the Libyan Sea. The last part of that road was finished in the 'fifties; and now another road enters the district from Rethymnon to the east along the coast. The buses are crowded and uncomfortable, the roads narrow and twisting, but in a few hours you are there. That is the mechanised part of the journey. The truly Sphakian part begins where the last road ends, for any community that gets a road begins to change at once. Here at the end of the road, where the mule-paths lead on into the wilderness of stone and scrub, travel begins to resemble those uncomfortable and leisurely journeys described in such detail in the pages of eighteenth and nineteenth-century travellers.

Our road ended at Anopolis, a plateau some two thousand feet above and to the west of Hora Sphakion. Riding up from the sea in the bus, ascending coastal bluffs of a steepness that ought to have defied all attempts at road-building, was like taking an elevator into the mountains. Beyond Anopolis the road expired amid knife-like stones: would it ever go any farther? The villagers of Ayios Ioannis, a thousand feet higher and several miles deeper into the White Mountains, hope that it will, but there is a seemingly impassable obstacle: the ravine of Aradaina. Afoot, we negotiated it without difficulties, and found ourselves in a practically deserted village on the western rim of the canyon. The former inhabitants had been such persistent feuders that the police had evacuated most of them—shipped them off to other islands. Often in Sphakia you get this feeling of walking through a ghost town or ghost district. Wars, feuds, revolutions and reprisals have sapped the population; Sphakians are scattered far and wide. One would never guess that in ancient times the area was thickly populated—Anopolis, for instance, today a collection of straggling villages with a total count of about seven hundred, once had seventy thousand inhabitants. In all of Sphakia, an area that extends some twenty-five miles from east to west, and eight or ten miles north-south, there are only three thousand people today.

The topography of Sphakia has protected it against all invaders —and we were learning how an area not actually large can expand

and throw up obstacles that are shown on no map, when you attempt to cross it. The whole district is a maze of ravines (hence the name, which probably derives from an ancient word for 'ravine', *sphax*—thus *Ta Sphakia,* 'land of ravines') and steeply rising peaks. One Sphakian mile can seem like two or three miles in a saner landscape. Thus, too, Sphakia expands in the imagination: reality, which is strange enough, being inflated in the semi-legendary aura that surrounds the place. Its reputation elsewhere in Crete, and in Greece, is formidable—perhaps 'notorious' would be a more accurate word, for its feuds and lawlessness are as well known as its tradition of fighting for independence against Turks and all other invaders. Even the Romans, it is said, never succeeded in penetrating the area, and it enjoyed virtual autonomy during Venetian times and for most of the Turkish period. The Sphakians have known freedom for thousands of years, and if they appear at times arrogant or haughty, and disdain petty restrictions imposed upon them by distant bureaucrats in Athens, one must admit that they have earned the right. It is incomprehensible to them that the government orders them to buy salt from the official monopoly, instead of harvesting it themselves from the rocky coves along their coast, as they have always done. The same with tobacco: they grow their own, as always—and shouldn't they, in the name of common sense? The absurdities of the tangled web of modern economic life have no hold here, where the simpler economy of a pre-industrial era still remains. The shooting of the now-scarce Cretan ibex, or *agrimi*—and occasionally of one's neighbour or a sheep poacher—are more debatable instances of exercising one's freedom, but they still go on, to the despair of the authorities. There are more national gendarmes stationed in Sphakia than anywhere else in Crete, and they are the gloomiest lot of policemen I have ever seen. Their job is impossible, and they know it; and they know also that the Sphakians are laughing at them behind their backs, and that doesn't help their morale either. We had been warned not to go alone where we were going, but we had laughed at these admonitions—one does not go into Sphakia to enjoy the dubious company and protection of the Tourist police. Furthermore, their warnings revealed an abysmal lack of understanding of the archaic mentality of the district: the last thing a Sphakian would ever do would be to harm a stranger who comes in peace. We were soon to learn of this first hand.

We climbed steadily after crossing the ravine, and the arid wastes gave way to a forest of pines and cypresses. The air was cool and refreshing—a delight to breathe. After some two hours, Ayios Ioannis appeared: stone houses with sod roofs, nestling almost out of sight among the trees in a sort of natural basin at the foot of high mountains. We wandered casually through the narrow lanes, enclosed by walls. We knew no one and had no idea where we might spend the night. It is the ideal way to approach a village or, indeed, any experience of life: open, uncommitted, fresh to new impressions.

We found ourselves in a small cobbled courtyard in front of a large house, typically Sphakian with its graceful arch and little wooden balcony. Under the arch a woman sat at a huge loom, with active fingers making the shuttle dance. A man of about sixty years sat on the long carved bench that occupied one whole side of the terrace.

'Welcome!' he greeted us, 'Come and sit with us. My wife will make coffee for you.' Which she instantly did, moving about her domain with silent grace. She gathered a bundle of sticks and a branch of dry thyme for kindling, lighted them, and heated the water in a long-handled *briki* —all at the open fireplace on the terrace in front of us. The man told us his name was Nikos Malephakis, and his wife was Katerina.

After coffee, Katerina produced a tin basin, a pitcher of water, soap and towels. Kneeling in front of Inga, she said, 'I will wash your feet.' And she did. We felt instinctively that it would have been graceless to refuse this ancient gesture of hospitality.

While that was going on Nikos announced: 'You will stay here. A week—two weeks—as long as you like.' And that was settled.

They gave us the best room in the house—the upper one with the balcony. Everything in it seemed to have been made by the skilful fingers of Katerina and her daughters: bed covers with rich embroidered designs, fringed pillow-cases, tablecloths, towels. The roof over our heads was supported by massive cypress beams that bore the axe-marks of some forgotten wood-cutter who had hewn them out of local timber. Perhaps he was one of those fierce ancestors who glowered at us from faded photographs displayed in heavy frames on the whitewashed walls. Sitting for a picture, then as now, had been a solemn occasion, and the men had arrayed themselves with bandoliers of bullets draped over their shoulders, silver-encrusted knives stuck in their sashes, and long-barrelled rifles in their hands. As for the women, they were black-coifed, with faces seamed by life and with a direct unflinching gaze upon a world they knew to be full of sorrow—the classic gaze of Greek women.

.   .   .   .   .   .

We stayed several days. We met everyone: relatives of our hosts, neighbours, friends. They came to look at us, and we went to their houses for meals and conversation. There was endless talk—the principal pastime in a land where manufactured amusements are totally lacking, where even newspapers are a rarity and magazines virtually unknown. Above all there was a sense of limitless time. Movements were leisurely; an invitation for a cup of coffee or a glass of *tsikoudia* could turn into an affair lasting several hours. During this spring season most of the men were high in the mountains with the flocks of goats and sheep that constituted the main livelihood of the community. Therefore it was mostly the women of Ayios Ioannis that we met during these days. There were Katerina and her daughters (only one unmarried girl remained at home, but three others had married into other Sphakian villages, and they came on visits). One of these daughters, Vangelia, had the straight nose and wide brow that are associated with the women of ancient times—and the dignity. Altogether, it was a happy and attractive family. We also got to know Iphigenia, a strong-willed, strong-faced woman from the Viglis clan of Samaria who had married into this village; Ariadne, her daughter; and many others. The movements of these women's lives seemed as deliberate and graceful as the steps of a *syrto* as they went through the rituals of kitchen and hospitality, of serving their men at meals (men and women never sat down at table together— the women ate later, by themselves), the care of their numerous children. Underneath, there were tensions and worries: gossip, quarrels, the ever-present fear of illness and accidents.

There was an afternoon when we sat under the great arch on the terrace of Iphigenia's house high above the village—all of us, guests and hosts and neighbours, sitting on the long wooden bench along one wall, while two youths plucked idly at a lute and a lyre. The scene was languid and peaceful: and suddenly, from somewhere among the lanes below us, came piercing screams and shouts. In an instant all had dropped what they were doing and had run out for a better look. What we saw was like a slow-motion film or a maddening nightmare in which you never get anywhere: a man was bending over an inert figure on the ground, and he was sy-stematically and rhythmically pulling at his hair and lamenting— 'He's dead! My boy is dead!' Others were beating their chests, and groaning loudly; women wept and called upon the Virgin. For several minutes they let the child lie there, until finally someone had the presence of mind to wipe his bloody face with a handkerchief and cold water. He moved, murmured, looked about—not dead at all! A miracle! they were saying, and giving thanks to the Virgin. And what, after all, had happened to cause this hair-raising outburst of panic? Why, a lad of seven or eight had simply fallen out of a fig tree and been knocked out. The instantaneous transformation of a peaceful scene into one of totally unwarranted hysteria—men and women alike jumping to the conclusion that the worst had happened —made one understand why the vendetta is still so prevalent: it springs from the volatile nature of the people.

The boy was shaken up and bruised, but clearly he would survive. A mule was saddled up and he was placed on it tenderly: he would be taken to Anopolis and thence by bus to the doctor in Canea the next morning. The little procession started out: several women accompanying the boy, and his mother walking beside the mule holding a large black umbrella to protect the child against the sun. We got word next day that he was recovering nicely in a clinic in Canea.

'But what did you do,' Inga asked, 'before there was a bus to take you to the doctor in Canea?'

Iphigenia answered: 'We just died, my child—we just died!'

* * *

Leaving Inga to absorb further feminine lore and gossip of the village, one morning I started out with Nikos before dawn and hiked high up in the mountains to the family sheepfold. The old man strode across the rocks with a rapid, swinging gait, erect and never flagging. The pace was difficult for me because our early breakfast of goat's milk had given me an upset stomach and nausea. But Nikos had a remedy for that: searching among the crannies of a cliffside, he plucked a green plant which he said was *spilinohorto,* and bade me eat some of its leaves. Skeptically, I did so; within minutes my discomfort had vanished. I attended with renewed interest as he pointed out various other herbs during the rest of our walk, telling me their names and their uses. Sage and marjoram were everywhere and high up in an inaccessible cliff sprouted a clump of silvery-green —the famous dittany (*origanum dictamnus*), an indigenous Cretan plant that was known in ancient times for its healing properties. More recently it has become known as a potent aphrodisiac (hence its popular name, *erondas*) and it fetches a high price on the market.

'But beware!' said Nikos, 'The *dictamo* you buy in Canea is not the real thing—they grow it down on the plains and it's no good. For real *erondas* you have to climb up there'—gesturing towards the cliffs—'and many people have been killed trying to get at it.'

The Archaic Face

After five hours' steady walking we arrived at the *mytato* (cheese-making establishment) which sat at the bottom of a treeless, boulder-strewn gorge. We were just in time for the morning milking. Niko's two sons, Manolis and Andonis, rounded up the animals with fierce shouts and whistles. Brimming mugs of warm sheep milk, that most nutritious and satisfying of drinks, were passed around.

Later, Nikos showed me the cool storeroom at the back of the hut where scores of round yellow cheeses were arranged neatly on racks for seasoning. Cheese-making, though arduous and exacting work, is fairly profitable as Cretan cheeses are famous throughout Greece and find a ready market in Athens. That evening I watched the entire cheese-making process. The milk was heated first in a huge cauldron, rennet was added and it was stirred rapidly with a long wooden ladle. Finally it was poured out into moulds and wrapped in cloths in the storeroom, with clamps tightened to press out the moisture. At nearly every stage of this lengthy process there was some tasty by-product to be sampled, such as warm curds of soft *myzithra* (similar to cream cheese) and later a drink of sheep buttermilk. It was nearly midnight when the work was finished. Long before then I had stretched out on one of the stone benches in a corner of the hut, wrapped myself in a thick goat-hair cloak, and dozed off. From time to time I would wake to see the young men and Nikos in the flickering firelight, silhouetted in smoke, taking turns stirring the cauldron: lean figures, *sarikia* askew, faces streaming with sweat. It was typical of them that they had insisted on my taking the most comfortable sleeping-place.

Early in the morning Manolis, the sixteen-year-old brother, and I set out for the village with *sakoulia* full of cheeses on our backs, leaving the father and the older brother to look after the flocks. The main concern of the goat-footed lad on this trek home was to look out for *agrimia* or Cretan ibexes. These rocky heights of western Sphakia and part of the Selino district are the last haunts of the graceful wild goats whose curving horns and slim bodies were depicted on Minoan gems picked up at Knossos. The law rigidly protects the four or five hundred that still roam wild, and there are two offshore sanctuaries for them on islands near Canea and Ayios Nikolaos. Manolis, I suspected, would have been only too glad to shoot one if he had had a gun. 'The best meat there is!' he declared enthusiastically and then, suddenly pointing down a ravine, 'Look! There's one!' I looked, and saw nothing—or I may have seen a reddish-brown flash; I couldn't be sure. This was their country, though; at the ice-cold spring of Zarani, where we stopped for a drink, they were known to refresh themselves.

(Much later, on a hiking trip to another part of Sphakia, I finally met an *agrimi*—a graceful little female who, they said, had been found in a cave. No doubt they had shot her mother, and wouldn't admit it. The shepherds had made a pet of her and had given her a nickname, '*Sanalaki*' or 'little *agrimi*'—*sanalia* being another Cretan word for them. She ran with the flock of sheep all day and came right into the fold with them at night. She was not expected to run away, as only males do that. During milking time she was very insistent about getting her share, and they had trained her to leap from one shepherd's back to another as they bent over the milking. Even at forty days, she had all the natural grace and dignity of a wild thing, and her little horns had started to come out. She would make wonderful sudden leaps into the air, and do pirouettes on her hind legs. I fell in love with her immediately, of course, and had it been possible I would have tried to take her away. They were trying to keep her a secret, but Cretans are not very good at that. At last report she was still up there doing very well.)

The next day we left Ayios Ioannis. Katerina and her daughters pressed upon us some of their handiwork: beautifully embroidered table-cloths and a handsome red-and-black *sakouli*. They urged us to return one day soon; and for our part, we knew that we would see this family again, but we did not know when, or under what conditions. Manolis accompanied us to the edge of the village, and his last shout followed us down the path: 'Come back! Come back quickly—and I'll shoot an *agrimi* for you!'

* * *

Several hours later, several miles eastward and some three thousand feet lower, we scrambled down the last slope and arrived by the seashore at the fishing port of Loutro. Ruins of many periods—Hellenistic, Roman, Byzantine—are strewn about the promontory that protects it from the west winds, but today Loutro is a sleepy place, where fishermen mend their nets in doorways that open directly on to the shingle beach that serves as the village street. We found a coffee-shop with outdoor tables under the pepper trees, where the congenial owner and his wife served us an excellent fish soup. This man told us that he is a descendant of one of Sphakia's greatest heroes, Daskaloyiannis or 'Teacher John', a merchant of Anopolis who led a rebellion against the Turks in 1770. (He wasn't really a teacher, but was given the nickname as a mark of respect.) Tricked into surrendering, the leader refused to sign a statement of capitulation, and paid for it dearly by being skinned alive in the main square of Herakleion. He endured this horrible torture 'without a murmur', according to the present bearer of his name.

That night in the coffee-shop Daskaloyiannis recited the peasant ballad that recounts the exploits of his ancestor. His glowing face told us that the story was as real to him as though it had happened yesterday, and the same feeling was reflected in the faces of the circle of villagers who gathered to listen. They must have heard it many times, yet their interest was still as fresh as though they were hearing it all for the first time.

As Loutro offered no other accommodation, the villagers obligingly allowed us to sleep on the floor of the one-room school-house. There, when we spread our sleeping bags in the aisle between the battered wooden desks, we gazed up at a gallery of Greek heroes, framed upon the walls: Karaiskakis, Kolokotronis, the heroine Bouboulina, ancient Achilles—and in a place of honour at the head of the room, Daskaloyiannis, the 'Teacher', in a real classroom at last. A hand-lettered placard proclaimed, truthfully: GREECE WILL NEVER DIE!

*   *   *

Frangokastello: the empty hulk of a Venetian fortress on a sandy shore; the arrogant Lion of Saint Mark over the main gate looking out over an unsubdued Sphakia. Ghosts as plentiful as asphodel on the blood-watered plain below the mysterious mountains: here the warrior clans used to gather to do their wild dances and to display their skill at arms. Hadjimichalis Daliannis, bull-headed Greek palikar, spurning local advice, here led his three hundred and eighty-five men to their death at Turkish hands in 1828; buried in the coastal sand dunes they lie, except for every May when they rise up and walk in the dawn mists—the 'dew shades' or *Drossoulites* as the frightened harvesters call them. It was not their time when we arrived—we were too early—but it was twilight, and a nervous wind was blowing down from the hills, whistling through the chinks in the fortress, sending chills down our spines. If ever a place was haunted, this was it—definitely tangibly realistically haunted—and yet somehow in spite of it we slept there, in a shallow cave under the brow of the bluff. We saw no ghosts, but we believed in them: impossible not to, in this land where the past seems almost palpable, where it presses ever closer, like the mountains that crowd against the sea all along the Sphakian shore.

* * *

We returned to Sphakia many times in the ensuing years. But, though we visited every other village in the district, we never made the trek back to Ayios Ioannis. Perhaps it was because we were always pulled on by the lure of the unknown, the unvisited place. Sphakia became for us the distilled essence of Crete, as Crete itself is of Greece for some people. We kept in touch with the Malephakis family, news of them reaching us via the efficient grapevine, for they were known all over Sphakia and had relatives in widely scattered villages. We would send our '*hairetismata*' or greetings to Nikos and Katerina through a daughter in Askyphou or through Katerina's brother in Hora Sphakion or through her old mother, and eventually greetings to us would sift back; and sometimes we would meet Andonis or Manolis in the market in Canea, that central meeting-point and news exchange for all of western Crete.

On our goings and comings we always made it a point to call on Katerina's mother, Kyria Eleni, in Hora Sphakion. She lived alone in a house at the top of the hill overlooking miles of coast. She could have stayed with any of her relatives, but she preferred independence. She was ninety years old, a complaining crone with a sure clutch on life, a cheerful hypochondriac who liked nothing better than to describe her numerous ailments in vivid detail. '*Panayia mou!* Charos will take me soon,' she would say—and then spit over her shoulder to make sure that he didn't.

Also in Hora Sphakion we used to visit Vangelia, the oldest of Katernina's daughters—the one with the classic features. She was a busy wife and mother, with children growing up and an active husband whom she seemed really to love—an unusual thing in this country of arranged marriages. On one of our visits we found her in black: it was for her father, Nikos, our host from Ayios Ioannis. He had been ill for several years—he must have been so even when I walked with him up to the sheepfold, though he made no complaints and devoted his attention to curing my minor attack of nausea. Even a trip all the way to Athens to the big hospital (his first time away from Crete) had failed to save him, and he had died while still in the sixties. 'He died young,' they said.

About a year later there was even more shocking news: Vangelia had become a widow herself, while still in mourning for her father.

Her husband had been out alone in the mountains, shooting birds and hares. When they found his body it appeared that he had slipped and the gun had gone off accidentally—but who could tell, in Sphakia, whether it had been a mishap or the work of some skulking feuder? He had been in his forties, the prime of life, with flocks of sheep and a growing family. No death makes a heavier impression in Crete than one like this. Old people can face their own deaths with good-natured philosophy and their relatives, though mourning, will say 'It was his time'. But the death of a man, a breadwinner in a community with none of the safeguards of modern society, no security save that of the family, is a shock to the whole community.

We had to go to the widow: it was an obligation. By coincidence we had arrived on the fortieth day after the man's death, the day of *mnemosyno* or formal remembrance. We climbed heavily up the hill, wishing we could avoid the visit. Children, sad-faced and subdued, led us to the house. In the yard the oldest son, a boy in his early teens, was chopping wood—manfully doing his duty as senior male. At the door we were met by Katerina, she was only a little changed by the intervening years since we had stayed with her at Ayios Ioannis: mellowed and softened by her own widowhood, but still radiant with life. She was glad to see us: clearly this visit which we, with our modern wish to avert our faces from death, had wanted to avoid, was appreciated by her and by the other women who sat in a black circle around the grieving woman. They were making the most of death as they do of everything: drinking its bitter dregs. The doors of that death house had been painted over black; the children were all in black; the table-cloth and even the bench-covers were black.

At the centre, Vangelia—quiet now as though ravaged by a hurricane of grief. The classic lines, the Grecian brow were still there, but all transformed by the weight of doom that had dropped on her. She had become sallow and drawn, had lost much weight and seemed to *want* to look ugly. (Had she pulled out hair or a tooth, defaced or scratched herself?—widow's practices in Crete. What screaming and panic there must have been when the news reached the house, when they brought the body down from the mountain.) Nothing was left to her now but her mourning; facing nothing but long arid vistas of grief, she seemed to be saying: 'All right, Charos—you wanted mourning, and so I will show you how to mourn.'

The effect on us was like that of tragedy: we felt pity and terror—and helplessness. Even the Greek ritual words for the occasion escaped us. But these people played their roles as though born to them. The daughter came silently with a tray full of cakes; she was thirteen and had her mother's classic features; now her ripening young form was already swathed in black—early preparation for her part as a Greek woman. But there was strength, too, in her movements, and one felt that her veins contained the strong blood that has enabled Sphakia and Crete to survive everything, to endure. And what of Vangelia? Would she ever attain the serenity of her mother and grandmother, the fierce acceptance of life in spite of everything? The basic steel is there. She lives her grief now and has done with it. She has children—joyous consolation. She will come through, but her life will never be the same; now still young at forty, she must begin those long indeterminate years of widowhood until finally she becomes another black-coifed complaining crone like Kyria Eleni. One day her portrait, too, will join the ancestral gallery on the walls.

13

Alarms and Diversions

It was a summer of alarms and diversions, and interludes of somnolence when the days passed like minutes, so lulled were we by the sun and the heat and the heavy damp air of our village— for by now we had discovered that 'Doc' had been right: this place did indeed have a bad climate, surrounded as it was by springs and marshes. But we were held by its beauty, as a man may be who continues a fatal affair with a woman he knows will ruin him.

The first alarm was an earthquake, or tremor, that swept over us during the calm hot days of early June, and was gone, leaving in its wake only the cold chills of premonitions induced by a sudden new awareness of our helplessness before elemental forces. It came upon us during the night; I awoke abruptly and felt the whole room in motion, like the deck of a ship during a storm at sea. Somewhere off in the night there was a dull rumbling, recalling ancient myths of the minotaur that lives in the bowels of the earth. I had no time to think, yet in those split seconds I was absolutely convinced that we were in for a real earthquake, and I momentarily expected the walls and roof of our concrete box of a house to come tumbling about our ears. What I did in those instants, out of pure instinct and with no time for thought, showed me that I had advanced at least one halting step out of the mire of selfishness from which we all start. I sprang across the room and threw myself over the bed where Inga lay sleeping. The gleam of intention that flashed in those moments was unmistakable: I wanted to protect her with my own body from the falling roof. I couldn't have been more astonished, for I had never dreamed that I would ever care to give my own life to save another. She awoke at the same time, and we clung together briefly, and then the tremor had passed; all was as before except that our illusion of security had gone —we realised with awful awareness how uncertain even is the ground on which we stand.

But in the bright sunlight midnight premonitions fade and are nearly forgotten. We were occupied by the endless diversions of village life, and by our own activities and outings. The even tenor of our life was upset by nothing more than minor, intermittent annoyances. The plague of scorpions, for example. Apparently they had their nest somewhere near our outside toilet, for we saw them often in and around the little building. Going there at night with a flashlight or a flickering kerosene lamp was a tricky business—the place had to be examined carefully before one dared to sit down. These little scorpions, which averaged about an inch and a half in length (though we saw a few two-and three-inchers), were said by the Cretans to be harmless, though it was admitted that the sting was painful, but unfortunately there was a dangerous variety too. The two kinds looked exactly alike except that one had five tail segments, and the other seven—I never could remember which type was dangerous, and in any case my first reaction upon seeing a scorpion is not to lean over and conduct a close examination. Though I never got ours classified, I did learn something about their habits. They were rather odd little beasts, liable to turn up anywhere—we had them over our beds, and in the kitchen, and in the washroom at various times. You never saw them coming or going: one minute there would be nothing, and then a scorpion would pop up. They were not aggressive, and their instinct was to run—and they could move surprisingly fast, though sometimes they seemed to panic and could only go round in circles. During our years on the island we saw a good many of them but we were never stung; a man who had been, told us that it felt 'like a hornet's sting' and hurt for about a day. The local remedy was spirits of ammonia, rubbed on the spot.

The curious thing was that most Cretans wouldn't admit that the scorpions existed. There is a sort of minor myth, assiduously cultivated by the Cretans themselves, that there is nothing poisonous on the island. Like many Cretan tales, it is not quite true, for besides the scorpions there is a kind of poisonous spider, the *rogalidà,* which is fairly prevalent in eastern Crete. There are not many snakes on the island but there is one variety, fortunately rare, that is poisonous; they are called *oxendria* and I take it that they are a sort of viper, though I have never seen one. So much for the story that Saint Paul cleared Crete of serpents, much as Saint Patrick is said to have done (with greater success) in Ireland. Everything in Crete is more complicated. On the whole, though, the island is free from noxious *beasts*; as one old lady told me, 'It is the sting of *people* you must guard against!'

She was right—the minute you lowered your guard you would get stung; you could not afford a moment's sentimentality towards the Cretans. The town merchants were, naturally, the cleverest at cheating and trickery, but the peasants tried it too—though usually in such a clumsy way that the results were merely laughable. Late that summer we got into a row with 'Madame Friday' about the rent. From the beginning we had always paid in advance, a month at a time. In paying the September rent, I happened to mention what month it was for, and the crafty old crone said, 'Oh, no—that is the *August* rent you are paying!' I insisted, she remained adamant, tempers bristled. We appealed to our neighbours—they all knew we had been paying in advance. Even the police were called in—but the old woman still insisted that we had never paid in advance. After a while it died down; we went on paying on the first of each month, re-enacting the same comedy each time. In the end we won out—she simply let it drop—but she had *tried,* as Cretans nearly always will.

The villagers were constantly being victimised by the pedlars who came through on their rounds of the country districts. Many of these itinerant merchants were quite prosperous, and drove about in cars or light trucks loaded with every conceivable kind of merchandise that a villager might want—with a heavy emphasis on trinkets and gew-gaws, plastic buckets and cups, artificial flowers (which were greatly preferred as a status symbol to the beautiful—but valueless—wild flowers that grew all around), cheap dresses, religious pictures, and so on. It was like the white traders selling to the natives. Their trucks were invariably mounted with loudspeakers and their arrival was announced far in advance by the blaring of *bouzouki* music (always scratchy, as they played the same records day in and day out as they bumped over country roads) and punctuated with occasional announcements delivered in a rasping voice. They actually were traders, who would accept olive oil or other products in lieu of money. Some of them engaged village women and girls to make tablecloths and other things for them, following cheap patterns provided by the merchant. Needless to say, the villagers were losing heavily on these arrangements, for they were never paid in cash for their labour or their oil, but always in goods—at a marked-up price, naturally. The women were always deep in debt to these pedlars, and never out of their clutches, for they were impulse buyers—I can't imagine a Cretan housewife calculating needs or making up a shopping list.

The merchants' visits were, in fact, social occasions—welcome diversions from the monotony of village life. The women would flock around, pawing the goods and engaging in banter with the pedlars. The successful tradesmen were the ones who could engage in salty exchanges with the peasants on their own level. Like the one who, seeing a yellowed crone of eighty hold up a pink, fringed nightgown against her blackened rags, called out, 'Well, grannie, do you want that for your second honeymoon?'

'Don't think I'm too old for that!' retorted the hag, 'But this isn't my colour—haven't you got one in black?'

'Oh, no—you need a light one, so your bridegroom can find you in the dark,' shot back the pedlar. The women all hooted with laughter —including the crone, who enjoyed it more than anyone. Not very subtle, but it was what they liked.

I once asked one of these traders, in a bantering way, why he always cheated. He rose to the occasion and instead of denying it, only grinned and said, 'It's not possible to make a living if you don't cheat. Isn't that true?' The circle of villagers backed him up —'Yes, he's right—an honest man gets no bread.'

* * *

There certainly is such a thing as the 'peasant mentality'—though it is not restricted to places like Crete: I have known Americans who had it. Tolstoy came up against it all the time, and was driven nearly mad by it; trying desperately to love his muzhiks, he nearly wound up hating them. In our village we never tried to love anyone, but took them as they were, and so most of the time we could be more amused than annoyed. We could never predict their reactions to anything; they viewed the world out of such depths of innocence. Unspoiled by the multitudinous information that reaches 'modern' people from so many sources, they saw new things with the freshness of children or of African natives. There was the young woman who, seeing our shelf full of books, asked, 'But why haven't you been able to sell them?' Knowing that I was a writer, she assumed that I had written all of the books and was trying to retail them, like the pedlars who came through the village. When she heard they were all by different authors, she crossed herself and exclaimed, '*Panayia mou!* You have enough books to start a school!'

You could never *tell* them anything—or rather, you could tell them until you were blue in the face, and they would nod and voice their agreement—and then the next day they would turn right around and do something that showed they had not listened. I went through this merry-go-round with the local 'postmaster', who was very much a peasant although he presided over an office. Once, upon going in to pick up some mail, I found him and his assistant with a pile of photographs spread out all over the desk. They were holding up the prints, passing them around to various loungers, and commenting on them. The pictures were indeed interesting—especially to me, for they were the rather expensive enlargements that I had ordered from a custom photofinisher in Athens. The envelope had been sent unsealed, so it had not been difficult to open it and take out the prints. No one offered any apologies or showed the slightest sign of embarrassment; the postmaster merely smiled and complimented me on my pictures as he gathered them together and put them back in the envelope. In as patient and courteous a way as possible, so as not to offend his *philotimo* or honour, I explained that I would rather not have these prints covered with finger-marks and mauled by many hands, as they were intended for publication. The next time I received pictures, would he please give them first to me, and then I would show them to him later? He nodded and agreed. Some time later, another batch of pictures arrived. When I went to the post office, he handed me the packet and said, 'That's a very good picture of Georgillis and Thea in their field.'

This time I showed more annoyance. 'Look, Russo,' I said, 'I told you before not to open my pictures and look at them before I get them.'

Instantly his face assumed an expression of outraged innocence. 'I? Open your pictures? Never—I never touched them.'

'But you just said . . .' I tried to say, but he overwhelmed me.

'It was the *customs house* in Canea that opened your pictures!'

The patent absurdity of this explanation, the barefacedness of the lie, were enough to disarm opposition—after all, a package sent within Greece obviously would not have to clear customs. I even felt a sort of grudging admiration for anyone who could lie with such a straight face. But by now I had been long enough in the labyrinth to know what tack to take.

'Of course, Russo, I know *you* never open packages. But if this happens again, I shall have to complain to my good friend, the Post Director in Canea, because those clumsy customs officials are ruining my best prints.'

It was obvious by the expression on his face that this point had registered solidly. After that there were no more thumb-printed pictures.

*   *   *

The idea that village life is 'simple' is an illusion of city people. We *tried* to simplify our lives, but at every point where we came into contact with the villagers, complications were sure to follow. There was the time, for instance, when Inga became involved in a dubious attempt to be helpful to some neighbours. A certain family, living on the outskirts, near the swamp, was so poor and shiftless that the whole village looked down on it. The father had been an alcoholic for many years, and never did any work. The mother, Polygeorgina, had been forced to scavenge for a living—to take odd jobs harvesting other people's olives or peanuts, to go out day after day picking wild *horta* and snails to feed her several children. They were receiving regular monthly payments from an American family that had 'adopted' one of the daughters; without this extra cash I don't see how they could have existed at all.

One day Polygeorgina came to our house, looking worried. Her husband was ill from too much drinking; a doctor had told him he was in danger of developing ulcers, and had recommended penicillin shots as a preventive. But she could find no one to give them; not even Madame Friday, the village wise-woman, would go near their house. She had got hold of a needle (rusty) and a syringe (filthy) but she couldn't give the shots herself. She was afraid. Would Inga do it?

Her story seemed a bit fishy (we had never heard of a doctor prescribing penicillin for ulcers), but she was insistent, and it was hardly possible to refuse. So Inga cleaned the syringe, boiled the needle, and plunged it into the groaning man's thigh, while the family stood around offering sympathy and advice. This went on every day for a week.

We lost caste immediately because of this. Our other neighbours blamed Inga for giving the shots, and me for allowing her to. 'Don't you know,' they whispered, 'that he hasn't got any ulcers—that's all lies—what he has is *gonorrhoea* that he caught from the bad women in Canea!'

Then one day I came upon Polygeorgina in the street. She was bent over, poking at something with a stick, and cackling with glee. When I took a closer look I saw that she was burning a toad—had poured kerosene on it and set a match to it, and was now reaping sadistic pleasure from its frenzied hoppings. It was charred almost to death, and there was nothing more that one could do for it except kill it—which I did.

'Aren't you ashamed of yourself?' I demanded.

'Why? It's only an animal! It was in the garden.'

I never spoke to the woman again. I went home in disgust and told Inga, 'No more shots.'

But that was not the end of the episode, for now word got around that Inga knew how to give injections and would do it for nothing. Everyone who had any kind of illness began asking for them. They obtained the penicillin, streptomycin, and so on, from pharmacies in Canea—without prescriptions, of course. We didn't like to say No to our friends, but we were worried lest some patient might suffer an adverse reaction to these powerful drugs. Also, it got us into further difficulties with Madame Friday because she regarded it as unfair competition—*she* had always been the only one who could give injections, and she charged for it. Finally Inga had to put her foot down: no more injections under any circumstances.

But these were small matters, indeed, compared with the night of the uproar.

One of our favourite local characters was the baker, a man in his late seventies who always wore a dirty bandanna wrapped around his head, with the two ends sticking up in front like horns. He had learned a few words of English during the war, and he invariably greeted us with them: 'Secret Service!' (delivered with an air of mystery, in a stage whisper) and 'Cows-boys!' (followed by a hearty laugh). He may have known more once, but his tongue had forgotten how to shape the words, so the sounds came out all garbled, like a phonograph record played at the wrong speed. He had served with the Resistance and had once been caught red-handed by the Germans, with all of his pockets stuffed with propaganda leaflets that he had obtained from the English. Incredibly, he talked his way out of this seemingly impossible situation when he went up before the German military judge—actually convinced the court that he had found the things lying in the road. This should illustrate the persuasiveness of Cretan lying. The honest Germans were out of their depth in this quicksand of evasions, omissions, half-truths and quarter-truths and no-truths; the Cretans were ahead of them by several thousand years of practice. Child's-play merely, for a Cretan to outwit them; but when he comes up against his fellow countrymen, that is another matter. For it seems that although our baker made most excellent bread, every loaf for some time had weighed just ten grammes less than it should have—that is, instead of the standard weight of one kilogramme, it weighed nine hundred and ninety grammes. The first to discover this trickery was our shaggy friend Georgillis. The baker couldn't have been unluckier. The old veteran of countless mountain feuds immediately went into a fury—egged on by 'Thea', his wife, who was even tougher than he was. The baker had to pass by their house to get to his place, which was out in the country, and this night he didn't get far. Georgillis and Thea and their son waylaid him in an olive grove and attacked him with stones and sticks. It must have been a grotesque battle, for three of the participants were well on in their sixties and seventies. The villagers said afterwards that it was Thea who inflicted the most damage—but it is doubtful if anyone knows exactly what happened. This much is certain: the baker was left unconscious, streaming with blood, with one eye hanging from its socket. The shouting and screaming and confusion during (and after) this battle can well be imagined. Luckily, there was a police station in the village— otherwise there might have been a repetition of that scene of carnage that occurred a few years ago in one of the Mount Ida villages, when a man killed another in a coffee-house argument, then the relatives of the slain man took instant vengeance on someone in the other family, and so on, the insane blood lust spreading like wildfire through the community, until at the end of an hour seven or eight people lay dead. But in this case the police were on the spot, and they arrested the Georgillis family, thus protecting them from any possible vengeance. The baker was taken to the hospital in Canea, where for weeks he hovered between life and death. Georgillis and his son were held in jail (Thea was released because someone had to look after the family sheep), and everyone assumed they would have to stand trial for murder. But the incredibly tough old baker lived through it. One day he returned to the village, squinting a bit, with a fearsome scar over his eye; and wrapped his bandanna around his head, and went back to making Bread—at a thousand grammes per kilo.

No charges were brought against Thea; Georgillis received a sentence which was immediately suspended because of his age and ill health; the son went to jail for a couple of years. But in the long run it was tough old Thea who fared the worst out of this incident During the fight, it was said, she had received a knock on the breast; there was soreness for some time and then a swelling which refused to go down. After some months she had to go to the hospital; and there, at last, she died of cancer. When they laid her out they found a pistol hidden under her nightdress.

*   *   *

Living in Crete revealed to us the rich contradictoriness of human nature. I believe that *all* human beings are inconsistent, that contradiction and paradox are inherent in our nature. But modern society, patterning itself after machines, which *are* consistent (or ought to be, when they're running properly), makes this insane demand that we should be all of a piece. In reality you find generosity and meanness in the same person; brutality and tenderness cheek by jowl; bravery and cowardice commingled. In Crete this is all open and exposed; no one has ever thought of trying to hide it, or to force themselves into a Procrustean bed of consistency. All of the participants in the violent little drama I have just related were friendly and generous people—if not precisely tender (but there is little tenderness anywhere on this island). Some of our best friends were thieves and murderers; and some of the very worst men (and not only in Greece!) were 'pillars of the community'.

It is not unusual in Crete to meet men who have killed once, twice, perhaps even three times; but even in this harsh land, a man who has committed fifty murders is something special. He is marked for fame, and for respect mingled with fear. High in the mountains to the south of our village, is a salient of the Sphakia stronghold, there lived such a man. There was, naturally, some disagreement about his actual score, and doubtless an element of exaggeration or myth-making, but all were agreed that it was in the neighbourhood of half a hundred. Many of his victims, to be sure, had been Germans during the war, when he was a hero of the Resistance, but many others had been fellow Cretans who had unwisely crossed him in one way or another—usually in disputes about animals and grazing rights. His name was Achilles, but the Cretans, with their flair for nicknames, had tagged him 'Bones' and thus he was known to everyone. That he had never spent a day in prison was due primarily to the fact that, until relatively recently, killings in blood feuds were considered 'family matters' and did not come up in the courts; also, no doubt, to his extreme wiliness in outwitting the authorities.

Having heard so much about this man, naturally I wanted to meet him—though, I must admit, I was not without some qualms as to how I might be received.'Just go there—he'll be glad to see you', said one of our neighbours, who had known him during the war. And that is what I did, when one of my summer outings took me to the vicinity of his village.

As I approached the gate a huge, ferocious dog leaped towards me with fangs bared. Fortunately, he was tethered, but the long chain had been adjusted precisely to a length that would bar any intruder. This beast was the first line of defence against any enemies who might have got it into their heads to seek vengeance for some of the man's earlier killings. The womenfolk—the housewife and two grown daughters—rushed out, silenced the animal, and invited me in. I had an excuse for being there: I had greetings from some friends of the family. It might have been a tenuous reason elsewhere, but in Crete it was sufficient to open doors and to entitle me to the full range of hospitality.

Achilles came from the backyard to greet me: a wiry, rather small man (for Sphakia, where six feet is average), with a leathery face and a painfully strong hand-clasp. There was nothing in his appearance, at first glance, to mark him out as a talented killer; but after I had been sitting with him for a little while I found the clue: his preternaturally sharp, cold eyes that were never at rest but always roving, always searching. In his movements, too, there was the lithe quickness of a cat. His manner was cordial, though he did perhaps less talking than might have been expected, and more watching. And once, when one of the girls dropped a plate behind him, he whirled and his temper flashed like a sword. The poor girl retreated to the kitchen in confusion, and he turned back to me, as affable—and as guarded—as ever.

Yet this obviously dangerous man showed unusual thought-fulness towards me. It was midday, and I had had a long, hard hike, and so after we had eaten he suggested that I might like to have a rest. He barked an order to the women—who stood ready to wait on him hand and foot—and they hurried to and fro, collecting bedding. At his order, they spread quilts under a shady carob tree in the yard, where I could enjoy the vagrant breezes. And not merely quilts, but clean white sheets and pillows with hand-embroidered cases. They made the bed with scrupulous care, and when all was ready Achilles bade me 'good sleeping'. Just as I was lying down, one of the daughters rushed out with a pitcher of cold water and a glass, placed them carefully on the ground beside me, and covered them with a white cloth. 'In case you're thirsty when you wake up', she explained. As a last gesture—perhaps necessary to insure my safety—Achilles came out and shortened the dog's tether so that he couldn't possibly reach me. He was very fond of the beast, who obviously lived for his master—and hated everyone else.

Achilles was the absolute dictator of his household. But if the woman and the older girls seemed little better than slaves (contented ones, I might add), the young boy was a prince: subject to strong discipline, yet always aware that he was the heir apparent. And from the nature of the games he played, it looked as though he might one day follow in his father's footsteps. That afternoon, after my siesta, I was startled to see the boy reach behind a door and pick up what I assumed was a toy sub-machine-gun; he levelled it at us and made 'rat-tat-tat' sounds. Achilles snatched it from him and put it back in its place—and I saw that it was a real gun, and loaded too.

Achilles was a strange companion, capable of animated talk and laughter at one moment, and in the next sinking into long silence for no apparent reason. He seemed to have an underlying streak of melancholy—something I had observed in many Cretans, including our friend 'Doc' of Ayios Nikolaos. These inexplicable Cretan depressions alternate with moods of almost manic gaiety and exuberance; it is as though these violent and even terrifying oscillations of emotional temperature were patterned after the unstable climate of the island. The manic-depressive dichotomy comes out in their songs and dances, which alternate between the dragging, somber *rizitika* ballads and the wild frenzy of the *pentozali* and *sousta*. And it also finds expression in their tendency to brood long over a grievance or an insult, and then suddenly to flash out in an act of violence or a 'night of long knives' against oppressors. It makes for difficult, unpredictable people—the Cretans as we knew them.

At the moment, however, it seemed that my host was brooding over nothing more serious than having his picture taken. After the evening meal he broached the subject that had apparently been on his mind all day: he had noticed that I carried a camera—would I mind taking his picture with his family? I was delighted to oblige him, and it was agreed that the portrait would be done the next day.

I had planned a hike to another village for the morning, but before starting out I told Achilles that I expected to be back in the afternoon, and we could set up the picture then. As usual, it was much farther to the other village than they had told me, and when I got there I fell in with some people who insisted that I stay for a huge meal. That took some recovering, and then it was really too hot to do any walking in the middle of the day, so it was late afternoon before I finally arrived back at the Achilles household.

As soon as I walked through the gate I sensed tension in the air. The children were crying and the mother shouted at them; everyone seemed out of sorts. The master of the house merely sat moodily in a corner, fingering the end of his moustache—detached from the proceedings. The woman was dressed in her 'Sunday best' or what passes for high fashion in a mountain village—including high heels that threatened to send her sprawling at every step. The children had been dressed up, too, but hours of play had smudged their fine clothing, and their faces and hands were dirty. I realised with horror that they had probably spent hours getting themselves ready for the portrait, and then had sat waiting for me most of the afternoon. I hastened to assure them that I would take the picture at once; an exposure meter reading revealed that the light was sufficient—if we hurried.

The mother rallied her forces: she called on the older girls to get out washtubs and draw water from the well, and the younger children were stripped down and given their second bath of the day —protesting at full voice over this cruel injustice. The son sulked and said he did not *want* to have his picture taken. Achilles perked up a little, and I saw him surreptitiously rearranging his *sariki*. But it was a long-drawn-out business; nearly an hour elapsed between my arrival and their announcement that they were ready. I feared there wouldn't be enough light, but I was prepared to go through the motions in any case—if I had tried to back out at this stage, for whatever reason, I think I would have become the killer's fifty-first victim.

They lined up against a wall, as though preparing to face a firing squad: Achilles, the kingpin, sitting on a chair in the middle, flanked by his woman and children. He wanted the dog in the picture—he seemed nearly as proud of him as of his son—and so he loosened the chain and brought the animal to sit at his feet. At the last moment they coaxed the unwilling boy into the picture.

I set the camera, focused, prepared to shoot—and then the dog broke loose. He rushed towards me, growling fiercely, and lunged at my leg with fangs bared. Somehow I managed to fend him off by putting my boot in his mouth; he bit and tugged at it—while Achilles just sat there with the faintest smile on his face. Then, languidly, as though there were all the time in the world, he rose and took the dog by the collar and pulled him back to the family group. I will always believe that he set that beast loose on purpose—to give me a fright, to test my mettle, perhaps as a revenge for my having kept them waiting.

The ordeal over, everyone brightened and relaxed. The fancy clothes came off within minutes, and the household went back to normal. I spent another night under their roof, and the next day trekked back to the lowlands.

The picture came out all right—properly exposed, albeit slightly grey. The woman looks tense, the little boy is scowling, the girls look awkward and nervous. The dog is looking angrily at the photographer, ready to charge again. But Achilles is superb: arrogant, serene, cock of the walk in his domain, gazing with cool insolence at the alien photographer upon whom he has just played a hair-raising trick. It was worth fending off that mad dog's attack just to get it.

* * *

Early in September we noticed groups of women passing through our village along the main road; most of them were barefooted and carried bundles over their shoulders. They were pilgrims and penitents, fulfilling vows to walk to the *panegyri* of the Virgin's Birthday at Myriokephala, a village in the mountains to the east of us, where there was a miracle-working icon. Many of our friends were planning to go, too—including Madame Friday our landlady, who declared that she would ride all the way on a donkey, over the mountains, and that she would ask the *Panayia* for one thing only: that she could see her daughter who had gone away to the New World. (Her request was granted within a year though not quite in the way that she had expected; she thought the girl would come back to her, whereas in the event it was she who made the long voyage across the sea, to establish a new home in her old age with her daughter and the man she had married. Thus are all our wishes granted—but in strange and unexpected ways.)

For those who had no walking or donkey-riding vows to fulfil, a fleet of ramshackle buses was laid on for the occasion. The afternoon before the festival we got on one of them and started out for Myriokephala. We saw at once that the driver was even more erratic than most, probably because he was crazed from over-work —the average village bus driver has to make only two trips a day, to town and back, and here was this fellow, ferrying busloads of pious women all day long. It was enough to set anyone's teeth on edge. We thought little of it, for we were accustomed to risking our lives with the maniac drivers of Crete; it was just another of the hazards of the country that we thought would never catch up with us, like diseases and natural disasters. The earthquake had shaken us slightly, but still we clung to our typically modern conviction that accident and misfortune always happen to someone else. The Cretans know otherwise, and every journey, every departure for them is a step into the unknown; they are fatalists and pessimists at heart—as well they might be, considering their history.

After crossing the plain of Dramia we turned off the highway, into a narrow side road. Going around a sharp curve, suddenly we were confronted by another bus careering towards us on the wrong side of the road. The other bus swerved and our driver panicked; there was a loud crash, the sound of glass breaking—and a large limb of an olive tree burst through the windshield. Shattered glass sprayed the interior of the bus. Inga and I, far towards the back, ducked to the floor. The women's piercing screams flew like particles of pointed glass through the air; several of them had the presence of mind to call on the *Panayia* for help. We saw that the olive tree—blessed olives of Apokoronas!—was the only thing between us and a deep ravine; had it not stopped us, we would have gone over for sure. The driver now committed another error: with a bus full of women and children, some of whom might have been injured for all he knew, he attempted to back away from the tree. But the machine wouldn't budge—the tree held it fast. The driver then recovered his presence of mind sufficiently to leap out—still ignoring the passengers—and to engage in fierce shouting and cursing with the other driver, who had also advanced to mid-road to take part in the word-battle. And there they stood, waving their arms and accusing each other of being cuck olds (the favourite Cretan term of abuse), until a gendarme, arriving in another bus, took over as moderator of the debate. Even he paid no attention to the passengers. Luckily, there were no serious injuries, only cuts and scratches and bruises. One woman with a weak heart had fainted, but she was revived with some water. Inga and I, unscathed but shaken, got out and walked the rest of the way.

News of the accident flew speedily to Myriokephala, and by the time we got there the crowds of pilgrims were proclaiming it as the first miracle of this year's festival—for, had not the women called upon the *Panayia* for help at the moment of the crash, the bus would certainly have landed in the ravine, and all would have been killed. Responding to the call, the *Panayia* had put out her arm—the olive branch—and had stopped the machine on the brink of the abyss. Pious survivors of the crash had brought a fragment of this limb to the church, where it was prominently displayed outside the door— perhaps already on its way to the status of a holy relic.

This was a religious fair out of the Middle Ages. There must have been at least five thousand people packed into the tiny mountain village, and a large percentage of them were hoping for a cure; they had brought along lame and sick children and the very old; mothers were shepherding idiot sons through the crowd; the blind were led up to kiss the holy icon. Tales of former miracles were current. The year before, it was said, a blind man had suddenly regained his sight, and a crippled child had walked.

The icon that was responsible for these cures was reputed to be 'over a thousand years old' and it had been painted, so the story went, by none other than Saint Luke himself: it is an exact likeness of the Virgin's face because the saint remembered just how she looked. The icon had been found by a monk called John the Hermit who had lived in a cave near Myriokephala. For fifteen consecutive nights he saw a light on a mountainside where he knew there was no one; finally he went to investigate, and heard a voice say *Edo eime*—'Here I am'— and there was the icon.

As with all such fairs, the religious and the commercial flourished side by side. Hucksters of religious pictures and trinkets, wheel-of fortune men, vendors of *souvlaki* and soft drinks were thriving. There were also two lyre-and-lute teams, and the *glendi* in the street outside the church became more and more frenzied as the night progressed. Perhaps everyone was stimulated by the cool mountain air. Many stayed up all night, while hundreds wrapped themselves in blankets and lay down in the churchyard, waiting for miracles. Inga and I, incorrigible sceptics, went up the hill and spread our sleeping bags under an oak tree. The next day we heard that, disappointingly, there had been no miracles this year—unless *our* narrow escape from the bus accident were counted as one. Which it probably was, in years to come.

Not believing that miracles can happen twice, and not considering our luck alone sufficient protection against the hazards of country buses, we *walked* home. We had gotten rather jittery, and had a feeling that our luck was running low. But Fate is not to be cheated, whichever way we may dodge. In one of the villages along our path we ran into a wedding feast, and of course we had to stop and partake of the hospitality; we couldn't have said No even if we had wanted to. Great steaming cauldrons stood on the terrace of the groom's father's house; an old man stirred with a huge ladle, and occasionally threw in another chunk of goat meat. Inside the rude stone house, it was like attending a feast of the Goths or Vikings. Rough boards had been laid over saw-horses to make a table, and rollicking peasants sat at long benches, while women came and went with plates of steaming food. The grandmother of the bridegroom, a half-demented bag of bones, lay on a pallet of filthy rags on a sort of scaffold above the room, and peered down intently at all the diners as though counting the cost of it all. Occasionally she would cackle a greeting to an old friend. This was one of the few times in Crete when I felt a bit queasy about eating food offered me, for I had a strong

173

suspicion that the chunks of meat left on some plates were served up to others later; and it is doubtful whether the forks and dishes were washed at all in the intervals between servings. Also, the table was black with flies. But it was better not to think of such things. To refuse to eat would have been a mortal insult; I considered it only for a fleeting moment, then gave up the idea and speared a huge forkful of goat meat while the onlookers beamed in approval. Inga, being a woman, was spared the need to make such a gross display of appetite. Once again we had made the necessary sacrifices to hospitality.

Just how great a sacrifice was to appear in due time. But for some days after our return to Georgioupolis all was peaceful. The first rains came, and alternated with bright sunshine; the Cretans now called it 'winter'. A blessed land, where 'winter' is the green season! I dug up a plot of ground in our back yard, and we planted our first Cretan garden. It was just coming along nicely when I woke up one day with a splitting headache, all dizzy and shaky, and Inga looked at me and said: 'You have turned yellow!' Madame Friday came and looked at me, and wanted to cut the tendon in my upper lip—the infallible cure for jaundice, she claimed. Weak as I was, I resisted her; and we went to Canea to look for a doctor.

14

In a Cretan Clinic

I was trying to read *War and Peace,* and it was getting very interesting: Natasha was attending her first ball, and Prince Andrey was about to meet her for the first time. But on the periphery of my consciousness there seemed to be apersistent murmur of voices; and although I was lying on my side facing the wall, many pairs of eyes seemed to be piercing my back. Natasha's charming face faded, and voices quite definitely took over . . . 'he is an American. . . all day long he reads in his big book . . . an educated man . . . a professor.' I turned slightly and peeked with just one eye over the top of the page: instantly a dozen pairs of dark luminous eyes focused on me, and I winced as from a glare of lamps. It was no use; I put aside the book, and once again faced the battery of questions. For what seemed like the four hundredth time I explained that I was, indeed, American; no, I was not a professor; yes, we lived in a village in Apokoronas. And I was lying here in a supposedly semi-private room in Dr Magoulades' private clinic in Canea; and I had infectious hepatitis, damn it all, and I was condemned to lie here for three whole weeks. 'Ah, hepatitis—the same as *icteros,*' said the self-assertive middle-aged man who seemed to be the spokesman for the group of people who had come to visit the man who shared the room with me—but who were ignoring the poor chap completely because they found this curious foreigner so infinitely more fascinating. He lowered his voice, 'Dr. Magoulades, of course, wouldn't want to hear about this, but . . . Have you considered having the tendon of your upper lip cut? You'll get well immediately—next day you'll be right up out of bed!' I went back to Tolstoy.

.   .   .   .   .

We were fairly lucky to have found a place in this clinic, for it seems that the Cretans are not quite so healthy as they look; in fact, there is a great deal of illness among them—especially of what the Rockefeller Report called 'filth-borne diseases' such as typhoid and hepatitis. (The clouds of flies at the last village wedding! Those unwashed plates! Now at last I began to see how great a sacrifice the guest must be prepared to make to the demands of hospitality. Now, truly, I was a 'prisoner of hospitality' condemned to lie on my back for I knew not how many weeks). There were not enough beds in the public hospitals and, as nearly as I could gather, only charity cases went there; all the others went to the numerous privately operated clinics. In a town of 34,000 there must have been at least a dozen private clinics, and they were all said to be doing a profitable business.

Dr Magoulades—sallow-faced, dynamic—had given me a thorough examination and ordered blood and urine tests. The results were very positive. But dynamic optimism was the doctor's stock-in-trade. 'I can cure you!' he announced with an encouraging grin, 'But it will take time—at least three weeks here, then another three weeks in bed at home. Rest is essential, and so is diet—you must drink much milk and yogurt and avoid fats and coffee.' Then most unappetising news of all: 'You must drink absolutely no wine, beer or alcohol for at least a year and a half.' In Crete, a paradise of cheap drinks, condemned to a teetotaller's dull life—it was almost the last straw.

At first the clinic seemed quite agreeable. True, it was rather dingy, and was bounded on one side by a large machine shop where tremendous hammering went on all day as the harried mechanics attempted to undo the ravages of Cretan roads and Cretan drivers on the battered bodies of trucks and buses. The other side was little better—a noisy street where boisterous youths paraded up and down every evening, shouting back and fourth to one another. But there were compensations . . . There were no restrictions whatsoever on visitors—every hour was visiting hour. The nurses and doctors actually urged Inga to spend her nights on a cot which they offered to set up at my bedside. They brought her meals on a tray, and were in general most kind and concerned about us. The extra meals and the free bed helped our economy, which seemed even more precarious now, with this illness stretching ahead. The cost of my bed, plus all meals and medical attention, came to the equivalent of $2.80 a day. The food was good and, so far as we could tell, so was the medical treatment. And during the first few days, when I was rather ill, I had a room all to myself, at no extra charge. All to the good. The drawbacks would appear later . . . .

The comings and goings in this clinic were a rich source of human interest that would have fascinated the author I was trying to read.

Tolstoy himself would have found material in these rude peasants, some of them exposed to doctors and medicines for the first time in their lives. There was my room-mate, for instance. They brought him in at four o'clock one morning, suffering from a violent kidney stone attack. He was a thickset, grey-moustached, prosperous country-man who had never before been sick in his whole life. With him came his wife, who proceeded to set an example of devotion. As there was no extra bed in the room now, she slept at his feet, curled up like a faithful dog. Before bed-time each night she would face east, kneel down and bow her head all the way to the floor, murmuring fervent prayers and crossing herself endlessly. She hardly ever left the room, and then never for more than a few minutes; she·took all of her meals in the room, and spent hour after hour in a chair by her husband's bed. When he suffered pain, and groaned, she suffered with him—I am convinced that she actually *felt* the pain in her own body. On the fourth day, the woman's daughter and son-in-law tried to persuade her to go out with them for a walk and a meal in a restaurant. After much coaxing, they finally got her out through the door. But once out in the corridor she uttered a little cry and broke away from them, and scurried right back to her lord's bedside. And there she stuck, without let-up, until he was discharged after two more days.

. . . . .

One day there was a flurry of excitement in the clinic. During the night an English patient had arrived. He was an elderly gentleman who, shortly before, had been luxuriating on a round-Africa cruise ship. Somewhere in the eastern Mediterranean, having passed through Suez, he was stricken with an attack of acute appendicitis. To make matters more dramatic, there was a violent storm blowing — those diabolical winds that have altered so many travellers' plans, including Odysseus and Saint Paul. Because of the rough sea, the ship's doctor didn't dare to operate, so they put the old gentleman and his wife off in the early morning hours, out in the Cretan Sea off Canea, on to a pilot boat, and they landed in Canea and were taken to Magoulades' medical establishment. Dr Magoulades, despite his many talents, was not a surgeon, but he sent for one, and the operation was performed without delay. The appendix had ruptured and there was a grave risk of peritonitis; the Englishman's life was in danger. But the operation was successful and the patient responded to therapy. Inga became friendly with his wife during this time. In a few days the danger had passed, the man was sitting up in bed and recovering rapidly. Our lives turn on coincidence, and this was to be a fateful one for us, though of course we had no suspicion of it at the time.

Dr Hasapis, the surgeon, came to see me and we had a friendly chat. His English was quite good, for he had done post-graduate work at a hospital in Yorkshire. Dr Magoulades, in the course of examining my liver, had noticed a tenderness on the right side that could have indicated a chronic appendicitis condition; this did not surprise me, as a German doctor had made a similar diagnosis some years before. Now Dr Hasapis, having heard about this, offered to examine me. After carefully poking and prodding for some time in the vicinity of McBurney's Point and other areas of my topography, he declared that I did, indeed, have an inflamed appendix and that I ought really to have it removed as soon as possible, because after having had hepatitis, the condition was probably worsened. He then offered magnanimously to do the operation himself—after I had recovered from my liver inflammation, of course—and it would cost me nothing at all except for the clinic fees and a small charge of ten dollars or so for his assistant. It certainly looked like a handsome offer, and I have never been one to look a gift horse in the mouth. True, I did have some doubts about the state of hygiene in the clinic, and possibly even about the surgeon's abilities; but a talk with the English couple resolved them. They were high in their praises of Dr Hasapis and of the care they had received in the clinic, declaring that they believed the old gentleman's life had been saved there. There had been some moments of doubt—especially when he had entered the operating room and had seen that it resembled the surgeries in old medical prints—but the main thing was that he had recovered. It did look as though we ought carefully to consider the surgeon's offer; after all, I couldn't go wandering about the White Mountains (as I was hoping, soon, to be doing) with a chronically inflamed appendix; and everyone said that nowadays an appendectomy is nothing, that you are on your feet a week afterwards. Dr Hasapis himself assured me that I would be able to go swimming two weeks after the operation. If anyone wonders why I didn't first go to Athens to consult another doctor, I should point out that at hardly any time during our years in Crete did we have even the boat fare to Athens, much less the money for expensive doctors and operations—and there was no possibility of raising this money by any conceivable loan, sale or act of armed robbery. We had chosen to live poor in Crete, and now we must accept the consequences—and we had no complaints. However, all this was for the future—my immediate problem was to recover from hepatitis.

After three weeks in the clinic I was considerably less yellow and my appetite had improved. Still, I was weak and shaky and my liver would start aching and twitching at the slightest provocation. Dr Magoulades released me, but warned me that I had to spend a further three weeks in bed. We were lucky in having some American friends—young teachers of English, and the only other foreigners in Canea at that time—to put us up during this period, as it did not seem advisable to return to the village. It was a black time for us, away from our own home, discouraged about my slow recovery. The full realisation of what a hard blow had struck us began to bite. Illness is bad enough any time, but when you are poor and in a foreign country the effect is multiplied.

Our room was high above the old Venetian harbour of Canea. Through the big window I could look out over thousands of red tile rooftops, with church towers and minarets jutting up among them here and there (one minaret had been converted into a church spire, with a cross on top instead of the usual crescent). Away beyond there were glimpses of green hillsides and white villages, and far, far up, at the end of every street, the culminating point of every perspective, the snow-white rooftop of the *Levka Ori*. I saw it in all colours and times of day; sunrise and sunset were especially lovely, when the old Venetian and Turkish houses round the quay would turn rosy-pink in the light reflected from the harbour water. There were storms, with torrential rain and lightning and thunder, and then the next day the air would be washed clean and clear, and the mountains snowier and more dazzling than ever in the winter sunshine. Nights were cold and raw and damp in the unheated room, but we had plenty of blankets. Mornings after a storm, the old men would be down on the quay shovelling up the masses of seaweed that the waves had brought in during the night. Horse-drawn carts rattled to and fro, going and coming from warehouses at the old port. At night the wailing lugubrious *bouzouki* music floated up from the waterfront cafés where sailors danced and drank.

Here we spent our third Christmas in Crete. Even in the best of circumstances I have always found this year-end season, when the sun has withdrawn so far from us, a gloomy and difficult time to get through; and it was worse than ever this year. But the day came when I was able to be up and out again, and at last we returned to our house in the village. We found it all fresher and lovelier than we had

left it, with the fields bright green from the rains. Our neighbours
were friendly and solicitous, though at first they seemed to eye me
with suspicion, even dread—almost as though they were seeing a
ghost. Inga found out the reason from the priest's wife: they actually
had thought I was dead! Village gossip had killed me off: the story
was that I had died and that Inga, not wanting to leave Crete, had
married a Cretan. Thus the myth-making web is spun around events,
even before they occur; and prosaic facts are embellished with the
romance of fiction.

* * *

We were home again, but our life was changed. I was unable to
resume normal activities for several months. Gardening and water-
carrying were too much for me, but our neighbours helped us with
those jobs. I was obliged to follow, a strict dietary regime, and it
upset our household economy, for it was supposed to include plenty
of meat and fish and other protein foods—always the most
expensive. And there were injections to be continued. Madame
Friday offered to give the shots, though she insisted they were
useless—that I would never be well until I allowed her to cut the
tendon in my upper lip. She claimed that 'thousands' of people came
to her for this cure. We were not among them; instead, we obtained
the necessary equipment, and Inga became an expert at giving me
injections.

Reading was our main activity during those months. We ordered
books from England, and it was always a great day when one of the
packages arrived—we would tear it open like children on Christmas
morning. Gradually my liver subsided, or toughened up, or
whatever it was supposed to be doing, and I went back to my
typewriter in an effort to pay some of the bills which this vexatious
illness had piled up. The greatest day that spring was when an editor
accepted one of my stories, paid a couple of hundred dollars for it
and asked for another. We would have been rich, by Cretan
standards, but our medical misfortunes were to eat it all up.

Came April—'the cruellest month', I should have remembered
that. Dr Hasapis examined me again, and declared that I ought now
to have my appendix extracted; I gathered that it would be hardly
more painful or difficult than having a tooth pulled. On a bright
morning, with the gorse in full blossom and all of Apokorona
gleaming like gold, we rode to Magoulades' Clinic in Canea, where
expected to spend no more than a week at most.

Our first premonition that all was not going quite right came on the morning appointed for the operation. I had been prepared for the knife, and been injected with morphine, and we assumed of course that I would receive a general anaesthetic—so the doctor had told us. But now suddenly he appeared in the room, all cheerfulness and confidence, and announced that because my liver was still in a weakened state, it would be better if I had a *local* anaesthetic. They would give me an injection and I would feel nothing, while remaining conscious. Inga said afterwards that the thought flashed across her mind that we ought to call the whole thing off right then; but the surgeon seemed so self-assured, it was inconceivable that he might not know exactly what he was doing. And he assured us that if I felt the slightest pain, I had only to mention it, and I would be given gas at once.

So I walked into the operating room under my own power, and they strapped me to the narrow cold table. Dr Hasapis and his assistant, looking strange and impersonal in their masks, loomed above me; but I noticed with surprise that one of the nurses and a third doctor wore no masks or gloves. The local injection was quite painful—it is not pleasant to have a long thin needle stuck in your abdomen. When they made the incision I felt nothing except a slight scratching sensation, and I relaxed, expecting to feel nothing more. But then they began a sort of clipping and tugging at my insides— *and I felt it.* I tried my best to relax and stick it out, but I couldn't and began to writhe about. I told them about it, but they just went grimly on. Soon the pain was excruciating, and I had to demand the gas that had been promised. No response—they just went on with their work. I don't know why I didn't faint, or scream, but I didn't. But I was writhing and covered with sweat and all the time a feeling of bewilderment possessed me; the same thoughts kept recurring: 'But why don't they give me the gas? What has gone wrong? Why is it taking so long?' The whole thing assumed the proportions of a surrealistic nightmare when the third doctor, who was there merely as an onlooker, leaned over me and asked in his halting English: 'Do you like pain?'

They had told me the operation wouldn't take more than fifteen minutes; actually, as I learned later, I was on the table a full hour— the surgeon said there had been 'many adhesions' of the appendix (attachments to adjoining tissues caused by former attacks of inflammation), and that was why it had taken longer. When they finally did get the appendix out, they held the bloody thing up in triumph for me to see, and then put it in a glass and dispatched a nurse to show it to Inga. This was common practice in Cretan clinics and the reason for it, so we were told, was that if the suspicious peasant families didn't actually *see* the thing, they would think the doctor had cheated them and left it in.

When the ordeal had finally ended and I was wheeled to my room, there wasn't much left of me—or so I felt. That day and night and the next day passed in a sort of daze. Inga said I looked like a man who has had a terrible shock—as indeed I had. Neither then, nor at any other time, did the doctors explain why they had not given me gas, and when we asked them about it they always managed to turn the questions aside; but I think now the reason was simply that they had none in that ill-equipped place. They had lied about it, hoping there would be no need for it.

Anyway, the worst was now over, we thought. I would mend quickly, and all would be forgotten when we returned to our eucalyptus grove in the warm days of late spring. But that, too, turned out to be idle optimism: after two days I ran a fever, and it was found that the operative wound had become infected. An antibiotic was tried; the infection seemed better; the treatment was dropped—and the fever recurred. After two weeks (and I had thought I would be swimming by then!) they finally got around to taking a sensitivity test to determine what medicine would work best against the infection. It turned out to be the most expensive one—each pill cost the equivalent of half a dollar, and I was taking them at the rate of one every four hours. All imported medicines are taxed heavily in Greece. What of the poor people, who simply can't afford such prices? As always, they must settle for second best—or nothing at all.

All through May I lay there. The wound refused to heal. I would be better one day, and worse the next. It was a fearful time for Inga. In many ways she suffered more than I did, for she had to be out and about, running to the pharmacy to buy the various medicines that were being tried (they did not supply them at the clinic), coming and going several times each day in the hot, dusty streets of the town. My inclination was to accept it all as bad luck, or fate, or whatever; certainly, having come to live in Crete under Cretan conditions, I was in no position to start blaming anyone. I knew, too, that antibiotic-resistant infections of the sort that I had are not confined to Cretan clinics. What *was* rather hard to take, though, was the striking change in the attitude of the doctors and nurses towards me. It became increasingly obvious that in some obscure way they blamed *me* for having caught an infection. Their whole manner seemed to say: 'What—are you still here? Couldn't you have the decency to get well and leave?' Nobody likes to be reminded of their mistakes—and I was a living reminder of theirs, a daily reproach to the doctors' *philotimo*. Towards the end they hardly tried to conceal their impatience and irritation.

Eventually the infection did clear up, and I was released—after a month in the clinic. But the wound still had not healed completely; one end remained open. Dr Hasapis said there must still be a stitch inside, and he assured me that it would work itself out eventually. He was right—it did come out, along with several other stitches—but only after six months. During those six months I had to keep a dressing on the wound, the daily changing of which became a ritual as familiar as brushing my teeth. I resumed sea-bathing (the doctor said it was all right) and we had a summer, of sorts, in our village. None of the villagers were surprised that the wound didn't heal; it seemed that surgical wounds hardly ever *do* heal quickly in this country.

Then there was the plague of boils, evidently a sequel of the wound infection. I had dozens of them, all over me, and some had to be lanced and were almost as painful as that miserable botched operation itself. There were more antibiotics to experiment with. But I shall spare the reader further trials, and draw a discreet veil over the rest of our medical misfortunes. Suffice only to say that they did continue, and that they made life in the village—beautiful, peaceful, but also isolated and unsanitary and far from doctors and medicines (unless Madame Friday and her witch's brews be counted as such)—untenable; and thus we were driven out of our paradise.

When the cheque for the second article finally reached me, I went to Athens—the first time in over three years that I had set foot off Crete—and there I found a good doctor who examined me thoroughly. He was an intelligent and articulate man, with a successful practice among foreigners and Greeks, and my tale of a Cretan clinic horrified him. In the first place, he said, it was extremely doubtful whether the operation had been needed at all, as these so-called 'chronic appendicitis' things are notoriously difficult to diagnose; and in any case, it should not have been done so soon after I had had hepatitis. Probably the strain of the operation and the ensuing infection, and the boils, had affected the liver, and that was one reason why I was still having trouble with it. As for the use of the local anaesthetic, he could only murmur, 'Shocking, cruel— but not surprising, considering that it was done by Cretans.'

'Oh?' I said, 'You know something about them?'

'I do indeed! I was an army doctor during the war, and there were many Cretans in my unit. I know them, with their ideas of being *pallikaria*—but they are not, they are cowards at heart! And fools. Do you know, they used to charge against enemy machine guns with their knives in their teeth! Of course they were mowed down—you might say that their methods were inappropriate in modern warfare. And then, when we had some simple examination to do on them, they were terrified like babies. And sadistic—we could never allow them to get hold of enemy prisoners, for they would do the most horrible things to them. They are like childish barbarians, and therefore dangerous. Oh, I could tell you a lot more about Cretans— you had better get away from that island before they kill you!'

There was nothing unusual in his views; Crete has, in Greece at large, about the sort of reputation that Texas or Mississippi has in America. There was some truth in what he said, but there was another side too. We had seen them at their best and their worst. It was a love-hate relation now—and no tie is stronger than this. We never considered leaving Crete. We could not imagine living anywhere else. I went back, and we continued as prisoners and victims of this impossible island that we loved.

15

Out of the Turkish Sleep

Halepa is a curious sort of suburb. It lies to the east of Canea, stretching up a hillside from a rocky shoreline. Here the town villas fade into the olive groves, and beyond there is nothing but open, bare country given over to thyme, heather, gorse and goats—but by then you are out of Halepa, on the Acrotiri peninsula. A rambling walk through half-hidden and unsuspected purlieus of Halepa brings faint reminiscences, like whiffs of scent on a light breeze, of Portugal or Spain or Mexico: a creeper of Bougainvillaea on a crumbling stone wall, hibiscus in a yard, houses washed pastel pink or rose or yellow, weatherbeaten shutters and the ubiquitous roofs of red tile. The whole area is criss-crossed by little ravines and gullies that reminded me of the *barrancas* of Cuernavaca. Everywhere the musty, stale odour of past glory long faded: the mansions lining the avenue that once were the consulates of the Great Powers —for this was the capital of an independent Crete—; the palace where Prince George lived during his tenure as High Commissioner in the first decade of the twentieth century; the fine house of Eleftherios Venizelos facing the little square that is named after this native of Canea who became the greatest statesman of modern Greece. A great place gone to seed is always a hunting-ground for the lover of the surrealistic, and Halepa was not lacking in this respect. You might be walking down a narrow side street and suddenly would catch a glimpse, through a gateway whose door hung askew, into a grass-grown courtyard where a painted statue of a bearded king holding a lyre held court to an audience of brambles and thistles. Closer inspection reveals an inscription: 'King David', Further penetration into the ramshackle building discloses the studio of an eccentric sculptor, a place full of satirical busts in clay—gargoylefaced women, birds and beasts with human features. The sculptor, it turns out, is a local fixture who has done the stone lions with rather perplexed faces that guard several of the rundown great houses.

It was to this suburb, rather than to the town itself, that we turned when we realised that life was no longer tenable for us in the village because of my persistent ill health, the liver trouble requiring special diets, and the rigors of the damp climate. To us, despite the evident drawbacks, Georgioupolis was still a kind of paradise, and it was bitter to have to leave it. On the day of departure we felt somewhat like Adam and Eve, driven out of their garden. However, we at least didn't have to walk—we had hired a truck from a nearby village, and on to it we loaded our household belongings and our cat (in a basket this time). All of the villagers lined up to see us leave, just as they had lined up to receive us a year and a half before. Then, with many a backward glance, off we drove along the eucalyptus road, and over the green hills of Apokoronas and along the shore of Suda Bay, and at last into Canea. Once again we had become town-dwellers.

When our driver saw the house we were moving into, he was so astonished that his mouth fell open, and remained that way for some time; it was one of the very few times I have seen a Cretan speechless. For we had found a vast ten-room villa that towered high above a rocky cove of the sea like one of those wave-girt monasteries of Mount Athos, a place with so many terraces, stairs, store-rooms, hidden alcoves and outbuildings that we could hardly keep track of it all. It had once belonged to the Swedish Consul; the present owner, an English lady who had married a Cretan, was now in Athens. The rent, amounting to twenty-five dollars a month, could hardly be considered excessive; we could afford it now, in the wake of my recent successes with magazine articles. What we liked about it was the privacy; although there were houses nearby, and even one or two rather close neighbours, the place was surrounded by walls and had its own iron grille-work gates that could be locked when one chose. I had always wanted to live in a *big* house, with plenty of room for my thoughts. But it was precisely all this space, and this inexplicable privacy—*monaxia* or abominable loneliness to a Greek —that dumfounded our driver. When he finally regained his speech, he kept repeating, 'But you will live here *alone*? Just the two of you in all these rooms?'—then crossing himself. He seemed very glad to get away from the spooky place. However, our cat Pushkin took to it at once: he cautiously pussyfooted up the stairs, poked his nose into every room, and sniffed every corner, and then went out and tried the terraces and walls, and finally pronounced himself pleased.

* * *

We moved in the autumn, just in time for the first big rains; and on stormy nights with the wind howling and the lightning flashing, and the whole house shaking when the thunder rumbled, it *was* a little ghostly. Or would have been, had it not been such a solid, well-made house. To stand high up on the top floor by a front window, looking out over the rolling sea, was like being in the pilot-house of a Great Lakes oreboat during a storm on Lake Superior; there were times when the illusion was so vivid that I felt a strong urge to reach for the wheel.

Now we learned new lore of the winds, the local peculiarities of the bay of Kydonia which we faced. The prevailing winds were the westerlies, and they could come up out of a calm sea and clear sky in a matter of minutes, with a force to slam shutters and knock over chairs left out on the terrace. Eventually we learned to spot the warning signs—wisps of cloud over the mountains of Cape Spatha that jutted far out to sea beyond Canea—that always indicated west wind. Of course, there were different varieties of west wind—and the fishermen had a name for every one of them. The worst was the *garbis,* the southwester, which was similar to a sirocco in its ability to induce headaches and restlessness. But there was one blessing— because of the White Mountains that loomed off to the south, blocking winds from that direction, the south wind came from the *east,* funnelled our way by Suda Bay, and greatly diminished by the hump of Acrotiri so that we hardly felt it at all. Of the north winds we saw many that winter; they blew for days on end, rolling great surf into our little cove and shaking the foundations of our house so that sometimes we feared the cliffside on which it stood might crumble away, and like the House of Usher our abode would disappear for ever.

I had never lived so close to the sea, right on top of it almost, and it was fascinating to watch it in its many moods. After the storms there were often splendid rainbows, visible over the whole span of their great arches that straddled the bay of Kydonia. There were blue-and-silver evenings, and golden sunsets over the spiny ridge of Spatha. Glorious, too, were the calm nights after all storms had subsided, when there would be the lights of many fishing boats out on the bay. Some of them would glide soundlessly right into our cove, with their bright carbide lamps mounted on the prows illuminating the transparent greenish water. They were spearing octopuses in which this rocky coast abounded.

We saw many sea-creatures. There were lots of fish, despite their numerous pursuers; I used to follow them when I had on my mask, paddling over the deep clear water like a sightseer. One day my swim was a short one, for I saw a small blue shark, and climbed quickly out to the safety of the rocks. He cruised right into our cove, making a wake like a ship's in the calm water, his high fin visible from far away. He came so close in—the water was twelve feet deep directly under our rocks—that I could look into his upturned eyes before he turned and made out to sea again. He was about four feet long, and was bright blue, shading to silver underneath. I had to admit that he was a beautiful creature—but I did not swim again that day. An old fisherman whom I questioned told me that there were many such small sharks, but they never harmed anyone and were afraid of people. I never saw another one so near, though I did see two or three together far out in the bay once.

Another time I saw a brown seal poke his snout above the surface, take a puff of air, and then dive. In a few minutes he reappeared within a few feet of the spot where he had first surfaced. I watched him thus for a quarter of an hour before he finally made off towards deeper water. There are a number of these seals in Cretan waters; I have seen them at Ayios Nikolaos, in the east, and in Suda Bay in the Canea district, and off the coast of Sphakia in the south.

One day the sea washed up strange testimony of the dramas that go on daily in its depths: a large eel that had obviously strangled to death trying to swallow a small octopus that was still wedged in its mouth. I was reminded of a Swedish short story, 'The Osprey and the Pike', by Sivar Arner, which tells how a bird and a great fish destroy each other. This story, I am told, was intended as an allegory of America and Russia; but I thought of a man and woman, locked to the death in a love-hate struggle.

Our seaside eyrie or marine observation post was, unfortunately, not quite perfect, for the sea at our doorstep was polluted much of the time. To east and west of us, along the shore, were rows of tanneries, and when they discharged their waste products the sea turned reddish-brown. The local people maintained that these effusions were harmless; still, they were not pleasant either. We were thus restricted in our bathing to the times when the water was clear: in the mornings, on holidays when the tanners weren't working, and when the wind blew in such a way that the pollution was swept far out to sea. There was also a smell from the tanneries, which the Halepa residents claimed was 'good for the lungs'.

However, town life did have its compensations. During our year and a half in the village we had done without electricity and running water, we never had proper baths, and in the winter we shivered. Now by this move we acquired a few of the household conveniences:

a bathtub, for which hot water could be obtained by kindling a wood-fire in the old boiler; lights at the flick of a switch; water that ran most of the time, and a private cistern to draw on when it didn't; an ice-box in the summer (a boy brought fresh ice every day). We decided now that we would not shiver through another winter, and bought a small iron stove that had been made in Salonika. Being a native Greek product, it was cheap; for the stove, and pipes, and installation, we paid only thirteen dollars.

It was one of the best investments we ever made. It kept us warm and cozy throughout the cold, damp, windy winter days; the smell of olive or pine wood burning was a delightful incense for our living-room; and I reaped the extra warmth and exercise of chopping wood. We were in luck here—underneath the house, in one of the many intriguing derelict rooms, there was a cache of dry, well-seasoned olive logs, and our landlord told us we could have them for nothing. I went into Canea and bought an axe; and that in itself was not so simple as it sounds, for first I had to buy the head in an iron-monger's shop, and then find a woodworker who could fashion a helve for it. I myself selected the piece of wood that he made the handle from, and it must have been a good guess, for that axe lasted over three years and was as good as new when I finally gave it away before leaving Crete. I became a confirmed addict of wood-chopping and came to regard it as a blessed tonic for body and spirit. Being still somewhat inclined towards 'liverishness', especially after a heavy meal or a little wine, I was relieved to find that these after-effects could be rapidly dissipated by working up a good sweat. There can be no better exercise than wood-chopping; but more than that, it is a fascinating skill requiring exquisite co-ordination of eye and muscle and an expert knowledge of the properties of the material. It is mentally stimulating, too, and often when I had hit some difficult place in my work I would go down and chop wood for awhile, and the solution would come to me easily. Even on the coldest days, with wind and rain and the sea roaring, a few minutes' wood-chopping would warm me up—and what a pleasure after-wards to go to the house laden with sweet-smelling olive wood for the crackling fire! This olive wood burned long and gave much heat; pine, though redolent, had the disadvantage of burning too quickly, and it was the same with cypress.

The only time the stove didn't work well was when the west wind was blowing. Then the smoke backed up in the room, and we would have to open all the doors and windows to air out. We tried caps and weathercocks and extra lengths of pipe, but all to no avail—one strong puff of west wind was enough to ruin all our arrangements. There is always at least one wind in Crete ready to wreck one's best-laid plans. The only thing to do is to try to live with them.

*   *   *

Canea itself, though styled as a capital, seemed to linger in a sort of 'Turkish sleep'—perhaps partly as the result of its languor-inducing climate, which is damp and heavy, with much rain in winter and humidity in summer. The plain behind the town, well-watered and rich in orange and olive groves and fruit and vegetable plantations, was an agricultural paradise, self-sufficient and somnolent. The fruits and vegetables found their way to the large *agora*, the municipal market, and that was about as far as they got—far enough to insure a sort of sleepy prosperity for the town and its satellite villages.

Language institutes, a museum, historical archives and a library constituted about the sum of Canea's intellectual resources. The language institutes, with one or two honourable exceptions, were outrageous clip joints masquerading as educational institutions, their sole purpose being to milk as much money as possible out of the students. It was sad to think that the parents of many of these young students had saved their drachmas to pay for courses that were nothing but a waste of time. The museum, archives and library were of good quality. The library was surprising; in addition to housing the large private collection of Eleftherios Venizelos, which had been bequeathed to it, it had shelves full of mathematical works in French, German and other languages, many of which had been donated by the governments of those countries. Whether there were any students in the town sufficiently qualified in both languages and mathematics to make use of them, I am inclined to doubt; but there were certain local boosters who were hoping for the eventual establishment of a university here, and this collection was to be the nucleus of its library. The Americans had contributed some boxes of paperbacks, which had been relegated to a top shelf in the depths of the stacks. While browsing among the shelves one day, I pulled some out and looked at them. Several of them were works of such blatant anticommunist propaganda that they would not have fooled anyone, not even a village idiot; but there were also some excellent titles by serious writers, in both fiction and non-fiction. When I mentioned this to the assistant librarian, who was following me around, he spoke contemptuously: 'Bah!—those books cost only ten

or fifteen drachmas each. Now, over here we have some *good* books.'
He pulled down a thick, handsomely bound volume of mathematics
that had been donated by the Germans. 'This one is worth over three
hundred drachmas! Here—just feel how heavy it is.'

The library had copies of Pashley's *Travels in Crete* and Spratt and
Dephner and other fascinating old books about the island, and I
spent many hours reading there. It was there, too, that I met 'the
flaming translator'. He was a civil servant with a shock of black hair
that stood on end, and a wild gleam in his eye; his passion was
translating from English to Greek, but his exuberant imagination
was chained to the mundane trivialities of technical manuals and
treatises on administration. Even here, though, he occasionally
found play for his creative abilities. As he put it, 'In translation, one
must use the imagination! For example, I am translating a passage
that reads, "The much-debated question is . . ." Much-debated? But
that tells you nothing of the excitement, the drama of controversy.
No! Something more is needed—the imagination flies to the rescue,
and I write: "The FLAMING question!" He had raised his voice
and his arms, and his eyes gleamed with mad delight as he repeated,
'Flaming—there is a word for you! That brings the whole passage to
life.'

* * *

One didn't have to go to the library to be entertained. The coffee-
houses, bars and tavernas provided human variety and endless
amusement. Our favourite haunt was a taverna on Hadjimichalis
Yianari Street which was nicknamed the *Vouli*—Parliament—
because of all the talking and debating that went on there. The
setting itself was irresistible: a huge barn of a place with a rickety
wooden gallery, long out of use except for storing things, and with a
row of great wine barrels ranged along the main floor. It was first
and foremost a wine tavern, but the excellence of the snacks that
went with the drinks had led, in recent years, to a considerable
expansion of the food side of the business. The specialites were
grilled pork chops, grilled liver and fried codfish; and for a mere ten
or fifteen drachmas you could have a meal second to none in town,
washed down with first-class Kissamo wine. All sorts of loungers
and hangers-on wandered in and out all day long, and after a while
we got to know quite a few of them—one always saw the same faces
there. There was the man with the kidney stones, whom I had met
first at Magoulades' clinic—he had been in very bad shape then,

ready to give up the ghost, but now here he was, red-faced, full of wine and pork, and praising the Lord that he had survived to enjoy more earthly delights. Then there was an old 'practical doctor' who used to drift in, carrying his lunch in a dinner-pail; he would order a glass of wine, generally on credit, and drink it with the meal. Lots of these characters brought their own food—there was never the slightest pressure to buy anything.

This superb tavern was run by the two Anitsakis brothers, Marcos and Christos. They presented a study in contrasting character. Marcos, who did all the cooking, had the artist's temperament that so often goes with good cooks; he was subject to fluctuations of mood, black depressions alternating with periods of good humour. When he was in a fine mood he was generous, easy-going and talkative; when he was out of sorts, it was best just to avoid him. A lot of his trouble came from too much success—his food was so good that in the winter season they generally had more business than they could handle. No assistant ever lasted long—inevitably there would be a quarrel. Marcos was remarkable in one respect; he had taught himself English and spoke it better, I think, than almost anyone else I met in Canea. And he had done it in opposition to his strongwilled father, who regarded the whole idea as absurd. I think perhaps that Marcos had experienced greater difficulties in his life than most people suspected, and that might have had something to do with his moodiness. His brother Christos was the most, even-tempered Cretan I ever met. No matter what madhouse of shouting confusion the tavern might be on a busy night, he went on his own way from table to table, unruffled, good-humoured, with an aura of male competence about him that silenced any rowdies who might have been tempted to cause a scene. These brothers became known to the few foreigners who drifted through Canea in those years, including some Englishmen who dubbed the place 'the British Embassy'—a mock title the brothers loved. A letter addressed merely to 'the British Embassy, Canea' once actually reached them. They took stray foreigners under their wing, stored their luggage free of charge, sometimes lent them money, gave them drinks or meals. I know of only one or two cases of their being taken advantage of and victimised; but this in no way altered their attitude. They just took it all as a kind of joke.

In the market and in the dark little shops of the narrow streets behind it lurked other characters of the town, ready to regale the chance visitor at any hour with tales of the old days and of their misadventures. Our favourite of them all was Socrates the bread man, who had a little stall in the main market where we used to buy dark bread. He was a sweet-tempered, friendly man who had emigrated from Asia Minor along with thousands of other Greeks back in the' twenties; he disliked nothing except the Turks, and them he disliked completely—even their language. 'Bread,' he would say, holding up a loaf by way of illustration, 'In Greece we have many words for the different kinds of it: *psomi, artos, koulouria, paximadia, starenyo*. But to the Turks it's all the same: *ekmek*.' He spat out the word with distaste—'*Ekmek*!'—shrugging his shoulders and rolling his eyes. 'Turks! What can you do with such people?' But he one day confided to me, in a low voice, that the Cretans are more like the Turks than the other Greeks are—a communication that surprised me only because it came from a Greek. The Cretans are more Turkish than they will ever know.

This large market building, shaped like a Greek cross, was a warren of tiny independent shops and stalls. The eclectic character of Greek trade was apparent in the variety of odds and ends displayed on the dusty shelves of these stores. You could find Moroccan sardines next to Southern Rhodesian corned beef; Danish caviar and French milk powder side by side. You might turn up a bottle of Chilean wine, perhaps imported illegally in the sea-bag of some world-wandering Greek mariner, or a tin of Japanese whale-meat. You had a choice of Nescafé from France or from the Ivory Coast— and the latter was three drachmas cheaper and much better. There was no consistency—things would appear one day and be gone the next, never to appear again. Of course, you had to bargain over everything—that was half the fun. If you didn't happen to feel like haggling one day, then you just had to resign yourself to paying extra.

As a gauntlet for the squeamish, one whole arm of the cross was devoted to butchers' stalls and the fish market. Red-aproned, black-moustached butchers swung their cleavers while live lambs, next in line, lay trembling and bleating plaintively. Entrails, sheeps' heads, testicles and other titbits were invitingly displayed. The butchers were aloof, dignified, difficult to deal with, but their neighbours, the fish-sellers, were raucous, exuberant and satirical. They waged epic battles of lungs with their rivals, and practically waylaid anyone walking past their stalls, waving fish or handfuls of shrimp before the noses of potential buyers. There was an eccentric woman who lived in an old house with a score of cats (twenty-three, she told me, but the number grew steadily, like the population of the world), and when she came to the market to buy food for her charges the air was filled with the loud meowing of the fishmongers' boys. Lively lads, these, full of pranks, wisecracks and a thousand tricks to pull with lightning speed on the unwary outsider.

. . . . . .

The old-fashioned ways of the town suited us very well; the last thing we wanted was bustle and progress. Canea, nominally the capital of Crete, had a population of only thirty-four thousand; it was half the size of Herakleion, and altogether lacked the commercial drive and vigour of that thriving tourist town and port. On a typical summer day the streets of Herakleion might swarm with five thousand or more tourists, including many who had but a few hours ashore from their Greek island cruise ships. On the same day the chances were that Canea had no tourists at all. Foreigners were such a rarity that they would be stared at by everyone, and sometimes followed through the streets. Living there was like living in a small town where everyone knew everyone else: slightly boring, but reassuring too.

But gradually a change began to be felt, it is difficult to say when exactly, but I think the key year was 1964, the year when a number of developments took place that began to alter the character of the town and to shake it out of its slumber. Not the least of these was the outcome of the national elections, when the right-wing party of Karamanlis lost out to the Centre Union headed by Papandreou. The Centre party included the Venizelists from Canea, and once in power they immediately began to proclaim great changes and improvements for their hitherto neglected home district. All of Crete, it was announced, would be built up systematically into a tourist paradise. An American survey group made a detailed study of the whole island and came up with many suggestions. A 'super-highway' would be built along the north coast all the way from Kastelli to Sitia; there would be hotels and motels and tourist pavilions. A lot of this was for the future, there being no money available at once, but a few things began to be put into effect. Construction on a new hotel started, the pinkish domes of the old mosque by the harbour were painted white and a modern restaurant was added to it, and the row of picturesquely dilapidated shops facing the market was torn down to make way for a big new building. The Cretans were not yet sophisticated enough to understand the potential tourist appeal (to say nothing of the historic value) of their old buildings. They were mortified to think that foreigners might judge them by the remains of the Turkish and Venetian quarters, and they would have dearly loved to tear down everything old and to replace it all with ultra-modern concrete-and-glass structures. Fortunately, they had not the resources.

About this time two huge new ferry-boats began to ply between Piraeus and Suda Bay and Herakleion. The island's trade was revolutionised overnight—all those fruits and vegetables, instead of mouldering on the stalls of the town markets, were shipped in great trucks to the mainland; the products became more expensive on the island of their origin. And now, too, travellers could drive right on to the ferry-boats in their own cars, and arrive some eight hours later in Crete. Many of them took advantage of this new convenience. Crete in general was becoming more motorised; creeping prosperity meant motor-bikes for many workers, and even cars for some of the more successful business and professional people. The villages were hardly affected; but the town was waking up.

This was the year, too, of an event that caused great excitement in Canea: a film company arrived to make a movie version of the Kazantzakis novel, *Zorba the Greek*. Suddenly women in fashionable dresses and boots—which looked very much like Cretan men's boots appeared on the streets and in the market. Film people buzzed along the old harbour front in hired taxis, and took over the Venetian arsenals as a studio. Even we, out in Halepa, were affected by the commotion. We had known ever since we moved there that our huge old villa was for sale, but we couldn't imagine that anyone would actually buy it. Now, with the arrival of Hollywood in town, certain self-styled real estate agents began to entertain wild ideas of vast profits from commissions. One of these operators, a returned Greek-American, got his eye on our house. He spoke to us one day, asking if he could bring some members of the film company out to look at it. We couldn't refuse, so we arranged a time.

Came the day, and a knock at our door. I opened, and found myself facing a huge man who stuck out his paw. It was one of the stars of the film, who had been talked into coming to look at our seedy mansion. The Greek-American, ingratiating and all apologies, followed.

'I hear you're leaving soon,' the actor said. I was surprised—this was news to me.

'Oh, I'm awfully sorry to intrude then—this gentleman said you were leaving.' He pointed at the agent, who contrived to fade into the background.

'What I want to know is, where do you swim?' the actor demanded. We walked on to the terrace, and I pointed to the sea cove among the rocks.

'Excellent swimming there,' I said, 'If you get there before noon.'

'You mean you gotta swim before noon?' he exclaimed.

'Yes—you see, after that the tanneries put out their stuff, and the water gets polluted.'

'Polluted—you mean the water is *polluted*?'

He wheeled suddenly and walked back into the room.

On the way out, he turned to the disgruntled agent, 'I expected a much bigger place—more land.'

That was one threat to our tenure in our polluted paradise, successfully averted. But we knew now that we were living on borrowed time, for a fever of real estate speculation had gripped the town, and people were buying up every old house or plot of land along the seashore that they could find, and prices were rising apace. We began to feel like squatters, living from day to day with the constant threat of eviction hanging over us.

*   *   *

Zorba the Greek, filmed in Canea, on the Acrotiri and out in one of the Cape Drepanon villages, became an international success and won several Academy Awards. In Crete it was a failure. The frank portrayal of harsh village morality and cruelty brought a storm of criticism—though in justice to the film-makers, it must be said that they were only following Kazantzakis's novel, and there was nothing in the film that couldn't actually have happened in Crete up to a few years ago. The film played for about a week in Canea and was a great disappointment to everyone; then the ecclesiastical authorities succeeded in having it banned. The general attitude towards it was neatly summarised by Christos of the 'Vouli' taverna, who told us, 'The film told lies about Cretans. We don't carry knives in our boots, and we are not thieves. We are not barbarians! And if that cuckold of a director ever dares to set foot on Crete again,—he drew his index finger significantly across his neck—'we'll slit his throat!'

When they finally sold our house from under us (we had been there just a year), we were ready with our plan of withdrawal. In good order, like soldiers in a well-organised retreat, we moved back to our prepared position at the base of the Acrotiri peninsula. There, at Ayios Mathaios, high above Halepa and within sight of our old villa.

we had found a humble but practical house, isolated in its own grove of pine trees. From its terraces one looked out over all of the Canea district, and the mountains loomed closer than ever. Here we enjoyed a winter of blessed solitude, near the town yet removed from it; more alone than ever we had been in Crete.

Progress, so-called, was creeping up even here: shortly after we moved the road-builders started cutting down great pine trees to widen a road already wide enough. But this proved to be a blessing in disguise, as far as we were concerned, for I was able to scavenge enough pine and cypress logs to keep our little wood stove supplied all winter.

Despite its proximity to Canea, Acrotiri was still a very countrified region, with shepherds and farmers living in villages that had a character of their own. Men had lived on this ten-mile-wide promontory for a long time: bones at least five thousand years old have been discovered in caves in the mountainous wall on the north side of the peninsula, and on the southern shore, facing Suda Bay, the Hellenic city of Minoa has been excavated. Elsewhere, scattered about Acrotiri, there are old monasteries from Venetian times, and Byzantine churches. That winter we walked all over the plateau, revelling in the finest display of wild flowers we had seen yet. The whole of Acrotiri is a natural rock garden where, each in due season irises, anemones, cyclamens, many kinds of orchids, and asphodel and gorse and heather and thyme colour the landscape with their distinctive hues. Crete has a hundred and thirty or more varieties of wild flowers that are found nowhere else; and Acrotiri is a showcase for quite a lot of them.

The raw outlines of Acrotiri's northern ridges, viewed in reddish morning light, have a primordial quality that strips the viewer of all his civilised layers, and brings him back to elemental innocence if only for a few moments. If spirits do indeed haunt places (and what a dull world if they didn't!) then this promontory that juts into the Cretan Sea must be one of the great haunted places and always will be, no matter what they do with it.

It was on one of my winter walks on Acrotiri that I received what I considered one of the finest compliments of my life: I was mistaken for a Cretan shepherd by an old man I met on the path. 'But where are your sheep?' he repeated earnestly, and I answered merely that I had none.

*   *   *

We noticed a gradual increase of military activity in the area. On one of our walks we were stopped suddenly at gun-point by a soldier who forbade us to go any farther. Acrotiri-based jet planes, having suddenly appeared at the commercial airfield, now buzzed over our heads frequently on their way to practise dive-bombing flights over the beaches west of Canea. It certainly was an effective way to discourage tourism, if that was what the military authorities wanted.

Then we discovered what all this had been leading up to: NATO and the Americans were to build a missile base on Acrotiri. Many people in Canea were against the base, for obvious reasons—it is not pleasant to sit on top of an arsenal that can blow you up at any time. But the project brought employment that they badly needed. Many of the poorer workers faced a cruel dilemma: stay at home and work on the missile base, or go abroad to Germany or elsewhere to work factories. There was much discussion of these questions in the tavernas.

'For years all we have asked for is work here in our own country,' one of the regulars at the 'Vouli' said, 'And now that they finally offer it to us, what is it? Missiles! We need schools, we need hospitals—but they offer us missiles.'

In the end, the consensus seemed to favour the base. It would bring the town the things it wanted. Having tasted of cars and motor-bikes and other fruits of modern life, they wanted more—and were willing to mortgage their home ground to get them.

All that we had sought to escape by coming to Crete had now suddenly been plumped down on our doorstep. We thought bitterly of Thoreau's words: 'But wherever a man goes, men will pursue and paw him with their dirty institutions, and if they can, constrain him to belong to their desperate odd-fellow society.' As foreigners living, so to speak, as guests of the country, there was no protest or demonstration that we could make—except to leave. It was time to look for another village.

16

The Whirlwind

The village was high up, next to the sky, and you were more conscious of air and light than of land or sea. It perched on the mountain out on Cape Drepanon, with the broad entrance of Suda Bay far below. The White Mountains—by now we couldn't live without them—were closer than ever, over the green foothills of Apokoronas to the south. The country around was a vast rock garden full of herbs and shrubs ready to flower in their season. Stone walls were draped at all angles, like necklaces, over the spiny country. The rocks were alive with colour and reflected light; at times even you thought they gave off sounds. Indeed, there was music and movement in this living landscape: the fig trees rang like lyres, the grapevines hummed softly and the mountaintops resounded like beating drums. We had achieved here at last the madness of perfection, and must bear the consequences, for perfection is for gods, not mortals.

As for the village itself (it was called Plaka)—it seemed more Provençial than Cretan, for instead of the flat-roofed cubes generally found in Cretan communities, there were substantial two-storey stone dwellings with roofs of red tile and outdoor stairways, and arched gates and high walls. Our house was such a one. It rose above the rest of the village, with clear views on all sides from its wide terraces. It belonged to the former village schoolmaster, who had moved to town. We fell in love with it at first sight: with the graceful entrance arch and the grape arbour that provided shade over the main cistern; with the high walls and gate that gave a sense of seclusion but not isolation; with the thick, hand-hewn, honey-coloured cypress beams that filled the interior with the fragrance of old wood.

We moved on the first of June, and settled in to a succession of tranquil days. By the time the sun rose each day over the tip of the cape, we were up too, and eating breakfast on the terrace that looked down towards the sea over vast grounds of silvery-green olives. The days were spacious and leisurely, our house providing ample room for each of us to pursue our own activities. Towards noon we would walk down through the groves to a secluded sea-cave where eons of dripping water had formed a solid pillar of rose-coloured stone, supporting the roof of an oval room where flickering sea-light played upon a pool of clear water. We swam naked, in coves of deep water among rock formations. Evenings, a bit of reading, and early to bed. A simple, healthy life. Inga started giving English lessons to several children, and their parents' gratitude took the tangible form of a steady flow of food offerings: fresh eggs, tomatoes, olive oil, wine—actually we had very little to buy ourselves. And I was working on a book that I had started to write.

If all this had a flaw, it was simply that it was too perfect. 'It can't last, something is bound to happen,' we would say, as though by saying it we could mitigate the danger. But we said it casually, as people will say such things, without any urgent sense of foreboding.

* * *

Looking back after a disaster, one always sees omens clearly that were overlooked at the time. There was the reaction of our cat, for instance. As soon as we took him inside the new house, he was taken by terror and went into a far corner with his hair on end. He cowered there for hours, and when finally we let him out in response to his pathetic meowings, he disappeared—never to return. He had been with us for five years and had lived in four other houses, and had never behaved thus before; on the contrary, he had always adjusted quickly to his new surroundings. We searched the neighbourhood for him, calling his name, and alerted all the villagers to look out for him—but he had simply vanished. We never saw him again.

It is too far-fetched to think that he might have been reacting to something in the spirit of the place? For, as we later learned, the house had a disquieting, even evil, history. Madness had run in the family, and in its hundred-year history the house had sheltered more than one maniac. The father of the present landlord, a wine merchant who had used the lower floor for storing his great barrels, and the upper floor for living, has suffered spells of insanity for many years, and in his old age had terrorised the village. Finally his wife had simply locked him out, and he lived out his last years with no fixed abode, wandering the roads from one village to another, sleeping out in the fields or in a corner of some coffee-house. After his death one of his sons, the village priest—who suffered from the same illness—had moved in with his family. One night sudden disaster struck: a fire broke out and the whole house went up in flames; only the thick stone walls were left standing. It was whispered that the priest had started the fire by upsetting a lamp, but no one really knew.

Our landlord, the teacher, rebuilt the house with his own hands, and lived in it before moving to town. But untoward and strange events still dogged the place. A man who lived next door developed a passion for a young girl employed as a servant in the teacher's house. One night he tried to rape her; she reported it to the teacher, who denounced the man to the police; and he was sent off to prison for two years. Upon his release he swore to kill the teacher; but instead, depressed by the ostracism imposed upon him by the village, he drowned himself in Suda Bay.

Nor were these the only reminders of death, bloodshed and evil in our village. We learned that a cistern in the square near our house had a gruesome history; during the wartime occupation a Cretan had killed two Germans and dumped them into it. The German Army would have burned the whole village in reprisal, but the war ended just in time to save it. To this day, no one drinks water from that cistern. The sea-cave that we thought so lovely had its bloody legend, too: a group of Turks had once been cornered there, and massacred on the spot. And the very place where we preferred to swim turned out to have been the suicide cove of the unfortunate neighbour.

We thought little about any of this, for in Crete there is nothing unusual about grisly stories; every village, every house-hold 'has them. Violence lurks beneath the apparently calm surface of life. The history of the island is one long series of wars, rebellions, feuds, murders—not to mention such natural disasters as earthquakes and plagues. There is a well-known *mantinada* that expresses it best:

'If you take up a needle, and probe the Cretan soil and stones,
Blood of warriors will stain it, and it will break on their bones.'

The only thing that we consciously found ominous was the odd haystack-shaped mountain that dominated our corner of Crete. It is impossible to say exactly what it was about it, but from the first we both agreed that we 'didn't like the look of it'. A large cave in its side had been used by the Germans as a work-prison and, it was said, place of execution during the war, but that had nothing to do with our feeling about it. It was just the look of it that made us uneasy; it was the only element in the landscape that wasn't quite perfect.

Winds of Crete

Often, in Crete, you get this odd foreboding about some topographical feature; you can be walking in bright sunlight down some narrow ravine, and suddenly it comes upon you so strongly that your hair actually stands on end, and your spine turns to shivering jelly. Why? Who could explain it? It is merely nervousness—or does some extra sense in the body react to an evil spirit of place? The ancients, too had such feelings,and they attributed them to the presence of nymphs or satyrs or demi-gods of the locality, or to Pan himself—hence the word *panic,* which exactly defines the feeling one gets at such times.

But our days passed peacefully; omens no bigger than the shadow of a man's hand were ignored in the great joy of having found at last just the right place. These tranquil days were even free of the winds that had bedevilled us so much in Crete. The idyll lasted exactly eighteen days.

The weather was odd on the eighteenth of June: it was sultry and heavy, and one felt something peculiar about the air pressure, though we had no barometer to verify this impression. We were on edge all day, on the verge of a quarrel. For the first time since moving to our new home we felt that paradise itself might pall; a faint, stale whiff of boredom, that deadly sin, seemed to have wafted its way into our life. A strange cloud hung low over the mountain; we commented on it uneasily to our neighbours, but they merely laughed and said it was nothing. The cloud didn't move an inch all day. When we went to bed at nine o'clock it still hung there in exactly the same spot. We tossed restlessly before falling into troubled sleep.

About three in the morning I awoke suddenly to a rumble of thunder. I got up and went outside to have a look. Several lightning flashes on the side of the mountain, very close, frightened me, and I ran back into the house, expecting a violent thunderstorm to break at any moment. In spite of that, I dropped back to sleep for a few minutes.

At 3:20 or a few seconds earlier (the clock stopped then and didn't start again until we had it repaired some days later), we were both awakened by a shutter banging upstairs. Thinking that the storm had arrived, I started up to close it. At the head of the stairs I was stopped short by a solid wall of air pressure. Try as I might, I couldn't move against it. 'This must be the strongest sirocco we have ever had,' I thought. And then all hell broke loose: the air full of flying sand, a tremendous roaring in my ears, loud sounds as of doors smashing open, glass breaking, heavy objects toppling over. There was a wrenching and tearing noise directly overhead.

I turned and struggled back down the stairs. There I found Inga, who had come after me and was calling to me; but I couldn't make out the words above the roaring of the gale. We clung together against the tremendous current of air that was rushing through our house.

Let's get through to the washroom!' I shouted.

Somehow we managed to fight our way across the room and through the narrow doorway. We took refuge in the corner behind the thick stone wall.

'I love you! I love you!' Inga shouted, and I answered, 'I love you too—hold on!' And hold on we did, for dear life, while that diabolical wind ripped off the roof and ransacked our house.

How long did it last? It is difficult to estimate time during such a crisis—probably not more than three to five minutes. Then it was over, and the whole world was deadly silent. Fortunately, I still held a flashlight in my hand. Timidly, tentatively—for we were afraid there might be another blast—we looked about. Total chaos: everything blown away, the house stripped of doors, windows, clothes, bedding. We looked out at the house across the street—it had been a solid two-storey stone building; now the top floor was entirely gone, simply blown away. Cries and screams drifted over from other houses: '*Panayia mou*! Aiee! *Kakomira*!'

There in the dark ruins, dumfounded, unable fully to grasp the destruction that had occurred in so short a time, we surmised wildly that perhaps war had come—perhaps an H-bomb had been dropped on the missile base at Acrotiri. But after a moment's reflection we guessed the truth: that these explosive effects had been caused by a tornado, the most powerful of all winds. As we later learned, it had swung up from the sea, mowing a swath about a hundred yards wide through the olive groves, flattening about a dozen stone houses in our quarter, then veering up the hillside and missing the rest of the village. Eventually it played itself out some five or six miles away. Miraculously, no one was killed. There were a few minor injuries but only one woman was hurt badly enough to require medical treatment; she was an old lady who lived across the street from us, and when her roof caved in her legs were injured and her daughter Sophia, a middle-aged spinster with strong arms, carried her out of the ruined house to shelter with neighbours. It was Sophia whom we had heard crying to the All-Holy Virgin for assistance and lamenting her bad luck.

It didn't seem possible that anything in our house could have survived such a wind. We assumed that we had lost all of our possessions, but the odd thing was that we didn't care: we were alive, we were not hurt, we had not lost each other. In the lurid light shed by disaster, a profound truth was illuminated, a truth that is usually obscured by our quotidian preoccupations: life is all, things are of no consequence.

But when we looked about, we saw that all had not been lost, after all. The kitchen was intact, for the freakish storm had missed that end of the house. Even glasses, cups and saucers were in place there —in striking contrast with the havoc that had been wrought in the other rooms. The walls and ceiling of the ground floor were intact, but everything in it had been blown away or smashed. The upper floor was harder hit: the tile roof, with its heavy supporting timbers, had been swept away. There were cracks in the massive, two-foot-thick stone walls, and one gable had collapsed, spilling great rocks on to the terrace. My work desk was covered with broken tiles and pieces of glass. A rock had landed on my typewriter; luckily, the metal case had saved it from total destruction. Dozens of my most valued books, notebooks and papers had disappeared. Several chapters of the book I was writing, that had been spread out on top of the bookcase, had blown away. The door of a large wardrobe, containing all our best clothes, had swung open and most of the contents had been carried away.

That was the first part of the disaster. After a few minutes the second part arrived: torrents of rain and hailstones as big as lemons. Our momentary unconcern about material possessions gave way to a desire to salvage what we could. Clad only in tennis shoes and pyjamas (which soon became soaked, so I discarded them and worked stark naked), I made countless trips up and down stairs, struggling to save the remnants of our books and clothing. The situation called forth hidden reserves of strength: I carried down a heavy trunk that I could hardly lift in normal times; it contained, among other things, the valuable camera outfit that I had feared was lost. We piled everything on tables and in corners of the kitchen— the only room not flooded, for it had a seperate, concrete roof that had not been damaged.

Finally we gave up and retreated—drenched, chilly and tired—to the kitchen. And there we sat, surrounded by what was left of our worldly chattels, while outside the downpour continued without let up for hours; and gradually the greyest, bleakest dawn of our lives crept in.

In the early morning light we went out to look at the village. What a sad and desolate place our former paradise now was! It looked as though it had been bombed. Under leaden skies people wandered in a daze, picking in·the ruins. Almond and apricot trees had been uprooted, the grape arbour shattered, the front gates flattened. I spent a dreary morning slogging through muddy fields, picking up items of waterlogged clothing. The capricious wind had tossed things in all directions. In a gully west of the house I found fragments of our tables and chairs, and a jacket of Inga's; on the hillside to the south I found some dresses that had blown half a mile and more. A Savile Row suit, relic of my pre-Cretan days that had hung in a closet all these years, had landed, still neatly arranged on its hanger, in a field several hundred yards away. A woman found it and brought it to the village, and I recognised it at once despite its layer of mud.

Scraps of my manuscripts and journals turned up in unlikely places—in the branches of trees, on rooftops, under piles of rubble. Word spread quickly that my 'book' had been lost; all the villagers were looking for it. But they didn't realise that it had been in manuscript form; they pictured a thick, bound volume such as the priest reads from on Sundays. Towards noon several of them came running. 'Your book—it's been found!' they shouted. Solemnly they handed me a heavy black volume. I opened it and looked at the title page: *Halleck's International Law, 1908.* What in the world was such a tome doing in a Cretan village? Then I remembered that an old house in the neighbourhood had once been occupied by a teacher, long since departed, who was said to have known English; doubtless it had been part of his library. But I didn't want to disappoint these people, so I told them, 'Yes—that's it.'

.   .   .   .   .   .

The shell of our house was barely livable. Once-white walls were streaked with yellow and were peeling from dampness. Masses of stones and rubble had spilled down the stairs. Mattresses, blankets, clothing were soggy. The upper floor was a total wreck, but with some improvisation we might still make use of the bottom storey. There was no question of spending the first night there, with the house in such a state. We sent word to a friend in Canea, who arrived in the afternoon in her little car, laden with food and clothing. She drove us back to town and put us up for the night. Many of our neighbours whose homes had been wrecked were taken in by relatives in the undamaged part of the village, others camped in tents that were brought in by a Greek Army emergency squad. Few of us had the courage to remain that first night in the area which seemed have been visited by some evil demon. Our friends in town urged us to abandon the house entirely, to find an apartment. in Canea. But we were drawn back irresistibly to the village; we returned the next day, set up cots and camped like refugees in the ruined hulk of our house.

Cleaning up after a tornado must be one of the hardest jobs in the world. It looked like a labour of Hercules, but it had to be faced: we rolled up our sleeves and set to work. Inga washed clothes, scrubbed floors, dusted and cleaned; I shovelled rubble. swept the terraces, gathered up scattered roof timbers with an eye to our wood supply for the coming winter. We spread all of our books and bedding out to dry in the hot sun. The yard and terraces were a shambles. Fragments of our lost books, clothing and household goods kept turning up from under the rubble. It was back-breaking, often heart breaking, work; yet both of us felt a strange joy, an intensity of aliveness that we had not felt during the leisurely days before the whirlwind. We had been shaken out of our growing complacency by the wind, into a new awareness of the joy and danger of living.

The capacity of living things for rejuvenating themselves amazed us, and gave us heart to carry on. The big grape-arbour was gone, but a smaller grapevine outside the kitchen window still lived, though it had been stripped of every leaf. Almost our first act after the disaster was to put up the vine and also the jasmine and honeysuckle bushes that had been blown down. Some people said they wouldn't grow any more; but they not only grew—they flourished, no doubt nourished by the heavy rainstorm that had followed the wind. Likewise the rose-bushes that had been denuded of their leaves; under our assiduous care and watering, they soon put forth tender new leaves. Within a few weeks we had dozens of roses in full bloom on our battered terraces. And thus in time the place became livable again. About a month after the storm the landlord came with a gang of masons and carpenters and put on a new tile roof, and set up the gates and installed doors and windows.

The high point of each day during those weeks of work came in late afternoon, when we would stow away everything for the night and then walk down through the groves to our beloved cove along the coast. The immortal Cretan elements were unaltered: olive trees with gnarled black trunks, stones shining like jewels in the dazzling light, violet blossoming thyme. Figs, melons, peaches ripened; we feasted on fruit and on sun and sea. We cleansed our dirty, aching bodies in the clear, blue-green sea, and told ourselves that we had done right to stay on.

The Whirlwind

The reaction of the villagers to the disaster was an altogether Cretan mixture of fatalism, laziness, opportunism and sheer enjoyment. Once the first shock was over, and they realised that no lives had been lost or serious injuries incurred, they relaxed. '*Things* don't matter!' said one of them. 'As long as we have not lost our lives, we have not lost anything.'

A rumour got about that the government was going to send in workers and bulldozers and heavy equipment to clear the ruins and build new houses for everyone; a million and a half drachmas had supposedly been allocated for this project. No one made any effort to clear the road of the masses of rubble and great pine trees that had fallen across it. There were plenty of able-bodied young men who could have done it in a few days—but why should they, when the bulldozers were coming to do the job so much more quickly and easily? The bulldozers became a myth that never materialised. Eventually a squad of sailors from the base at Suda cleaned up the worst of the mess.

The natives had more important things to occupy them these days. The village was invaded by thousands of curiosity-seekers. This was said to be the only tornado that had ever struck Crete—at least within living memory—and Cretans are insatiably curious about all natural wonders. They had never heard of a wind capable of knocking down stone houses and snapping thick tree-trunks, and they wanted to see the effects for themselves. They came in chartered buses and in taxis from the towns, and on foot and on muleback from other villages. They walked up and down the lanes and in and out of people's yards. Never before had the little community received so much flattering attention from so many strangers all at once. The people welcomed them with open arms, offering them drinks, acting as unpaid guides, telling the story of the storm over and over again. They seemed to feel that it had been worth a tornado to be able to enjoy all this; it was a taste of heaven for the gregarious Greeks. For us, with our northern love of privacy, it was unmitigated torment, far worse than any natural disaster. Our gates were down, and we were at the mercy of the sightseers. We began to feel like animals in a zoo. They would come right into our house and look around, pointing at us and murmuring. 'Ah, these are the tourists!' It never occurred to them that in this context *they* were the tourists.

One day some representatives of a charity organisation arrived and announced that they were going to distribute clothing. The people were assembled in the church where they heard a lecture from a priest, the main theme being that God is good and will provide, and that we should accept gratefully. Perhaps some of the listeners took his words too literally. Pushing, shoving and shouting, they attacked the piles of clothing and grabbed all they could lay hands on. Sometimes two women would tug at the same dress or skirt, threatening to tear it asunder. The horrified charity women, assisted by the priest, finally managed to restore order. A new method would be tried; all the clothes had to be put back in the original pile and the people would wait outside to be called in one by one. This worked better, though it failed to satisfy anyone: they would have preferred picking and choosing for themselves. One old man who had lost his house and all his possessions in the storm expressed great displeasure at the items selected for him—they were second-hand, they wouldn't fit, and so on. Finally he simply turned around and walked out. I knew for a fact that he had nothing in the world but the clothes on his back, yet he still possessed enough pride to look a gift horse in the mouth and say No. His gesture had a noble arrogance about it that seemed infinitely superior to the hat-in-hand, foot-shuffling humility that too often seems to be expected of charity recipients. The Cretans are always aware that to accept someone's gifts is to confer a great favour on him. And since they are so often lavish in their own generosity, it is only natural that they should expect the same from others.

With the passage of time the stream of visitors shrank to a trickle, then dried up entirely, much to the disappointment of the villagers who could never get enough of it. Hardly any of them had made any effort to clean up after the storm, preferring to leave everything just as it was, as a sort of exhibit for the sightseers and for the government officials whom they believed would come to assess the damage and allocate money for rebuilding. They were, in fact, quite annoyed with us because we set to work so soon; it seemed inappropriate to them that we should do such heavy work at all. The schoolmaster said to Inga, 'But why does your husband, an educated man, do such things? He works like an ordinary labourer, out there with his shirt off!' The teacher, like the village president and other notables, was one of those who did absolutely nothing. But now at last, as the summer waned and no government help was forth-coming, the people looked about, saw what had to be done, and reluctantly began doing it. They had extracted the last drop of novelty from the situation, and now the dirty work must begin.

The Whirlwind

Our own personal trials were not yet over. One day while working in the yard I cut my thumb; it became infected, the whole hand and then the arm swelled up, and I had to go to a doctor to endure a most painful lancing operation. For ten days I was without the use of my right hand. After it healed, we hoped to get a breathing spell at last. But one day I came down with a high fever and chills. After a few days in bed, I was examined by the district physician when she came by on her weekly round. Typhoid! It was like a last blow from the evil demon that had hung over us all summer—a delayed effect of the whirlwind. The disease was blamed on polluted water in cisterns that has been blown open during the storm. Chlorine was added to the cisterns, and the children were inoculated. Fortunately, Inga escaped it, and my own case was a relatively mild one. Even so, I was in bed for two weeks and remained weak for some time before recovering completely.

All we wanted now was to reach September—September became the mountain peak that we had to climb; once we reached the summit, all would be well. And so it turned out. By September first, and not before, we had recovered our health and strength and peace of mind. Our house and our spirits had been restored. The sightseers had gone. Blessed quiet reigned again in Plaka.

*   *   *

I am sitting in my airy workroom now, looking out towards Kokkino Horio, the next village, and the mountain, which from this angle resembles Cezanne's Mont-Ste-Victoire. The ominous charge that hung over it all has gone; now it is merely beautiful and peaceful. It is as though our sufferings and labour had exorcised whatever spell it was that hung over the place. The grapes have ripened and the vineyards are full of people picking them. They carry them up from the fields by the sea in wicker panniers strapped to the donkeys' sides. Barefoot men, streaming with sweat, tread the grapes to wine on their terraces every evening—they must do the work at night to avoid the thousands of wasps which, they say, presage a hard winter.

In this ripe season I pause, and look back, and I am glad that we stayed on—glad of our work and struggle. That faint whiff of boredom during the first perfect days in the house was more terrifying than any tornado. Perfection we no longer have or desire. The scars of the storm pockmark the walls of our house, as I carry the scars of Crete—literally—on my body. We have lived and felt intensely, and shared a terrible experience. It is well: for change and challenge, search and struggle are the elements in which we humans thrive. The pure air of perfection is too rare for us to breathe. The Greeks, masters of makeshift and improvisation, know this instinctively; we had to learn it. I know there are more disasters ahead, more trouble and pain and sorrow—as well as joys unimaginable. I accept all of it; I have no complaints; I welcome it in advance.

A small figure all in black is jogging along the road towards Kokkino Horio: the village priest. He is riding on a donkey, perched atop a beautiful deep red blanket. He sits side-saddle; the west wind has started blowing, and he reaches up to adjust his stovepipe hat. The donkey's pace is infuriatingly slow—or so it would seem to me —but the priest doesn't seem to mind; he just sits there in his Cretan sleep and jogs along. Eventually, the donkey will get there; the west wind is blowing but eventually it will stop. The priest—the Cretan— is in tune with this country, a part of this landscape, in a way that we will never be. His figure is in its place, part of the scene; his ancestors for hundreds, thousands of years have been Cretans. Let the west wind, the *garbis,* blow; never mind if it swings to the south, and becomes a *sorokos*; or if the cold north wind, the *boreas,* starts blowing and ushers in an early winter. The Cretan is ready for all of them, ready even for the whirlwind or for any disaster, including the ordinary ones that all of us can expect in the course of life. He has learned to live with the winds.

Epilogue

We stayed on in Plaka for more than a year after the tornado. We had gone to Crete in the first place expecting that, even with the most fantastic luck, we could not manage to remain more than a year, and we had stretched it out to nearly six years. We might never have left if circumstances had not finally forced us out. For some reason, the government became suspicious of foreigners who had lived for long periods in Greece, and revoked the residence permits of a number of them. The tortuous Byzantine mentality of Levantine officialdom had no doubt begun to suspect that they were spies. Eventually our turn came. After all, we were living in a village near Suda Bay, where an important naval base was located, and we looked across to Acrotiri, where the missiles were. I had a *beard*—almost proof positive of espionage. And why did we live in a *village*, when any sensible person would have preferred the amenities of a town? At the beginning of our second summer in Plaka we ran into trouble when we tried to renew our permits: were granted only three months instead of the usual six. We managed to get an extension, but by autumn they were insisting that we really had to leave the country. The officials in Crete could give us no reason for the expulsion— only that the orders had come from Athens.

Even then, we could without a doubt have talked our way into staying. It was a question of going to Athens, finding the right official, pulling the right strings. Other foreigners were doing it. But we were disinclined to do so; we had not come to Crete to wheedle and plead with bureaucrats. If they wanted us to leave, very well, leave we would. We took the view that one should always be alert for the signs and portents that life, that nature, throw out for our guidance. This refusal of our permits probably meant that the time had come for us to leave. Then there was the question of Inga's heart condition. Although she had sent X-rays and electrocardiogram reports to her doctors in Sweden, after so many years there was a definite need for a more thorough examination. (When she finally did have that checkup after our return to Sweden we learned that her

211

condition was exactly the same as it had been before we went to Crete. She was advised to wait for some years more before undergoing an operation. Apparently the life in Crete, despite its hardships, had been good for her!)

It was not until we stood on the deck of the ship that was to take us away from Crete that the reality of our departure hit home to us. As the ship moved away from the dock, Inga could not bear to look, and went down below decks to our cabin.

and went down below decks to our cabin. But I wanted to see the retreating shoreline of the island that had seeped into our bloodstream and become part of our flesh. I did not want to flinch from the pain of this departure, for it, too, was part of our life, part of what Crete had done to us and made of us. So I stood there in the twilight watching the receding island, picking out my favourite peaks from the massif of the White Mountains—the ones I had climbed or watched in changing light through the seasons from our various terraces—and picking out the tiny points of light high above the bay where our village lay. I stood there long after darkness fell, until I could no longer see Crete but could only feel it, and finally I went down and joined Inga in the cabin.

Cretan girl harvesting olives

Shoreline of Sphakia near the Venetian fortress of Frangokastello, where

The Venetian fortress of Frangokastello in Sphakia

The pace of Loutro, a village with no roads, allows the fisherman ample
time for his siesta
Old windmills at the entrance to the Lassithi Plateau

Georgillis and Thea
harvesting wheat

Winnowing the harvest

The crowning of the bride and groom, by the priest, during the wedding ceremony

Wall painting in a
Byzantine church,
Alicampos

Virgin and child – part
of a Byzantine wall
painting at Alicampos

A priest of Sphakia holds the Bible to be kissed by villagers

Faces in the crowd during the Easter services

Women at their eternal spinning

'He was a kingly man'

A Sphakian with typical 'archaic' beard trim of the region

Inga, camped out on the old Hellenic site in an olive grove at Souyia

The author

Sphakian girls on their way to the well

Index

CRET

GULF OF
KISSAMO

GULF OF CANEA

Canea

ACROTIRI

SUDA BAY

CAPE DREPANON

• Kastelli

Suda

Plaka

Vamos•

Rethymnon•

Georgioupolis•

Kandanos•WHITE

THE OMALO

•Alicampos

•Arkadi

Koustoyerako•

MOUNTAINS

Askyphou

•Ayios Ioannis

•Amari

Spili•

Spili•

Paleochora

Souyia

Ayia Roumeli

Loutro•Anopolis

Yerakari•

AMARI VALLEY

Mt Kedros

Hora Sphakion

Frangokastello•

•Tir

GULF OF MESSARA

LIBYAN

Matala•

YUGOSLAVIA
ALBANIA

BULGARIA

BLACK SEA

GREECE

AEGEAN SEA

TURKEY

IONIAN
SEA

CRETE

MEDITERRANEAN
SEA

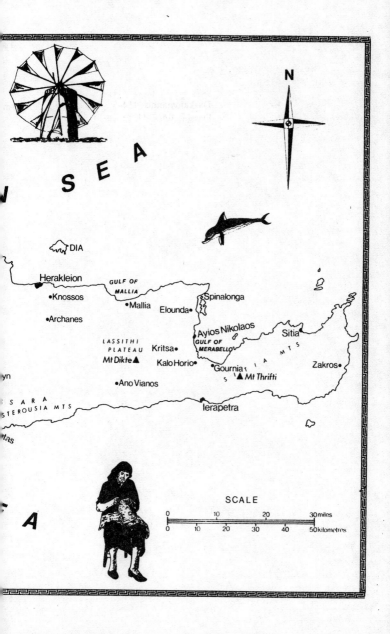

N

S E A

DIA

Herakleion GULF OF MALLIA

•Knossos   •Mallia Elounda• •Spinalonga

•Archanes

LASSITHI PLATEAU Kritsa• •Ayios Nikolaos Sitia•

Mt Dikte▲ Kalo Horio• GULF OF MERABELLO

yn •Gournia ▲Mt Thrifti Zakros•

S A R A •Ano Vianos

STEROUSIA MTS Ierapetra

tas

A

SCALE

0   10   20   30 miles

0   10   20   30   40   50 kilometres